D0609260

Hide & Seek

Potomac Books of Related Interest

Counterspy: Memoirs of a Counterintelligence Officer in World War II and the Cold War by Richard W. Cutler

Imperial Hubris: Why the West Is Losing the War on Terror by Michael Scheuer

Insurgency and Terrorism: From Revolution to Apocalypse, Second Edition by Bard E. O'Neill

Sacred Secrets: How Soviet Intelligence Operations Changed American History by Jerrold Schecter and Leona Schecter

Silent Warfare: Understanding the World of Intelligence, Third Edition by Abram N. Shulsky and Gary J. Schmitt

Spymaster: My Life in the CIA by Ted Shackley with Richard R. Finney

Stealing Secrets, Telling Lies: How Spies and Codebreakers Helped Shape the Twentieth Century by James Gannon

Who's Watching the Spies: Establishing Intelligence Service Accountability edited by Hans Born, Loch K. Johnson, and Ian Leigh

Why Secret Intelligence Fails by Michael A. Turner

Winning the Un-War: A New Strategy for the War on Terrorism by Charles Peña

Hide *&* Seek

Intelligence, Law Enforcement, *and the* Stalled War *on* Terrorist Finance

John A. Cassara

Potomac Books, Inc.
Washington D.C.

Copyright © 2006 Potomac Books, Inc.

Published in the United States by Potomac Books, Inc. All rights reserved. No part of this book may be reproduced in any manner whatsoever without written permission from the publisher, except in the case of brief quotations embodied in critical articles and reviews.

All statements of fact, opinion, or analysis expressed are those of the author and do not reflect the official positions or views of the Central Intelligence Agency or any other U.S. Government agency. Nothing in the contents should be construed as asserting or implying U.S. Government authentication of information or Agency endorsement of the author's views. This material has been reviewed by the CIA to prevent the disclosure of classified information.

Library of Congress Cataloging-in-Publication Data

Cassara, John A., 1953–
  Hide and seek : intelligence, law enforcement, and the stalled war on terrorist finance / John A. Cassara.—1st ed.
      p. cm.
  Includes bibliographical references and index.
  ISBN 1-57488-998-2 (hardcover : alk. paper)
  1. Terrorism—Finance—Prevention. 2. Money laundering—Prevention. 3. War on Terrorism, 2001– 4. Cassara, John A., 1953– I. Title.
  HV6431.C378 2006
  363.325'7—dc22

                                                    2006001248

Printed in the United States of America on acid-free paper that meets the American National Standards Institute Z39-48 Standard.

Potomac Books, Inc.
22841 Quicksilver Drive
Dulles, Virginia 20166

First Edition

10 9 8 7 6 5 4 3 2 1

In memory of my father, Lt. Col. Joseph R. Cassara, U.S. Army, a casualty of the Cold War.

In memory of the April 18, 1983, victims of the bombing of the U.S. embassy in Beirut and casualties of the War on Terrorism.

And to the grunts of the U.S. Civil Service who toil to protect us in the backstreets and the back cubicles in the United States and around the world, thank you for your *service*.

Contents

Illustrations

Preface

The failure of the U.S. intelligence and law enforcement communities in the September 11 terrorist attacks has been well documented. Congressional committees and independent commissions have detailed many of the government's shortcomings and inactions. However, the committees and commissions used the bureaucratic institutions themselves both as vantage points and as the primary sources of information for their critiques.

Unfortunately, little attention has been focused on what I call the stalled War on Terrorist Finance. Historically, U.S. law enforcement has found that "following the money" often leads to the leadership of organized crime. Yet, there has been little discussion in the public domain about how the system of financial intelligence put in place during the War on Narcotics is inadequate for the new War on Terrorism.

To help explain today's stalled War on Terrorist Finance, this book describes personal experiences and the progressively related issues of fighting the Cold War as a CIA operative, posing as an undercover arms dealer, targeting Italian-American organized crime in Rome, investigating money laundering in the Middle East, sounding an early alarm on the growing threat of "alternative" methods of laundering money and financing terrorist operations, and battling bureaucratic myopia in Washington, D.C. It was designed to bring true-life insight to many of the issues, procedures, and decisions that resonate today.

This book is *not* meant to be a comprehensive primer on money laundering and terrorist finance. For the most part, it focuses only on methodologies, events, and policies of which I have direct personal knowledge. Moreover, this book is not written for my peers; it is written primarily for the layperson. Many of the issues involved in terrorist finance are complex, and I hope that by telling a story and using real and varied examples from a unique career, I have made the subject matter easily digestible. The incidents and issues discussed are also designed to give the concerned and curious citizen one public servant's perspective on what it is really like out there. Many of the examples given are symptomatic of larger issues that have not yet been addressed by various post–September 11 reforms. And although this book chronicles both success and failure, it will, I hope, be an overall positive testimony to the importance of government *service*.

I will be pleased if my recounting of incidents of the last twenty-five years provides insight for the reader. If in the telling of tales I embarrass certain individuals or agencies, I apologize. That is not my intent. I am not trying to settle scores but to revisit events as they unfolded in an intellectually honest and factually correct manner. On June 6, 2002, President Bush appealed to employees of the intelligence and law enforcement communities to report suspicions of threatening activity and bureaucratic inertia and appealed to managers to "continue to think and act differently to defeat the enemy."[1] Over the years I repeatedly tried to push within the system. But the system hasn't worked. This book, written immediately after my retirement, is a final attempt to act differently, outside of normal channels, to help bring attention to issues that are important in the War on Terrorism. Many of these issues have never before surfaced publicly. After a long career in government, I have come to realize that some bureaucracies are either unwilling or unable to reform themselves. Outside pressure must occasionally be applied.

Another reason for writing this book is purely personal. I want to impress upon today's youth that government service is worthwhile and that they should not "weary in doing good." I also want to give my children an idea of what their father did with a large portion of his life. I know too well after a career in the government that "If it is not written down, it did not happen."

I would like to thank my family for their love, support, and understanding while I wrote this book. *La famiglia é la più grande ricchezza nella vita.*

Many people deserve public recognition for their insight and assistance with the manuscript. Likewise, others truly helped with their friendship and encouragement. For a number of reasons, it is best that these people remain in the shadows. They know who they are, and they have my deepest respect and appreciation.

I would like to thank the editors and staff at Potomac Books, particularly Don McKeon, vice president and publisher, for his early and continuing support, patience, and experienced editorial eye.

Introduction

I felt as if I had failed. On September 11, 2001, as television coverage reported planes slamming into the World Trade Center, the Pentagon, and a field in Pennsylvania, I felt the anger and outrage of all Americans but also deep personal defeat and frustration. The successful surprise terrorist attacks on the U.S. mainland symbolized the failure of the U.S. intelligence and law enforcement communities. I had spent more than twenty years of my life in those communities both as a case officer in the Central Intelligence Agency (CIA) and a special agent in the Department of the Treasury. I knew well the entrenched culture of the bureaucracies that in some ways enabled the attacks. In that sense, the attacks were not a surprise.

Although there has been much post–September 11 fanfare about the inadequacies and misplaced priorities of the CIA and the Federal Bureau of Investigation (FBI), the attacks also represented another failure that thus far has not received much attention. They demonstrated the weakness in America's current system of financial transparency that is used in the "War on Terrorist Finance." The potential of financial intelligence has received much hype. To paraphrase President George W. Bush in the days after September 11, "We are going to kill or capture the terrorists and take their money." Others can debate the success of the former tactic. However, to put it charitably, America's mostly silent War on Terrorist Finance is stalled. And the stakes are huge. Although completely eradicating terrorist financing is impossible, better success in following the money could be more important than any tactical battlefield victory. Historically, investigating the money trail has been one of the most significant law enforcement techniques in attacking various types of entrenched criminal activity. Following the money often leads directly to the top of a criminal organization. Cutting off channels of illicit finance deprives a criminal organization of its lifeblood.

Understanding the complexities of terrorist finance and its somewhat inverse partner, international money laundering, are daunting. These two criminal activities overlap with a variety of international and law enforcement and intelligence issues. The chapters following describe many examples of real-world difficulties in the War on Terrorist Finance. Unfortunately, easy fixes do not exist. There are not just a few large faults that can be singled out and remedied. Rather, both before and after September 11, a series of wrong decisions and misplaced priorities were facilitated by bureaucratic cultures and entrenched ways of doing business. But most important, as the 9/11 Commission notes, the bureaucracies failed to prevent the terrorist attacks in part because of a "lack of imagination."[1] By examining one insider's career in the intelligence and law enforcement communities, this book will attempt to provide additional insight into many issues of continuing concern and to give examples of policies and decisions that exposed such a deficit of imagination.

I labored to make this book as accurate as possible. The narrative, comments, and opinions expressed are mine; they are not affiliated with any government agency. I did not include classified information, specific financial intelligence, and on-going case information. Although at times I changed certain sensitive information and identities to protect intelligence sources, methods, privacy, and reputations, this does not take away from the veracity of the story. I was candid during my career, and I will be candid now. For the sake of brevity and chronological flow, many additional incidents and examples could not be included.

Portions of this book were subject to prepublication review and edited by the CIA, Department of State, and the U.S. Secret Service. Postemployment publication policies by the Department of Homeland Security and the Department of the Treasury were also followed. The CIA heavily edited chapter 1, in particular. I apologize to the reader if portions of the chapter and some later references to the intelligence community seem to lack adequate description and clarifying information.

The intersection of international law enforcement and foreign intelligence collection, particularly in the areas of money laundering and terrorist financing, will be increasingly important for all of us to understand in the years ahead. To make positive advances, we have to understand the background of current issues and the culture of the bureaucracies. Thus, the first few chapters of this book, before discussing money laundering and the finance of terrorism, introduce a progression of related issues, countermeasures, and intelligence and law enforcement tactics and tools that first surfaced in the Cold War and the War on Narcotics. These chapters give the reader a foundation and a real-world perspective on issues, procedures, and policies that continue to surface and to suggest how the community can be improved and better positioned to fight the new type of war America has found itself in.

There has been some success in the War on Terrorist Finance. The U.S. government is developing some innovative tools and procedures. Departments and agencies are being reorganized. Bureaucracies are becoming much better at sharing information. Progress has been made in providing training and technical assistance and helping countries help themselves. We need to understand that some of the money-laundering and terrorist-finance methodologies and techniques our government is confronting do not have realistic or cost-effective solutions. In addition, as we learned combating money laundering in the War on Narcotics, U.S. adversaries readily adapt to countermeasures.

Money is the necessary ingredient for terrorist organizations. Simply put, without money there is no terrorism. Unfortunately, nearly five years after the September 11 terrorist attacks, despite a variety of initiatives, countermeasures, regulations, and reorganizations, there is no doubt that terrorist networks retain access to hidden financial sources and can move and transfer both money and value to finance the next terrorist plot.

1

A Sense of the Street

W orking with Carlos was always a pleasure. He spoke English, was the consummate gentleman, and provided the best human intelligence in the U.S. intelligence community on the Angolan target. And he was always on time. I hated waiting for agents to make a meet. If an agent didn't show within fifteen minutes of a scheduled meeting time and place, we reverted to an alternative meeting plan that depended on various forms of communication. Most of my commo plans required the use of a public telephone. Trying to find one that worked in the old but beautiful European city where I was stationed was always a challenge.*

Turning the corner on a major street, I downshifted in my battered little white Honda Civic and scanned the area both for Carlos and for anything that was out of place. I could see he had just pulled into a parking place himself, and as he looked into his rearview mirror, our eyes met. I pulled up beside him, and Carlos gave me a big smile. I opened the door, his bulky frame settled into my passenger seat, and off we went. Searching both the chaotic traffic and the Honda's mirrors for possible surveillance or anything out of the ordinary, I drove and listened as Carlos related the latest intrigues in the communist Angolan Central Committee. Carlos wasn't a member of the politburo-type committee, but over the years he had certainly demonstrated his "access" to information and people that were of interest to the U.S. government. He was a very skilled agent and consistently managed to report information that proved very useful.

At the end of our car meeting, I reviewed, or "recapped," the information Carlos had just given me to make sure I got everything right. I gave him some intelligence reporting requirements or questions for future reporting that I had recently received from headquarters. We re-

---

* In order not to reveal classified information, location and operational cover cannot be disclosed.

viewed our commo plan. Finally, I passed him an envelope that contained his monthly salary and had him sign a receipt. For the most important human source we had on Angola, the sum was not a lot. It certainly did not come close to compensating him for the risk he was taking. He knew better than I did that if he were caught in Angola he would be executed. It was that simple and that real. But another reason I enjoyed working with Carlos was that he did not help us for the money. Carlos was an agent for the Central Intelligence Agency (CIA) because he believed in the United States and what we represented and because he hated the Soviet Union and what the communists had done both directly and via proxy to his country. During the Cold War, agents who cooperated because of ideology always seemed to be the most motivated.

After dropping off Carlos near his parked car by the grounds of the university, I cut through some backstreets on the campus heading back to my apartment. As I continued my countersurveillance route near the university, I felt that the hustle of campus life seemed much more familiar than my new life as a spy. I was not much older than most of the students I saw, having graduated from college myself in the United States just a few years before.

I had attended college in southern California, where my passion for surfing competed with my studies. While I completed my graduate degree at the American Graduate School of International Management in Phoenix, the CIA hired me to be an analyst. I reported to CIA headquarters in Langley, Virginia. A short time later I found out about the agency's career trainee program, which accepted a tiny cadre into the clandestine service of the CIA known as the Directorate of Operations (DO). By early 1980 I had completed the DO's case officer school and was assigned to Africa (AF) Division at headquarters, where I dealt with Angolan issues. One day, as I was standing at a urinal in a headquarters restroom, the chief of AF Division asked if I was ready for my first assignment overseas. Fewer than eight months later, I was undercover collecting foreign intelligence.

My apartment was located in an area of the city that could have been the setting for a tourist postcard. The buildings that lined the narrow alleylike street on which my apartment was located were so close together that at certain points you could spread your arms and touch the sides of the white and pastel-colored buildings. The windows and balconies were alive with flowering geraniums, and every balcony seemed to hold a little old lady dressed in black enjoying the view, the sunshine, and the refreshing breeze coming up from the river that led to the sea. Most balconies also had canaries in cages that serenaded the hustle and bustle of life in the street below. At the entrance to my apartment, a tile figure of a nineteenth-century soldier was plastered into the wall and stood like a permanent sentry by the staircase leading to my door.

My small one-bedroom apartment was furnished primarily with antiques that belonged to the landlord. Returning from my meeting with Carlos, I put on a tape of Mozart, sat down at the nineteenth-century desk, and pulled the chair close to my manual Underwood Five typewriter. As I wrote an intelligence report based on Carlos's information, the chattering keys seemingly kept time with the music. I had been taught at the Agency's school for spies, commonly known as the "Farm," to write intelligence reports while a meeting was still fresh in the mind. I took pride in my reports because that was my primary mission, the production of foreign intelligence or "FI." I drafted and tweaked the words until my report was clear, concise, and written in the approved Agency format. Putting the intelligence report aside, I next wrote a contact report memorializing my actual meeting with Carlos, documenting commo plan updates, his receipt of monthly payment, and other administrative and operational details. I knew both the CIA station chief and AF Division in headquarters would be pleased with my report on the latest political developments in Angola.

✳

Before the War on Terrorism and the War on Narcotics, there was the Cold War. Many of the tactics, capabilities, procedures, and bureaucratic structures that existed in both the intelligence and overseas law enforcement communities on the eve of September 11 were legacies of the Cold War, a confrontation that existed primarily due to the articulated communist quest for worldwide domination. Unfortunately, much of the bureaucratic and structural Cold War legacy proved inadequate to fight the later challenges of the asymmetric War on Terrorism.

With the hindsight of history, it would have been possible to project the eventual collapse of the Soviet "evil empire." But when I joined the

CIA in the late 1970s, the Soviet Union appeared strong and represented a very real threat to the security of the United States and its allies. Vietnam had invaded Cambodia, consolidating Soviet power in Southeast Asia. The Sandinistas had taken over Nicaragua, which joined Cuba as a Soviet outpost in the Western Hemisphere. With the toppling of Iran by the radical Islamists led by the Ayatollah Khomeni, combined with the Soviet invasion of neighboring Afghanistan, America saw aggressive threats developing in the Middle East and South Asia.

In 1980 Africa was also one of the premiere areas of confrontation between the Soviet Union and the United States. As the former colonial powers of England, France, Belgium, and Portugal pulled out of Africa, new powers had rushed into the vacuum left behind. The continent was a bubbling cauldron of competing political agendas and struggling "liberation" movements. Many of the countries that had recently obtained freedom from their colonial masters soon became immersed in civil wars. Many of the wars had as their origin historical tribal animosities that had existed in Africa before colonization. These tribal conflicts were made worse by the artificial borders of many African countries, which had been drawn by European colonial powers without regard for native historical, tribal, ethnic, religious, and linguistic differences. As a CIA African division colleague once told me, "The secret of understanding Africa is to understand tribalism. It is the root cause of most of the conflicts in Africa." Over the years I learned this is true for much of the rest of the world as well. For example, many of today's conflicts, including those in Afghanistan and Iraq, are fueled, in part, by tribalism.

Africa's attempt to achieve rapid modernization and to play catch-up to the rest of the world exacerbated the traditional conflicts caused by African tribalism. Some of the colonial powers left their former colonies with decent economic infrastructure and education and a competent civil service. As late as the 1950s, Africa was a net exporter of natural resources and commodities. It had a balance of payments surplus. Other colonial powers took advantage of their colonies, exploited their resources, and gave back very little in return. When they finally left Africa in the 1950s, '60s, and '70s, they often left nascent countries unprepared to enter the global family of nations. Into the void stepped new and unscrupulous native leaders and would-be leaders who, in many cases, had as their real agenda personal aggrandizement and wealth. The tradition of tribal chiefs easily evolved into the new ritual of national dictators. Many times the power grabs were under the guise of "pan-African socialism," "national liberation," or "socialism with an African face." Undoubtedly, there were some true believers in socialism and the promise of the common good. But the altruists simply lost to competing interests. And unfortunately, Africa's mistakes in postcolonial development that are so apparent today were not so obvious forty years ago.

In the struggle for the hearts and minds of Africa's awakening peoples, the Soviet goal of world communism and domination also played a part. Direct Soviet influence via commerce and aid were often coupled with security services, weapons, port privileges, and proxy military troops and advisers. The Soviet Union would target an area of strategic importance and political vulnerabilities, and then it would sponsor a socialist party or leader, help the party obtain power, and finally, through "fraternal assistance," work to maintain socialist power. The new African socialist government would become dependent on the Soviet Union and would often grant the world power a physical presence, political influence, and confiscatory trading rights. Nowhere was this more apparent and more troubling to the United States than in the former Portuguese colony of Angola.

The bloodless Portuguese revolution of 1974 overthrew the country's conservative right-wing dictatorship. The new socialist/communist-leaning government that came to power immediately moved to liberate its African colonies. With the departure of the Portuguese from Angola in 1975, Angola had a power vacuum that the Marxist Popular Movement for the Liberation of Angola (MPLA), the conservative Union for the Total Independence of Angola (UNITA), and other lesser parties such as the National Front for the Liberation of Angola fought to fill. The resulting civil war, influenced as much by tribalism as ideology, soon became a proxy battlefield in the Cold War then raging between the Soviet Union and the United States.

By October 1975 the Angolan factions favored by Washington were losing the war. But on November 4, 1975, Cuban President Fidel Castro, without informing Moscow, decided to send soldiers to Angola.[1] A few months later the Soviet Union came on board with Castro's agenda and began to airlift Cuban troops to Angola. The arrival of thirty thousand Cuban troops totally changed the dynamics of the Angolan civil war.

Angola not only became a battleground in the Cold War, but it also soon became a battleground between the U.S. Congress and the executive over primacy in foreign policy. The memory of Vietnam was fresh in the minds of Congress. The 1970s were a time of distrust of the government and fear of being embroiled in another third-world quagmire. In December 1975 the U.S. Senate passed an amendment to the Department of Defense appropriations bill terminating covert assistance to anti-communist forces in Angola. A short time later the Clark Amendment attached to a foreign aid bill extended the ban. Once the bill was passed the CIA had to operate under its constraints.

So, despite the constant demand by Washington policymakers for intelligence on Angola, the CIA was forced to operate from afar. Angola was considered a "closed environment" because the United States did not have a diplomatic presence in the capital, Luanda. Because the United States had no embassy there, there was no State Department reporting from Luanda. To fill the intelligence void, the CIA attempted to recruit from a distance agents who had access to information of interest. It was not easy then nor is it today: just as the CIA struggled with the closed environment issue during the Cold War, it has likewise been challenged more recently during the lead up to the war to topple Saddam Hussein's Iraq and still today with the need to collect intelligence in closed environments such as Iran and North Korea.

In the case of reporting on Angola during the Cold War, the challenge was to identify, or "spot," an individual who lived and worked in Angola and had access to intelligence of interest. Most important, the potential agent had to be able to communicate with the outside world after his recruitment. Agents who had excellent access to information would serve no purpose unless they could report that information. So during the Cold War years, the Agency looked for potential agents who periodically traveled outside of Angola and could be personally met and debriefed. If this were not possible, the Agency would recruit agents who had the necessary skills to communicate via systems of "impersonal communications." Some Cold War techniques were not much changed from the way international espionage was practiced in the eighteenth century.

When I was ready to deliver my report to my boss in AF Division, Andy Peterson, I couldn't just call him on the phone from my apartment and ask to drop the document off. Our phones could possibly be monitored by security services. Good tradecraft called for me to use a public telephone to place the call. That day I walked a few blocks from my apartment looking for a public phone that was in working condition. It seemed like all the phones had been ripped out of the booths or had had objects wedged into their coin slots by vandals. Eventually, I found a phone that functioned and placed my call. The conversation was short, pleasant, and innocuous. At the end I said, "Andy, let's have an espresso at the usual place Thursday at 2:00 PM." There were many variations on the theme, but between Andy and me, having an espresso was code for passing the report in a previously agreed upon place and manner twenty-five hours later than the time mentioned over the phone. We knew we would be meeting Friday at 3:00 PM. And since it was already midday Friday, I had to get going.

Practicing countersurveillance techniques and cutting through the backstreets, I finally emerged on a broad boulevard near where I would be meeting Andy. I bought a newspaper at a corner kiosk, ducked into a café, and ordered an espresso. Looking at my watch and the window, I counted down the minutes until it was five to 3:00. Taking the intelligence report out of my backpack, I discreetly inserted it into the newspaper and rolled them into a paper baton. I left the café and headed toward the American embassy. Sure enough, I saw Andy at exactly 3:00 PM walking toward me on the other side of the street. Cutting across, we passed each other on the crowded sidewalk. Now Andy had the rolled-up newspaper. I knew my intelligence report would soon be on its way to Washington.

✣

The mission of a case officer during the Cold War was in one sense a very tiny subset of the overarching U.S. intelligence cycle. The cycle is as applicable in combating today's threats of terrorism and terrorist finance as it was a generation ago in obtaining information about the Soviet Union and its proxies. The intelligence cycle has not changed. In the intelligence community, the cycle still drives the way information or intelligence is generated, collected, and analyzed.

The intelligence cycle is the process of developing, collecting, and analyzing information from a variety of sources, thereby turning that information into finished intelligence.[2] The intelligence product is used by policymakers to assist them in making informed decisions or to help other consumers of intelligence products frame issues under review. The "consumers" of foreign intelligence include the president, the National Security Council, Congress, and major departments and agencies of the government.

The first step in the cycle is planning and direction. In this step, intelligence officers identify the target for intelligence collection and draw up either specific reporting requirements or the types of questions that the intelligence is supposed to answer. Because it is a cycle, the first step is also the last step because the intelligence collected will probably generate more questions and new requirements.

The next step in the cycle is the actual intelligence collection. Many different sources of information are available. They range from "open-source" material in the international press to technical collection from highly sophisticated electronic intercepts and overhead satellite imagery to information that spies, such as Carlos, collect on the ground.

The third step in the cycle is processing the information. This step is becoming increasingly complex because in the information technology age the amount of information collected and available to analyze has grown almost exponentially. For example, today, in dealing with terrorist finance, the Department of the Treasury is drowning in the over 13 million pieces of financial intelligence that are collected every year. As we will see, this is simply too much data to analyze properly.

The fourth step in the intelligence cycle is the analysis and production of all source intelligence. Often contradictory information is reviewed and analyzed. Intelligence analysts evaluate the information by considering source reliability and validity. The information is finally collated, formatted, edited, and submitted as a final report or product sometimes called "finished intelligence." And finally, the last step in the cycle is the dissemination of the information to the policymakers or others who initiated the original intelligence "tasking."

The CIA DO uses its case officers overseas primarily to collect human foreign intelligence. "Collection" was the part of the intelligence cycle I was most involved with while I was overseas operating as a case officer in the Cold War. Today collection remains the most problematic step in the cycle for the United States in venues such as Iraq and Afghanistan and combating various international terrorist threats. Intelligence from human sources (humint) is vitally important in putting together the jigsaw puzzle of an intelligence product. For example, while overhead imagery can take "spy-in-the-sky" pictures of weapon systems on the ground, humint provides policymakers answers to the important questions such as: What is the intended use of the photographed weapon system?

As a case officer in the early 1980s, I was responsible for obtaining humint from agents who would provide answers to the intelligence taskings received on Angola and other subjects of concern. The taskings were sent to officers from CIA headquarters. To get the vital humint, I was trained to recruit agents, or sources, who had access to the desired information. In other words, I was taught how to convince people to commit espionage so that they would agree to provide information to the U.S. government. Once they agree to do so, they are considered "recruited" assets or agents of the U.S. government.

Just as there is an intelligence cycle, there is also a recruitment cycle. The first step in the recruitment cycle is spotting somebody with access to the desired information. The next step is to "assess" the target's susceptibility to recruitment. This generally entails judging the potential agent's vulnerabilities and desires. The case officer next "develops" the target by building a personal relationship and then finally delivers a recruitment pitch that is based on the assessment. Agents might agree to spy for varied reasons, but experience has shown that the major reasons are greed, revenge, ideology or strong personal belief, recognition, and even adventure. Often, it is a combination of two or more factors.

Although the recruitment cycle was conceived during a Cold War that no longer exists, human nature remains the same. In that respect, it doesn't make any difference whether somebody is being recruited to work against the Soviet Union or being recruited to work against today's terrorist threat. The personal challenges a case officer faces and the bureaucratic steps and procedures involved in the cycle have likewise not changed too much over the years.

✳

My primary role as a young case officer was to "handle" agents and maximize their reporting potential. I had been sent to my post to help relieve Andy of much of his workload. By handling a variety of agents, I also was given the opportunity to develop my skill sets, language ability, and confidence in preparation for later attempts at recruiting my own new agents. I enjoyed working with agents and helping them improve their ability to provide information of interest by having them address the questions in their intelligence reporting: who, what, when, where, why, and how?

My case officer assignment was also my introduction to "the street." My operational cover allowed me to spend time walking the city and observing people in an environment that was very foreign to me. I soaked up the new culture, lifestyle, and manner of doing business. I forced myself to overcome my natural reserve and hesitancy to use a foreign language and to meet and cultivate an ever-widening circle of contacts, essential practices in the world of intelligence gathering. In addition, familiarity with my environs enhanced my operational security, communications, and tradecraft.

One of the things I most enjoyed about being a case officer was obtaining foreign intelligence and sending it back to Washington, where, I hoped, policymakers would see it. On numerous occasions, information that I provided was included in the *Presidential Daily Brief* (PDB), a synopsis of foreign intelligence that the CIA prepared every night and delivered to the president early the following morning.

Even without specific reporting requirements from the intelligence cycle, by staying well informed and studying political winds and issues of concern, I could construct questions for my agents or pursue topics that would have a receptive audience. For example, in response to such questions during a meeting with a well-placed Angolan source, I learned that Angolan students and young professionals had been sent to a communist training academy located on the Isle of Pines in Cuba. Reportedly, the Angolans had rioted over perceived discrimination by the Cubans and poor living conditions. The event demonstrated a bit of a split between the two "fraternal" communist partners. I dutifully reported the information to Washington.

About a week later I was pleased to note a short article in the *International Herald Tribune* that reported the same Isle of Pines revolt. This was very welcome news for a case officer: press or open-source reporting confirmed my earlier classified reporting. It also confirmed what my agent had reported, adding to his credibility. It was a nice little development, though, frankly, I didn't think too much about it until a few days later when I got an immediate operational cable from headquarters. Apparently, the information that I had reported was included in the PDB. The Reagan White House had loved it. The political ideologues, always trying to score points against Castro's Cuba, couldn't control themselves with news embarrassing to Cuba and had leaked the information to the press. An investigation was undertaken to try to uncover the individual who leaked the intelligence, and I was directed to immediately contact my source and advise him of the leak. Headquarters had justifiable concern that the information provided, now in the public domain, could help opposition counterintelligence services identify the reporting source, and I was concerned because I constantly assured my agents of operational security. The White House leak made case officers look hypocritical. Of course, the investigation into the leak's source never bore fruit; no one was held accountable. But if the investigators had identified the source of the leak, I would have suggested that the culprit in Washington accompany me to the next meeting with the betrayed agent and have him explain what happened.

While case officers report facts and do not get involved with policy, the reporting of foreign intelligence can be politicized, as in the above example. Foreign intelligence consumers sometimes use the information in ways it is not intended, for example, to advance political agendas. The same issue is in the news again today: congressional investigating committees are examining whether pre–Iraq War intelligence assessments on Saddam Hussein's weapons of mass destruction were molded to fit agendas rather than objective analysis of the facts. And as we will see later, after September 11 law enforcement and intelligence services felt initial pressure to use intelligence in ways not originally intended so that the U.S. government could aggressively move forward with a program of financial "designations."

During my first few months overseas, I became increasingly proficient at handling a wide variety of agents and at writing intelligence reports. Andy was very happy that I had been able to relieve him of much of his bureaucratic burden. My next professional and personal challenge was to get my first recruitment. Securing a recruit was a professional challenge because, although the name of the game in the DO is to produce intelligence, a case officer's reputation came from recruiting sources.

It was a personal challenge because it takes a certain amount of nerve to ask somebody to commit treason, particularly when you are doing the asking in a foreign language.

I had received some information about a technician from Angola, Francisco, who was visiting his family in the city I was stationed in. I gave Francisco a call, and buying my friend-of-a-friend ploy, he agreed to meet me for lunch. I was very impressed by Francisco when I met him at the restaurant. He was sophisticated and quite intelligent. Over a lengthy lunch with lots of excellent wine and brandy, I elicited from him details about his work in Angola and his possible access to information of interest. Finding that he traveled regularly, I became quite interested in pursuing the courtship.

After lunch Francisco invited me back to his apartment to meet his family. During the next few weeks I continued to develop our relationship and assess whether Francisco might be able to produce intelligence. When he passed all of my tests, I began to figure out how I might structure an effective recruitment pitch. In my apartment and during my long walks through the city, I would rehearse my lines and try to imagine his possible responses. If they have made proper assessments and their pitches are skillfully delivered, good case officers should almost be able to know beforehand that the answer will be yes. If they believe the answer will be negative, the attempt should not be made. I believed in my gut that Francisco would say yes, and over the years, in many diverse circumstances, I learned to trust my gut feelings. I felt Francisco's motivation to cooperate would be based on equal parts ideology, money, and a spirit of adventure. Therefore, I practiced phrasing my lead-in conversation and pitch so that they would hit all of the right buttons. I also had to structure how I would drop my cover and let him know I was secretly working for the CIA. My biggest challenge, however, was to deliver the pitch in a foreign language. I kept my dictionary by my side as I practiced and rehearsed just the right words and grammar over and over again.

But first I had a few bureaucratic obstacles to overcome. For good reasons, I was not allowed to unilaterally decide to try to recruit my first agent. I had to discuss the possibility of recruiting Francisco with my superiors and then send operational cables to headquarters asking for approval. In short, I had to recruit the bureaucracy before I could try to recruit the agent.

I also gave a lot of thought to where I would deliver the pitch. I finally decided that I would arrange lunch at a restaurant in the part of town in which I felt the most comfortable. There were many different ways to get in and out of the area quickly, and even though this part of town was a prime commercial center, I knew a few quiet locations where we could talk. I thought that after our lunch, we would stroll outside to a nearby park where I would deliver my rehearsed lines. In a worst-case scenario, if Francisco became loud and indignant or even started ranting about being manipulated by the CIA, I could at least get away from him quickly. I even identified a kind of escape and evasion route I could use if I needed to get away from the park in a hurry. On the day of the meeting, everything went as planned. After a nice lunch and our stroll in the park, Francisco agreed to become an agent for the CIA and report information that he observed while he was in Angola. He became a very good foreign intelligence source, and information he collected often became part of the intelligence cycle.

Francisco was the first of several to follow. I became adept at collecting intelligence and writing intelligence reports. And I enjoyed the hunt of the recruitment cycle. By pure chance, I realized my best recruitment several months after Francisco became an agent. Enlarging my social network of acquaintances, I met an individual of potential interest who was visiting the city for a few months before going back to work in Africa. Vitor originally struck me as a bit of a nerd. Obviously very bright, his reserve initially masked his strong feelings and frustrations about his work situation. He mentioned he worked in the telecommunications industry; those were magic words.

While I developed our relationship over the course of several get-togethers, Vitor confessed that he had no desire to go back to his homeland. He was disgusted with the poor living conditions, and during his visit to the European city, he had been enjoying the comparative good life. It was obvious he needed money, and he talked derisively of his country's corrupt leadership. In today's language, he would be termed a "disgruntled employee." He was wearing recruitment vulnerabilities on his sleeve, but what access to information of interest did he actually possess? Becoming more and more proficient at my craft and the language, I began to slowly move out of character and drop hints that I was more than what I seemed. Taking the bait, he let me know that he had with him some manuals that would in effect open the door to a very important information system. One thing led to the next, and I recruited Vitor and secured copies of his manuals.

Headquarters was delighted with the development. This one recruitment more than paid back their investment in my hiring, training and first overseas assignment. The National Security Agency (NSA) was also thrilled. NSA has many functions, but one of the foremost is the production of foreign intelligence through the interception of various forms of foreign communications signals. After Vitor was officially recruited, NSA analysts were dispatched to meet with him and further his debrief. The subject matter under discussion was frankly over my head, and I was only too happy to let NSA fully exploit my new source. The information Vitor provided gave the U.S. intelligence community a unique window that they hadn't had before and resulted in new opportunities to monitor developments in a country of concern.

Despite my growing experience and success, life as a covert operative overseas was hard. I believed in my mission, but everyday I was confronted with the reality of working effectively overseas in my chosen occupation. I also discovered that it is one thing to travel to a country and stay a few days or a few weeks but it is quite another matter to put down roots and actually settle in a foreign environment and culture.

I was almost entirely on my own. I received very little logistical support. I had to find a place to live. I had to deal with a landlord who over time became increasingly suspicious of my cover story. I had to buy a car. I had to figure out how and where to pay utility bills and then spend countless hours in line every month paying them. I had to open a bank account in the city and then other accounts elsewhere to, in effect, launder my paycheck into my foreign bank. I had to register with the foreign government. In 1980 my host country was still considered rather backward for several reasons, including its stifling bureaucracy. It seemed like every time I turned around I was required to get an official paper with a tax stamp, a requirement for countless mundane day-to-day tasks. And when the arrival of my shipment of household effects from the States was delayed almost six months, I had to struggle to try to find clothes and shoes that would fit my rather large American-size frame. And everything I did required me to speak a foreign language.

Before I was selected by the Agency to become part of its clandestine service, I had been given a language-aptitude test. I failed it. Miserably. Yet somehow I still made it into the DO program. Although the exam showed I didn't have an aptitude for language, I did have the desire. I spent countless hours in my apartment trying to memorize words and conjugate verbs. I started with readers for schoolchildren. Later I tried to study newspapers, listen to television, and, of course, be alert for useful phrases, expressions, and mannerisms during my daily excursions in the streets. I had studied the language a few months before leaving Washington, but I found a great difference between the grammar and accent I was taught and the actual language spoken in the country I was assigned to. I made horrendous and, at times, comical mistakes. But I kept trying.

Any case officer or State Department foreign service officer will agree that there is no substitute for being able to speak the language of the country in which he is assigned. Language impacts everything, both the professional and personal. All will likewise agree that learning a foreign language is a daunting challenge: the more one learns of a language, the more one realizes how much more there is to learn. That is equally true of a foreign culture. And only proficiency in a language will begin to unlock the intricacies of the culture. True fluency is almost impossible for nonnative speakers to achieve. Cinematic portraits of sophisticated American spies easily switching from one language to another or masquerading as one nationality or another are rare in the real world. Americans are simply at a disadvantage learning foreign languages because in our culture we are rarely exposed to other languages. Functioning as a spy was not my biggest challenge overseas, but rather it was trying to successfully speak and understand a foreign language. Through sheer hard work I learned enough to succeed. However, I always regret never being able to become truly proficient.

The other major challenge I continually confronted was boredom. It seemed that my work was either feast or famine. I was running about a dozen agents; that was considered quite a workload. But very few of my agents were actually based in my city. Most traveled back and forth and could be gone for months at a time. For some odd reason, many of the agents seemed to consistently return to the city at the same time. During those periods, there were not enough hours in the day and night to meet, debrief, train, and keep up with all of the paperwork involved. At other times very few agents were in town, and outside of monitoring clandestine impersonal communications from my agents in Angola, I had little to do.

Trying to make a positive impression with my superiors, I would take advantage of these dry spells and identify possible sites around the city suitable to covertly pass communications. I also identified countersurveillance routes and otherwise ensured that I practiced good tradecraft. But despite my efforts to keep busy, frequent bouts of loneliness and boredom would not go away. Regardless of the fiction portrayed by Hollywood, being a CIA spy is not glamorous work. It's lonely. For most of the first year of my tour, the highlight of my day would be the *International Herald Tribune* delivery in the evening to various news kiosks. In the days before CNN, I was starved for English-language news. I spent my evenings in restaurants, with a bottle of wine and the *Herald Tribune* as my only companions. I obviously needed some human interaction.

To help improve my language skills and relieve the boredom, I got the Agency to agree to fund occasional language lessons. As I walked into the classroom the first day, a pretty young lady with striking eyes and a beautiful smile met me. Looking at me for the first time, she blushed. My first thought was, "These lessons aren't going to be so bad."

The language lessons became secondary. I devoted my attention to the teacher. The conversational lessons became an excuse for me to get to know her. Cristina was twenty-two years old and a recent graduate from the university. She had the equivalent of a master's degree in languages, and in addition to her native language, she was quite fluent in French, German, and the Queen's accented English. She was very bright and personable and knew what was going on in the world. She was working part-time at the language school giving lessons to earn some extra money. Cristina was very proud of her country and culture, and I soon discovered she delighted in answering my many questions about them. The second lesson I asked her to lunch. When she refused, I asked her to dinner. She had never met an American before and was curious. Maybe that's why she said she would make an exception to her policy of not going out with her students.

The first dinner evolved into many others. I had come to love the city, and Cristina was quite happy to show me aspects of it that only a native truly knows. We found little hole-in-the-wall restaurants, talked for hours over coffee at the beautiful sidewalk cafes, and explored much of the area's vast historical and cultural treasures. Cristina introduced me to her friends—all young professionals—and as a group we went to the movies and other events. I was becoming more and more enmeshed in the local way of life. Cristina and I became friends and then best friends.

During the following months, when I would pick Cristina up outside her parents' apartment, she would meet me at the door and never invite me in. At first I thought nothing of it, but over time I became increasingly concerned that she was embarrassed to introduce me to her family. I didn't know if it was something about me personally or if it was because I was a foreigner. When I finally asked her, she demurely explained that in her culture, bringing me home to meet her family would mean the relationship was serious. I had come to a crossroads.

The Agency had an up-and-down policy about its employees' involvement with foreign nationals. In a certain context, one could argue that the personal lives of employees aren't the employer's business. But the Agency was obviously not a typical employer, and it rightfully had a need to know if an employee could possibly be co-opted by outside influence. Accepting this logic, when I started to date Cristina I asked the Agency to run background checks on her and her close family. I knew she was not a threat; the background check was simply one of those things one does to protect oneself in a bureaucracy. I also told my bosses that I was dating her. They were quite happy for me and glad to hear that I had found a social outlet and that I was active in the local community. However, a "serious" relationship brought everything to another level. At the time, the Agency didn't prohibit marriage to a foreign national, but it was not looked upon favorably. In any event, I had to choose which road to take. I told Cristina that I would like to meet her parents.

When I next rang the bell at the door to her apartment, her mother Rosina greeted me. She was a very tiny lady; she kept tilting her face upward, searching for my eyes. She ushered me in with a big hug and a little kiss on each cheek. I met Cristina's family. Then I met the neighbors' families. And then came the food.

Being away from my home for so long, I delighted in being invited into a family life. I could usually find Cristina's father, Eduardo, at his desk with the afternoon newspaper or staring out the window to the street below. He and Rosina had only two children, Cristina and her older sister. But with so many neighbors and friends bustling in and out it seemed like one big extended family. Even though I was from a different culture, I was immediately accepted and almost overwhelmed with their hospitality and generosity.

✻

Life was good. Professionally, things got even better with the arrival of my close friend from headquarters, Nick Jones. He and his wonderful family were another source of stability and a much needed lifeline. Moreover, Nick and I worked well together. We delighted talking ops by the hour and planning recruitments.

Shortly after Nick arrived, headquarters forwarded a directive from policymakers to increase CIA coverage of the situation in Mozambique, the former Portuguese colony, which, similar to Angola, had drifted into the Soviet orbit. Subsequently, we were asked to try and recruit reporting sources on Mozambique. A few days after we received the directive, I noted in one of the local newspapers that an individual active in Mozambique political affairs was currently touring. Using the alias of Joe Roberts and a ploy about conducting a marketing survey about possible business opportunities in Mozambique, I called the individual and met him in the lobby of the Sheraton Hotel. We had a pleasant conversation, but I think he suspected I had some type of undefined contact with the U.S. government. He mentioned that his son, Antonio, was also visiting. Antonio was a mid-level official in a Mozambique government ministry. One thing led to the next, and I met and subsequently assessed and developed Antonio over a series of meetings. I finally gave him a loose pitch structured in such a way that his acceptance would entail an introduction to a friend who worked at the American embassy. Of course, the entire scenario had been worked out in advance with Nick. A few days later Nick and I met Antonio for dinner in a nice seafood restaurant. After a pleasant conversation over appetizers, I gave Antonio my apologies, pleaded a pressing personal matter, and left him alone with Nick to finish dinner. Nick recruited Antonio. And later I had a good chuckle when Nick told me that when I left the restaurant, Antonio remarked that he really liked Joe Roberts but "he is a little naive."

Looking back I don't take any pride in case officers' manipulation of Antonio, his father, and countless others. Of course, the recruitment targets might have been playing case officers for their own purposes as well. Regardless, my work on Mozambique was a good example of how the system should work, i.e., the intelligence cycle, operational tasking, the recruitment cycle, close operational coordination, and the resulting production of foreign intelligence. Headquarters was pleased.

While these events were taking my time and attention, I was also closely following a sensitive Agency operation deep in the heart of the Angolan bush. By 1982 the only viable anticommunist force in Angola was UNITA, headed by Jonas Savimbi. Savimbi's forces were primarily based in the remote southeast corner of the country, an area from which they ventured out to conduct both guerilla-like raids and occasional deployments in force against the communist government's military forces and their Cuban allies. Despite the Clark Amendment, which prohibited U.S. government agencies from aiding anticommunist forces in Angola, policymakers were tasking the Agency to closely follow military and political developments in this hot battlefield of the Cold War.

I never really entertained thoughts of not volunteering for this new mission, which was certain to be an adventure on a grand scale. I would be literally transported into a totally different world. I hoped I would be able to use my background and training and to contribute to a different kind of Cold War battlefield. At the time, operations and opportunities like this in the Agency were extremely rare. Of course I wanted to go.

I also had practical reasons for volunteering for the operation in Africa. After almost two years running primarily Angolan agents, I knew the issues involved probably about as well as anybody in the U.S. government. The operation had risks, but it could advance my Agency career. And I thought that if the operation were successful, the Agency would be hard-pressed to oppose my plans to marry Cristina. During a trip back to headquarters, AF Division's director of personnel personally assured me that I should not have any problems with the Agency bureaucracy should I decide to marry Cristina. But I always had my doubts. I was particularly troubled because the new director of the CIA, William Casey, had ordered a review on the entire issue of marriage to foreign nationals.

I returned to the Washington, D.C., area in September 1982 and began training.

❋

Although his image and legacy have been tarnished over the last few years, in 1982 Jonas Savimbi was a larger-than-life figure at the top of the UNITA organization. Savimbi commanded the absolute loyalty of his native Ovimbindu tribe, of which he was both military commander and tribal chief. He dressed in camouflage fatigues, wore a green beret, and sported matching ivory on the handles of his cane and revolver. For good measure, he usually had a bowie knife tucked in his belt. I have kept to this day an autographed picture, inscribed to "Mr. John," of Savimbi decked out in the above regalia. The Angolan communist MPLA government called Savimbi a "bandit" and "terrorist," but conservative circles in Washington and elsewhere described him as a "freedom fighter" fighting the Soviet-proxy government in Luanda. Savimbi was strongly backed by the Reagan administration.

Still, about a month into my training regimen, the operation was terminated. I was truly disappointed. To this day I regret that it never materialized, though the cancellation wasn't anybody's fault. I comforted myself with the knowledge that it is quite common for risky special operations to be cancelled. In fact, if it were possible to keep score, I would wager that far more operations of this nature, held hostage to funding, timing, imagination, logistics, people, and politics, are cancelled than actually take place. Years later I would find that sensitive law enforcement operations suffered often-similar fates.

When the operation was cancelled, things started moving quickly for me on both professional and personal levels. I was invited to return to CIA headquarters for an assignment in AF division. And because I would no longer have to disappear into the African bush for a couple of years, I felt I could proceed with my plans to marry Cristina. Almost as soon as I received word that the assignment was cancelled, I filled out the appropriate Agency form, which included a mandatory pro forma offer of resignation clause, detailing my plans to marry a foreign national. I was assured that all of this was standard procedure and that the bureaucracy just wanted a chance to review my record. Told that it was just a "coincidence," I was concurrently summoned by the CIA's Office of Security to undergo their standard polygraph examination, which is administered approximately every five years to Agency employees. Naively, and just "in from the cold," I thought I had nothing to fear either from submitting my plans to marry a foreign national or in taking the exam. I sincerely felt that I had nothing to hide and was in fact proud of my record. Moreover, I took the Agency at its word that we were all "family."

The polygraph has long been the subject of much controversy. The CIA has a legitimate need to protect its security, and the polygraph is one of the chief tools that the Office of Security uses in its quest for truth and security. However, it is a mistake to believe the polygraph can somehow divine the truth. It is amply documented that honest people have failed the polygraph while dishonest people have passed.[3] The polygraph is actually a somewhat simple instrument that measures and records physiological activity; it cannot peer into the heart, soul, and mind of a subject. A blood-pressure cuff is wrapped around the upper arm and inflated. A tube is tied tightly around the torso to measure respiration. To detect changes in skin resistance brought about by perspiration, electrical leads are attached to two fingers. In theory, lying or deception induces nervousness or fear, which in turn creates stress, which reveals itself in measurable changes in cardiovascular activity, the rate and depth of breathing, and sweating. The success of the test rests on the ability of the operator to interpret the "arousal" reactions, or significant changes from the baseline recordings that are established as the norm in each of the recorded areas at the beginning of each polygraph or chart. If the machine is calibrated properly and the measurements are accurate, there should be discernable reactions to questions that pose problems for the examinee. But the results of the test also depend on the skill of the operator and the actual interview or interrogation.[4]

Carl, my examiner, seemed to pop right out of the Office of Security mold. He was a cross between a caricature of a grade-B movie detective and Sergeant Friday in the old TV series, *Dragnet*. Carl's job was to identify security threats to the CIA and America via the machine he had hooked to my body by asking personal and invasive questions. He seemed to enjoy it. He offered no idle chit-chat or humor. Carl was all business. That was fine with me. I had worked with his colleagues over the years as they administered polygraphs to many of my agents. I thought I knew exactly what to expect.

The first few questions were a walk in the park. Then Carl asked, "What foreign national knows of your employment with the CIA?" Having nothing to hide, I told him about Cristina. The machine had lots of physiological sensors, but I didn't hear any bells and whistles. It didn't matter if they didn't sound. Carl reacted like he had hit the jackpot at the lottery. Still not concerned, I started at the beginning and told him the story of my assignment, the recently aborted clandestine operation in Africa, and my decision to tell Cristina the truth about my employment because we had planned on getting married and I wasn't going to base our relationship on lies. My assignment to Africa would have meant that I would literally disappear for the next two years. I would be completely incommunicado. I told him that my relationship with Cristina was common knowledge both at my previous posting and at headquarters.

The story and my explanations fell on deaf ears. From that question on the polygraph exam went rapidly downhill and my stress levels went up. The regulations said I could not divulge my true employment to a foreign national and that was that. The operator was not going to get involved in debating the merits of policies and procedures or listening to real life reasons why I found that in one case it proved impossible to comply with the regulations. Carl could read my arousal reactions from the machine, but as a now-seasoned ops officer, I could also read him; I didn't need a machine. Before the exam I had anticipated understanding and common sense. I came to realize that I was going to get no quarter.

Office of Security types are rated, in part, on the number of "scalps" they collect, just like case officers are rated, in part, on their recruitments. It can be an adversarial relationship. Seeing an opportunity in me, Carl started to move in for the kill. Both my assignment and the African operation were sensitive. I didn't try to deny it.

"Put yourself in my situation," I said. "I know it is a technical violation but do you know how many covers I have had in the last five years? When I was hired by the Agency out of college, where much of the student body was foreign, I was told I could tell people that I worked for the CIA. First I became an overt analyst. After I was selected to the DO, I was told to tell everybody that I worked for another government agency. After completion of the career trainee program and anticipating that I was going to be assigned overseas with an official cover, I was told to use yet another agency as a cover. During my assignment overseas, my operational covers continued to change. I didn't have an office or any semblance of a normal business routine. I would disappear at odd hours. I was told to stay away from Americans and encouraged to make foreign friends. I found a very special friend. Cristina helped me get through that tour. Over the long time that I've known her, it was either tell her the truth or because of my crazy routine have her think that I was trafficking in narcotics. I certainly didn't tell her everything, but she was aware of my Agency employment."

My explanation made no difference. Carl used it the way an executioner would move to sharpen the axe. He was convinced there was more. In fact, Carl acted like he had uncovered a major counterintelligence threat to the United States.

I was still seated in the polygraph "hot seat." Carl told me to stay put. He said he wanted to examine his readings but would be "right back." He asked me to further examine my conscience. I was left alone in my disbelief, although probably monitored through a two-way mirror. I couldn't yet believe the Office of Security was making such an issue of disclosing the true nature of my employment to my fiancée. My disbelief then turned to focusing on my discomfort and then to feelings of anger. Carl had left me strapped in with the blood-pressure cuff and sensors attached to my body. After waiting over thirty minutes I realized he was not in any hurry to come back. Was this another stress test? Between the interrogation and the physical discomfort of being strapped in, I was rapidly losing patience. I finally decided that if he wasn't coming back I was going to look for him. I unhooked myself from the machine's sensors and wires. He wasn't outside, and I couldn't find anybody else from the Office of Security. I decided to go upstairs to his unit chief's office.

When I arrived at the office, the door was ajar. I looked in. Almost twenty-five years later I remember the scene clearly. I felt I was witnessing a Keystone Cops movie. Office of Security operatives were scurrying back and forth. They were all talking at once, and all were talking about me. It was apparent they thought they had discovered a major security breach. Lawyers were being called. Interrogation tactics were being discussed. Notifications to management were being prepared. At that moment, reality finally hit me. The Office of Security wasn't just trying to collect a scalp; they were after my head. My career with the CIA was in jeopardy. With a sick feeling in my stomach, I left the Office of Security and headed toward the office of the chief of AF Division, Dorwin Wilson.

Dorwin ushered me into his office. I didn't have to ask the question. I could see the hurt and disappointment on his face. "Dorwin," I said, "Have you heard what happened?"

"Have I heard? I've been given a blow-by-blow description. Look, nobody is accusing you of cooperating with foreign intelligence services. You didn't abuse government property and haven't used drugs. I think I understand what happened with that girl and why. But the Office of Security is a force to be reckoned with. I've already spoken with Mike Harvard, the Office of Security supervisor in charge of this inquiry. He is asking that you go home, get a good night's sleep, and come in tomorrow and finish the exam. Then we will see where we are."

Leaving Dorwin's office, I looked at other AF Division staff. Nobody would meet my gaze. Word traveled fast. I was already marked. My friends and colleagues were told to stay away from me.

Despite Dorwin's advice to get a good rest, I simply couldn't. My mind kept replaying the scenes. I honestly didn't know what I could have done differently. I knew if it weren't for Cristina, I might not have been able to make it through my tour. She became my best friend and the woman I wanted to marry. Looking past my emotions, I had also been trying to objectively assess her ability to function as an Agency spouse. It wasn't easy to find a partner with the personality, smarts, strength of character, and perspective necessary to help me live a double life in the far reaches of the world. She became my most important recruitment while I was overseas. She was innocent of all this intrigue. I could understand the prohibition of getting married to a Soviet or perhaps even someone from the East bloc. Why couldn't the Office of Security understand? I told people what was going on. Why were there double standards? The deputy chief had been living with a European diplomat. That apparently was OK, but marrying a local foreign national was not? A victim of poor tradecraft, another case officer operating at my post had been wrapped up by the local security services. If I was so "insecure," why did I have such a successful tour? My internal debate was finally resolved with the acceptance that, come what may, I would continue to be completely honest when the polygraph exam resumed.

The next morning I was back "on the box." This time Carl opened with tact and pleasantries. According to him, all he wanted was "the truth." And that is what I gave him. For hours I answered his pointed questions and told him all I could recall. His pleasant demeanor changed to more aggressive tones as he kept prodding, telling me the machine was showing signs of deception. Then he accused me of lying. He disregarded my protestations of innocence. He wasn't interested in context. My appeals for common sense went unanswered. At the end of a long day Carl finally felt that he got all he could from me. He did not prepare a summary of findings, and I wasn't asked to review and sign a statement. I was not offered counsel. The bottom line was that I had told the truth about my employment to my fiancée. For that breach of security, the Office of Security was prepared to throw the book at me.

Carl escorted me upstairs to Mike Harvard's office, the same office in which I had observed the Keystone Cops' routine the previous day. Harvard was sitting behind his desk as I walked in. As he pushed back his chair, he almost tripped on his sense of self-importance. In my opinion, Harvard seemed to be a self-appointed guardian of the CIA and all that it stood for. He didn't waste many words, telling me that I represented a major security threat to the United States and, as a result, I was to be put on administrative leave, with pay, pending further investigation. He directed me not to talk to any of my colleagues and said they would be directed not to talk to me. He gave me a telephone number that I was to call everyday to report in. Otherwise, he suggested I should stay home and not leave the greater Washington, D.C., area. My punishment was nothing more than a form of house arrest, courtesy of the Office of Security.

Harvard dismissed my explanations with a wave of his hand. "You'll get your day in court but first we need to review your case. After that it will go to the DDO [deputy director of operations]. He'll be the judge."

Confined by the dictates of the Office of Security, I could do nothing but wait for the Agency to make a ruling. Everyday, I dutifully called the telephone number I had been given to report in. Otherwise, I was left alone with my thoughts. My mind raced. My emotions were up and down like a roller coaster. What saved me was my knowledge that I had done nothing wrong, regardless of what the CIA thought. The Agency psychiatrist who had evaluated me prior to my joining the DO told me I was "disgustedly well adjusted." I certainly needed a level head to survive this ordeal. Although embarrassed in front of others, I could still look at myself in the mirror every morning. I knew exactly what had happened and why. In retrospect, I probably should have done more to bureaucratically cover myself. However, being a young officer it just didn't dawn on me that it was necessary. When I was in my DO training class, I had the nickname of "Polyanna." I had believed it when the Agency representatives told us that "we are family" and "our people are our most important resource." But even though I felt betrayed, I still held out hope that the Agency I loved would realize its mistake and make things right.

Barry Banks, a close friend in Washington, D.C., who had his own undeserved run-ins with the Office of Security and the polygraph, was sympathetic to my plight. He let me know that I was not unique. "John, this city is filled with the walking wounded, those who have suffered at the hands of the Office of Security and its misuse of the polygraph." A scholar in Soviet studies and a true gentlemen, he told me that those most likely to fail the polygraph are often the most innocent, those with a strong conscience and who exhibit strong responses to any accusation of wrong-doing. We both agreed that the scandalous behavior exhibited by the Office of Security must do horrible damage to the dreams and aspirations of young applicants and that many of the conscientious people who fail are exactly the type the Agency needs. Years later Agency contacts told me of their growing realization that one, albeit small, contributing factor to September 11 was the CIA's overreliance on the polygraph as a screening mechanism for personnel. The Agency suffered in the 1990s because the only case officer recruits that seemed to pass muster with the Office of Security were those that lived very sheltered lives—exactly the wrong kinds of people to send into the back alleys of the world where today's threats are found. Moreover, even the heavy-handed use of the polygraph had not prevented the long-running Aldrich Ames espionage case that surfaced in 1994 and other entrenched in-house scandals. Still today, security officials in the CIA and, to a lesser extent, the FBI love to champion the very real success stories of the polygraph. However, little is ever revealed about the Agency's overreliance on it as a security tool, its abuse in practice, and the need to balance security policies with common sense. The polygraph remains an intrinsic part of the CIA's culture.

For almost two months I waited under "house arrest" until I finally received word that the DDO, John Stein, wanted to meet with me and review my case. Stein headed up the Agency's clandestine service. He had a distinguished career and a background as a case officer. I hoped that if anybody could understand the realities of my assignment it would be him. I also hoped that the DDO would have the gravitas to stand up to the Office of Security. I used to be in awe of the Agency's ruling hierarchy, but the last few months had given me a new perspective on things.

Accompanied by Dorwin Wilson and other AF officials, I was very calm and delighted to finally "have my day in court," when I met Stein.

Stein started off the meeting by announcing that he had reviewed my file and that he wanted to say at the beginning that my record as a young case officer was "outstanding." Nevertheless, he was troubled with the report he had reviewed from the Office of Security. He asked me to explain to him why I divulged my Agency employment to Cristina. I did so. But this time, instead of talking to myopic technocrats in the Office of Security, I spoke to peers in the DO. They understood the realities of the field. They understood that things are not always black and white. I explained the facts of my cover considerations. This was made easier because some of the AF officials present had actually visited me in my overseas apartment. Stein nodded with understanding and then said, "John, what would you say if some of us have come to the conclusion that you divulged information to Cristina because you were trying to impress her." Without hesitation I responded, "I'm insulted." His face registered surprise. He was obviously not expecting that rejoinder. After I again explained my reasons and rationale, Stein said that he accepted my explanation. In his capacity as the DDO, he told me I could maintain my job with the Agency. But he wasn't sure what position I would have. I was filled with relief. I then asked whether I could marry Cristina. The officials answered that bureaucratically speaking, there wasn't anything standing in my way. When I left, I shook Stein's hand and gave him a sincere thank you. He had renewed my faith in the Agency. I never saw him or heard from him again.

Within a few days I flew back overseas. I formally proposed to Cristina while she sat on a park bench on a hill, which enjoyed a beautiful panoramic view of the city. We were married a month later. The ceremony took place on a gorgeous winter's day in a five-hundred-year-old church not far from Cristina's home. Although the Agency would not allow any of my friends and former colleagues to attend the ceremony, I spotted Nick Jones, my former colleague, observing the wedding scene right outside the church. Only Cristina, my family, and Nick and his family were aware of what had happened since I left many months before. My new parents-in-law, Rosina and Eduardo, and all of Cristina's family and friends were completely unaware she had married a CIA case officer. Almost twenty-five years later, they are still unaware.

As happy as I was, I was very anxious to finally get back to work. After a short but sweet honeymoon, Cristina and I together moved to the United States. We settled into our townhouse in Reston, Virginia, not too far from CIA headquarters. A few days after we returned, I went into the office expecting to hear about a new assignment. Instead, I was surprised to be escorted back to Mike Harvard and the Office of Security. True to form, he didn't mince words and he didn't congratulate me on my marriage.

"We are accepting your resignation from the Central Intelligence Agency." Dumbfounded, I asked him what he was talking about. Harvard reminded me that when I applied to get married to a foreign national, I had signed a document which stated I would offer to resign employment pending security review.

The old feelings came flooding back. "I thought that is exactly what the polygraph exam and the two-month security review were all about. The DDO reviewed the case himself. He told me I could remain with the Agency. He was supposed to be the judge."

Harvard replied, "I don't care what Mr. Stein said. I represent the Office of Security. You no longer work for the CIA. The director [William Casey] just instituted a new policy for agency employees who choose to marry foreign nationals. For security considerations, it is prohibited. You are the first employee who falls under this new policy. If you wish, you may appeal either to the director or the deputy director. That is your right. However, I don't think it will do much good."

Harvard was right. Despite the promise made to me by John Stein, the director of operations, and my later appeal to the deputy director of central intelligence, I was soon out of a job. I learned that nobody wanted to expend the political capital to confront the all-powerful Office of Security over a junior ops officer. I was being jettisoned because it was politically and bureaucratically expedient to do so. It was part of the Agency's way of doing business. Just like its overreliance on the use of the polygraph, political posturing and positioning were part of CIA culture. William Colby, a former director of the CIA, once wrote a book about the Agency and the culture that it generated called *Honorable Men*.[5] I had wholeheartedly believed in that culture. But there was nothing "honorable" about the way I was treated. Five years of loyal service under sometimes-trying circumstances counted for nothing. I was newly-wed and unemployed.

2

Undercover Agent

Even though I was forced to leave the Central Intelligence Agency in 1983, I wanted to continue to serve and participate in the challenges to U.S. national security. I also wanted to try to go back overseas. I felt like I had left behind a lot of unfinished business. So before my final departure from the Agency, I had a meeting with the Office of Security in which I insisted that the Agency not blackball me from future federal employment. The Office of Security admitted there were no grounds to keep me from working elsewhere in the government. To me that once again proved how hollow their stance was on the so-called security threat.

My immediate problem was to find work. While the long appeals process continued, the Office of Security had prohibited me from shopping my résumé. I resorted to the kind of work I became familiar with while going to school: I literally knocked on people's doors asking if they wanted me to mow their lawns or paint their homes. I had to support my new bride.

Cristina had a hard welcome to America. Nevertheless, her talent with languages soon helped to get her a job with the Department of State as an interpreter for visiting foreign officials and heads of state. In this position, she escorted many official delegations around Washington, D.C., and the United States. She even interpreted at a White House state dinner and other White House and Vice Presidential Mansion functions. She worked directly with President and Mrs. Reagan and Vice President and Mrs. Bush. I was very proud of her, but at the same time, her work just reinforced my views on the ridiculousness of CIA policy. One agency of the government, the CIA, had dismissed me from employment because they deemed my marriage to a foreign national a security risk. Meanwhile, another agency of the same government, the Department of State, had given my wife a job and sensitive assignments interpreting for the president of the United States!

Finally free to shop my résumé and apply for jobs, I applied to the Federal Bureau of Investigation, Drug Enforcement Administration (DEA), and Secret Service. I received a fairly quick job offer to be a supervisory analyst for the FBI in their new counterterrorist center at FBI headquarters. I accepted because I needed immediate employment. However, the position was dependent on a successful full-field background investigation. While waiting for the time-consuming background check to be completed, I continued with my other applications and I applied to become an FBI special agent.

There is a type of caste system of operatives and analysts in the U.S. law enforcement and intelligence communities. Since September 11 analysts have received increased respect, which is long overdue. The CIA initially hired me as an analyst before later selecting me to be part of the clandestine Directorate of Operations. I have always been thankful I had that first job at the Agency because it gave me some insight and empathy into an analyst's trade. But it was apparent many years ago, just as it is today, that prestige, adventure, and the ability to get things done still reside with those who are out in the field, i.e., the case officers and special agents. If my career path was taking me to federal law enforcement, I wanted to be a criminal investigator or special agent.

Counterintelligence, particularly attempts to monitor the Soviet espionage efforts directed against the United States, was a huge issue for the FBI. I reasoned that I would be an attractive candidate for the Bureau because as a former spy, I could possibly provide insight on how to help detect opposition spies. I successfully passed the FBI written exam, but when I telephoned to make an appointment for the oral exams, I was given bad news. Possible counterintelligence insights notwithstanding, because I was not an accountant, lawyer, woman, or minority and did not speak a foreign language of interest they were not interested.

During the subsequent Secret Service interview process, a team of Secret Service special agents actually came out to my house to interview Cristina—not because she was considered a security threat but rather because spouse interviews were part of the application process. They wanted to meet the perspective employee's spouse and let her know the kind of lifestyle that a Secret Service agent would have, that is, a lifestyle not conducive to family life. Cristina and I both appreciated the visit. I could only contrast the Secret Service's courtesy with my recently concluded ordeal with the Agency. In that case, not one CIA official even had the common decency to meet with my wife. I was convinced that if someone in the Office of Security had just taken the time to chat with her, the security issue would never have developed.

A job offer finally came, and on December 27, 1983, I reported for duty at the Washington, D.C., field office of the U.S. Secret Service. I was a special agent, at a grade of GS 7, step 10, with a salary of $21,527 a year, plus overtime. My appointment to the Secret Service was a five-grade demotion from my CIA rank. I didn't care. I just wanted to work in the field again.

❋

Today the Secret Service is part of the new Department of Homeland Security (DHS), but when I joined, it was part of the Department of the Treasury and boasted a long and distinguished history. The Secret Service, or Service as it is often called among the rank-and-file, was actually started in 1865 at the close of the Civil War. At that time it was estimated that almost one-half of the money in circulation was counterfeit. On April 14, 1865, then–Secretary of Treasury Hugh McCulloch proposed forming a federal anticounterfeiting unit to President Lincoln. Lincoln gave McCulloch the OK to proceed.

The official conversation with Secretary McCulloch was one of the last Lincoln had.[1] He was assassinated that same evening at Ford's Theater. The young Secret Service Division of the Department of the Treasury was successful at helping to curtail the epidemic of counterfeit currency and, as a result, was given additional responsibilities to combat fiscal fraud against the government. In the late nineteenth century, Secret Service agents at times were detailed to protect dignitaries, including the president. In 1901 President McKinley was assassinated while visiting Buffalo, New York. With Lincoln's assassination also still fresh in the nation's memory, there was a hue and cry from both the American people and Congress to take steps to protect the president. At the time the Secret Service was the only viable federal law enforcement agency that could take on the responsibility full-time. It moved in to fill the void and in 1906 was given statutory authority to protect the nation's commander in chief.

The mission of the Secret Service has continued to evolve over the years, but its core mandates of combating various types of financial crimes and protecting the president and other "protectees" designated by Congress remain. Investigation and protection are actually complimentary. The Service has found that their criminal investigations help prepare their agents for protective responsibilities. During investigations, agents learn to read people, size up situations, and if necessary react quickly and decisively. These are all necessary attributes for protection. Coming from the clandestine service of the CIA, I found it immediately apparent that the name "Secret Service" is, in part, a misnomer. There is very little "secret" about it. It does, however, very much execute a public trust or "service." I was very proud to carry its badge and be one of approximately two thousand special agents.

I reported on my first day with six other newly hired agents. Many of them had some sort of previous law enforcement experience. I had no background in criminal justice or investigations and didn't know what to expect. My formal training began many months later at the Federal Law Enforcement Training Center in Brunswick, Georgia, and was followed by another few months of training at the Secret Service Academy at Beltsville, Maryland. My on-the-job training began immediately. Like most of the new agents, I was assigned to the check squad, called the fraud squad in the Service. But because I was reporting to duty in Washington, D.C., I was also immediately considered a fresh body for ever-demanding protection details. Just as real-life CIA spies or case officers have little semblance to the fiction portrayed by Hollywood, my life as a Secret Service special agent was far different from popular belief.

For about three-and-a-half years, I rotated between investigations and protection. I cut my teeth in law enforcement, primarily learning how to investigate the fraudulent use of checks issued by the U.S. government. Reporting to the check squad, I was immediately assigned a number of open cases. Some could be solved rather quickly or even administratively closed with a few telephone calls and simple interviews. After a few weeks of on-the-job training, the scope and complexity of the investigations I was assigned soon increased. I learned to prepare and file my reports in the approved Service style. Law enforcement report writing is clear, concise, factual, and generally chronological.

I made my first arrest after having tracked down a small criminal group that processed stolen and forged U.S. Treasury checks. I conducted the "payee interview" and the "victim endorser interview," located and interviewed the suspects, took sworn statements and handwriting exemplars, and finally presented the investigative findings to an assistant U.S. attorney (AUSA) in Washington for prosecution. Criminal caseloads are so high for AUSAs that certain thresholds have to be met to get prosecution. If an AUSA declines prosecution, the federal agent can often try to get state prosecution. In this case, the suspect met with the AUSA and, as a result, entered into a plea-bargain agreement. Prosecution was declined for the other principal suspect because of his lack of criminal intent. The suspect pled guilty before a federal magistrate of the misdemeanor charge of "uttering," or passing a stolen U.S. check. He was sentenced to two years probation and restitution for the full amount of the seven checks. There were dozens of similar investigations that seemingly only varied in the details. These investigations provided much street and sometimes court experience. And just like a case officer is rated—in part—on recruits, I found that a special agent is rated—in part—on arrest and seizure statistics.

Pursuing the investigative leads in the check cases generally took us to the roughest neighborhoods of Washington, D.C. There I received quite an education. Some D.C. neighborhoods seemed as foreign a culture to me as anything I had seen overseas. I obtained a new kind of "street sense." The poverty and lifestyle were hard to believe. Crime, primarily caused by the prevalence of organized criminal narcotics networks, was all encompassing. The members of the check squad always teamed up with a partner when they ventured into the rough neighborhoods. We wanted a witness during our interviews, but we also wanted the extra security. Guns were commonplace in certain neighborhoods. In those days Washington, D.C., had one of the worst homicide rates in the country.

At the time the standard issue for Secret Service agents was a Smith and Wesson revolver, .357 caliber, model 19, 2.5-inch barrel, with a blue-steel finish. I was given lots of training in its use. Professional instruction, great training facilities, constant practice, and mandated monthly qualification standards make Secret Service agents some of the best shots among federal law enforcement personnel. It is a tremendous responsibility to be a badged law enforcement officer and carry a concealed weapon. Thankfully, only very rarely does an agent actually have to use a weapon in the field. In fact, most plain-clothed federal agents, whether the Secret Service, FBI, DEA, Internal Revenue Service, or today's DHS, never actually fire their weapons except at a training facility. Guns are, however, a necessary tool of the trade. They are there in case things go horribly wrong and to protect oneself or the public in exigent circumstances.

While it was very common for agents in the Secret Service's Washington field office to work all day in the depressed sections of the city, at night the same agents could be assigned to work protection events at the Kennedy Center, a five-star hotel, or a private residence. The protectee, politicos, and often foreign dignitaries and Washington glitterati would be in attendance. Often, as I stood guard, or "post," in the opulent surroundings, I could not help but think of the poor and dispossessed I had dealt with just hours before, only a short distance away. Their daily struggles to survive in the same city made a strong impact on me. It was hard to witness such poverty and despair coexisting with such affluence in the capital city of the richest country in the history of the world.

Shortly after participating in the 1984 presidential campaign as a member of protective teams that jumped or leapfrogged from place-to-place ahead of the candidates, I was switched from the check squad into the protective intelligence (PI) squad. As the name implies, PI is concerned with gathering information that represents a threat against a Secret Service protectee. Unfortunately, many of the individuals that cross the Secret Service's radar screen are mentally ill. There have been thirteen attempts to assassinate or harm a U.S. president. Twelve of those attempts have involved people judged to have had some form of mental illness. Other times potential PI subjects suffer from serious mental disorders that render them unable to function in the real world. Schizophrenia is the most common form of psychosis and sometimes causes delusional or hallucinatory thought and actions. Paranoid schizophrenia is particularly troubling because it can result in hostile or aggressive behavior. A paranoid schizophrenic is generally unable to engage in relationships and is overly suspicious. Of course, "normal" or mentally stable people, motivated by nonpsychotic disorders, also can become subjects of PI investigations. For example, a man in a bar could make an insulting and threatening remark against a Secret Service protectee. If somebody overhears the remark and it is reported out of context, an investigation may be initiated.

The White House is a magnet. Tourists come from all over America and the world to go on White House tours or to stand outside the wrought iron fence that circles the property to snap photos for the folks back home. Likewise, the White House can be a magnet for the mentally deranged and people who feel they are directed by outside forces to personally deliver messages to the U.S. president. These people also come from all over the country and all over the world. Normally, they approach one of the gates of the White House and demand to see the president. When that happens, the Uniformed Division of the Secret Service calls the PI squad of the Washington field office and a special agent is dispatched to conduct an interview. During my time with PI, the special agents didn't receive a lot of specialized training in recognizing mental disorders. Rather, they were requested and encouraged to use their interview skills and street sense to assess and evaluate the individual. The primary goal during the interview and possible subsequent investigations is to determine if the subject represents "a danger to himself or others." It is a credit to the Secret Service agents that they rarely make a mistake.

I interviewed dozens of PI subjects around the White House who suffered from nonpsychotic causes of frustration and also those who suffered with various types of mental illness. Every PI interview required an extensive report and generally follow-up fieldwork by the appropriate Secret Service field offices. There were many sad stories. Most of those suffering from mental illness had been previously diagnosed and had left the institution at which they had been receiving care. Many came from long distances, somehow making it to the White House. Whether coincidence or not, I found it interesting that most of my PI interviews took place during full moons. One subject told me that the CIA had kidnapped him and implanted a microchip in his brain. He believed he had consequently been receiving messages from the Agency ordering him to go see the president. One elderly lady was convinced she was Queen Victoria and had come to the White House to pay her respects to the U.S. president. A rather attractive young lady had a crush on Ronald Reagan and tried to get his attention by going to Lafayette Park across Pennsylvania Avenue and flashing her breasts; she then made threats against the first lady. Unfortunately, on a few occasions I had to make the decision that mentally troubled subjects could not be sent away safely and represented a possible threat; these people were sent to St. Elizabeth's mental hospital for evaluation.

One factor that contributed to the large number of mentally ill and homeless people visiting the White House was that in the mid-1980s, society abandoned many of those who had been in mental institutions, returning them to the community. The people returned were not considered dangerous to themselves or others by psychiatrists and lawyers. Having good intentions, these professionals thought their former patients would be happier on the street. The deinstitutionalization of the mentally ill was supported both by liberals and by fiscal conservatives.[2] When I was on the PI squad, I saw up close and personal what deinstitutionalization does. I got to know many of the mentally ill quite well. They could be found bathing in public fountains during the summer and warming themselves on steam grates in the winter. Outside of an institution, they didn't have the incentives or the reminders to take their medication. Typically, they also suffered from self-delusion. They believed they weren't actually sick and didn't need medicine at all. But schizophrenia and manic depression require medical treatment. Some of the mentally ill people who visited the White House did not politely approach a gate to chat with a Uniformed Division officer. On a number of occasions, I was confronted with "gate jumpers" and others who exhibited more aggressive or hostile intentions. Incidents occur very quickly, but it is an additional credit to the Secret Service, both the agents and the Uniformed Division, that very rarely do they escalate out of control.

Despite some wonderful adventures and the honor of serving in an outstanding organization with some great people, I eventually realized the Secret Service was not for me. Frankly, standing post or guard on a marble floor at 3:00 AM and counting the holes in acoustic ceiling tiles, trying to stay awake, is not a lot of fun. Moreover, I felt I was constantly waiting for nothing to happen. I never served in the military, but I imagine peacetime military service is comparable. After a while, training gets old. Agents are thankful when nothing happens, but at the same time they want some real action. I felt I was going brain-dead standing post. Perhaps, if I had started in another field office that dealt more with investigations, rather than in Washington, D.C., with its emphasis on protection, I would have stayed. I enjoyed being out on the street doing casework. But assigned to Washington, D.C., I was usually just another body, another post stander.

I was told I was a good agent, a high form of compliment in the

Service. Because of my foreign language experience, I traveled to a number of countries with Presidential and Vice Presidential Protective Divisions advance teams. During my interaction with the Presidential Protective Division, I was asked about joining the detail—an elite assignment but one that also meant I would constantly be on the road. By this time, Cristina and I were expecting our second child. During the initial interview process, the Secret Service warned us about family pressures. I didn't understand then, but when I actually had a young family, I didn't want to become an absentee husband and father.

Over the years I had heard about the U.S. Customs Service. Like the Secret Service, Customs was part of the Department of the Treasury. In fact, it had an even longer history within Treasury, and its accomplishments were also very impressive. When they think of Customs most people think of inspection and control at airports, seaports, and land-border crossings. Although important work, it doesn't sound glamorous. However, Customs also had an investigatory side staffed by special agents, which dealt primarily with U.S. transborder cases. Customs investigators didn't get a lot of public recognition, but within law enforcement circles, they were well respected. The agency's involvement in international issues appealed to me, so I applied.

Because I was already an agent for the Department of the Treasury, the application process wasn't very painful. The Customs office in the northern Virginia office of Reston, which conducted my preemployment background investigation, was at the time initiating a new undercover weapons investigation. The Customs special agent who was the chief "undercover" needed a partner. He heard about my background in the CIA and thought I would be a natural fit. I was asked if I would consider Reston as my office of assignment. I was excited about the possibility of joining Customs, and having an immediate opportunity to participate in a law enforcement undercover operation sounded very adventurous. When the formal offer came, I accepted. I stopped working for the Secret Service on Friday and reported to work at Customs the following Monday.

✳

The U.S. Customs Service was justifiably proud of its mission, history, and heritage. Congress recognized the importance of Customs early on, in 1789, when it passed the Customs Organization Act. In fact, until the income tax became a permanent feature of the U.S. tax system with the passage in 1913 of the Sixteenth Amendment, the U.S. government depended on customs duties as its primary revenue source. The mission and organization grew. By the mid-1980s, the average traveler returning to the United States from a trip abroad would encounter Customs inspectors. There were, at that time, approximately six thousand personnel, who staffed roughly three hundred U.S. ports and border crossings. Customs also had an Office of Enforcement, which consisted of about three thousand special agents and other support personnel. Enforcement was responsible for various investigative programs, tactical interdiction, and intelligence support. The Customs Office of Enforcement was charged with enforcing over four hundred laws, more than the FBI handled. Although the focus at the time was the War on Narcotics, just about anything that had nexus to the border came under the Customs domain. Long before September 11 the U.S. Customs Service was part of this nation's first line of defense.

The Office of the Resident Agent in Charge (RAC) in Reston comprised about a dozen special agents. The agents were divided into groups that focused on various customs violations. Primarily because of my overseas background and experience with the CIA, I was assigned to the strategic group that focused on the illegal export of U.S. weapons and high technology to prohibited end users.

I learned that manufacturers and exporters of certain categories of U.S. exports were required to have licenses issued by the governmental entity that controlled the commodity they manufactured or exported. For example, the Department of State issued licenses to manufacturers and exporters of strategic or sensitive munitions items, and these manufacturers and exporters were required to register with the Office of Munitions Control. Periodically, the Department of State published a munitions list identifying articles that require such licensing. The Department of Commerce regulates the export of critical and sensitive U.S.-manufactured technical items under the Export Administration Act. Individual validated licenses are issued by the Department of Commerce upon application by an exporter. No commodity or technical data subject to the Export Administration Act regulations may be exported without the proper approval and license.

Weapons and technology with military applications that is engineered, produced, and manufactured in the United States have a ready market around the world. During the Cold War, there was a tremendous demand from the Soviet bloc for state-of-the-art American weapon systems. China, Iran, Libya, and other nonfriendly players were also very active in their attempts to procure desired weapons and technology. Decisions as to which countries could receive U.S. weapons became instruments of U.S. foreign policy. For example, during the Iran-Iraq War of the 1980s, the United States gave support to Saddam Hussein's Iraq. The United States also ensured Israel's survival by providing weapon systems that would defeat anything the Israeli armed forces would confront on a battlefield. In addition, during a time when apartheid South Africa was viewed globally as a pariah state, U.S. arms sanctions against South Africa were lodged in concert with a United Nations (UN) arms embargo.

In this environment a shadowy underworld of international arms dealers and brokers thrived. They operated everywhere from sophisticated office suites in European capitals and high-rise towers in Singapore to colorful Arab *souks*, or markets, and on the fringes of never-ending African conflicts. Their tools were the telephone, fax, and telex. The arms dealers' success was dependent on their ability to network their international contacts. The lure was an occasional hefty commission, which was obtained by locating and brokering items for sale against buyers' requirements. Many of the brokers represented clients who were simply fronts and cutouts of governments and their intelligence and military services. Into this milieu stepped Don Bludworth, special agent, U.S. Customs.

During the Vietnam War, Don had won distinction as a "tunnel rat." Because he was rather small in size, he had the physical ability—and courage—to burrow into the Viet Cong's tunnels and hiding places. Years later, when he joined Customs, his ballsy nature made him a natural undercover agent. By the time I joined him in April 1987, Don had already had a series of successful undercover stings that targeted the underworld of arms brokers. The previous undercover operations he was involved in while assigned to the Reston office were rather limited in scope but did result in arrests and convictions. This time Don convinced the office management and the Customs bureaucracy at the regional and headquarters levels to mount a more complex operation, which was code-named Project Wayward.

In short order, I was named Don's partner in this fledgling undercover operation. Ideally, undercover operations have at least two govern-ment participants. The partners act as overlapping witnesses, cover one another's backs in case something goes wrong, and backstop the techni-cal monitoring of undercover conversations. In addition to my role as an arms dealer, I was also asked to double as the administrative project man-ager. I handled the books and wrote the checks for the approximately $100,000 project. Harold Gay was named the case agent. He wrote the case reports, coordinated surveillance teams, and did the many other tasks necessary for a successful operation.

Don was very welcoming, and we immediately hit it off. He took me under his wing and started giving me tutorials in Customs, the use of undercover operations as a law enforcement technique, and the inside world of arms dealers. I had a lot to learn.

Customs recognized that the greater Washington, D.C., area was a natural location for "strategic" investigations. In addition to being the center of government, Washington was rapidly becoming a major locale for defense and high-technology representatives and manufacturers. Cus-toms had pioneered "Gemini" outreach programs to educate the muni-tions and tech industries on illegal attempts to procure their products. Some industry contacts who participated in the Gemini programs be-came valued sources or informants who discreetly provided very useful information to U.S. Customs. Don had a stable of industry informants who had helped him develop promising targets of investigation. These insiders also provided Don with useful industry insight and scuttlebutt. In undercover investigations, particularly those targeting arms dealers, credibility is the name of the game. As I soon found out, the bottom line in being a successful undercover operative was having the ability to make the target believe that I was who I said I was.

Our undercover "storefront" was located in a prestigious business development near Georgetown in Washington, D.C. The name of our front company was Military Armaments and Communications (MARCOM). Don had the main MARCOM office, which was a welcom-ing but generally nondescript room with a desk, chair, couch, and plenty of natural lighting and lamps. He displayed some pictures and potted plants to give the office a little warmth. Late one night Don and I accompanied Customs technical support staff as they installed audio and video record-ing equipment. Hidden in Don's office were microphones and microlenses, which provided audio and video coverage of our meetings. I had the adjoining office, which also contained basic office furniture in addition to a cabinet full of the electronic monitoring and recording devices. The other tenants in the building were completely unaware that an undercover Customs operation was in their midst. Only the building manager was aware of the true nature of MARCOM.

Because of the backlog of new special agent recruits, I wasn't sent to the Customs training academy for another year. However, I did receive some tutorials in the law enforcement aspects of undercover Customs operations—which were quite different from my undercover experiences with the Agency. Included in the tutorials were discussions with an AUSA based in Washington, D.C. In particular, the attorney tutored me on entrapment. Undercover law enforcement agents engage in a kind of courtship with a target. Everything depends on an agent's ability to gain credibility, set the hook, and consummate the transaction. Yet courts have ruled that a target is "entrapped" when he is induced or persuaded by law enforcement agents to commit a crime that he had no previous intent to commit. It is not entrapment if the subject is ready and willing to break the law and law enforcement provides only an opportunity for the person to commit the crime. If evidence leaves a reasonable doubt as to whether the person had any intent to commit the crime prior to inducement or persuasion by a government agent, the person is not guilty. As a result, surreptitiously recorded undercover conversations become an extremely important record for both the government and the defendants. The recorded conversations become the primary record of intent. From a law enforcement perspective, playing back the suspect's own incriminating words in a court of law is wonderful evidence.

Undercover investigations are just one tool in the U.S. federal criminal investigators' toolbox. Other law enforcement tools and techniques such as surveillance and following the paper trail are also employed to support investigations. But over the years U.S. law enforcement has found that undercover operations are in some cases the only method available to successfully penetrate a criminal organization. Once an agent is inside, invaluable intelligence can be obtained and the eventual takedown of the organization can be orchestrated. In contrast, many countries around the world do not allow undercover operations. Some foreign governments are concerned about rogue operations or the possibility of "agent provocateurs," who incite incriminating action. U.S. law enforcement acknowledges these concerns by operating undercover investigations with numerous safeguards, oversight, and checks and balances.

Before I joined Project Wayward, Don had identified possible targets for the undercover sting. Some of the targets had surfaced, but had not been pursued, in his previous investigations. Others had been referred to him by informants. But in reality we weren't planning to rely solely on these targets. An undercover operation can be compared to throwing out a net; you never know what you might catch. Don and I soon put the finishing touches on the MARCOM office. We were ready for business. The net was out. Don, under the alias Donald Gordon, contacted potential targets to let them know that he had a new business and a new partner. My alias was John Costa. I chose an undercover background that dovetailed with my previous work overseas. I learned in the Agency, and it was confirmed with law enforcement, that an undercover operative should choose a cover with which he is familiar.

One of Don's previous targets was Kenneth Dobson, a resident of the Republic of South Africa who had made inquiries regarding the purchase and resale of various items of U.S. military equipment. If the sales Dobson inquired about were completed, they would have been in violation of both the Arms Export Control Act and the Comprehensive Antiapartheid Act that was then in force. With the establishment of MARCOM, Don again renewed contact. The South African again made inquiries about the acquisition of various items on the munitions list. But inquiries are not a violation of law. And talk and telexes are cheap. Bullshitting is the name of the game with arms dealers. We didn't believe that Dobson was serious or that the inquiries would go far.

However, a number of months later, a rather young, brash, and enthusiastic individual arrived unannounced at the MARCOM office and introduced himself as Frank Rizzo. Rizzo said he was the president and CEO of a Washington, D.C., trading firm and a former member of the U.S. Navy special forces SEALS. He was accompanied by an attorney from the United Kingdom. Don and I were thankful that when they unexpectedly showed up at MARCOM, we were both there and in role. I quickly ducked into my office, turned on the equipment and slipped in a recording tape. After I made sure everything was working properly, I joined the group back in Don's office.

Rizzo was aggressive. He was a self-styled soldier of fortune and given to braggadocio. He was of medium height but packed a powerful build. His eyes darted as he spoke, checking out MARCOM, Don Gordon, and John Costa. He told us that ever since he had left the SEALS, he had been active in the arms business. He explained that during the course of his business, he had completed some minor transactions with Ken Dobson in South Africa and Dobson's partner, Pierre Blanc. He added that it was Blanc, also known as "Frenchman," who was well connected in South Africa and that the requirements they were pursuing resulted from those contacts. Rizzo had heard about MARCOM from his South African associates and freely admitted that he had stopped by to check us out. Don parried his inquiries with aplomb and gave the visitors the impression that we were viable brokers. We elicited enough personal information so that the two men could later be fully identified in our law enforcement databases. We had to find out specifically who had just entered into our net.

Over the next few months the checking and courtship continued. Don and I established a good working relationship with Rizzo. We discussed numerous possible deals, nothing illegal. Inquiries primarily involved obtaining spare parts for C-130 aircraft for Nigeria. It was obvious Rizzo was trying to get to know us. He wanted to feel comfortable with whom he was dealing with. Conversely, as undercovers, Don and I were trying to reinforce our credibility while waiting for Rizzo to take the bait and propose an illegal transaction. Because of the entrapment guidelines, we were very careful not to generate the idea of committing a crime or to persuade him to do so.

All of our conversations had to be a matter of record. When we spoke with Rizzo or other potential targets on the telephone, the conversations were recorded. Our meetings with targets at MARCOM were likewise recorded. Sometimes we met with Rizzo or other targets in a bar or at a restaurant. In those cases, I carried a concealed recording device on my person. Although the technology and techniques have changed, at the time I found what worked best for me was to secure the recording device in my groin area and tape the microphones to my chest. Suffice it to say this was uncomfortable, but I wore the device below the belt for a reason: sometimes, in the macho and suspicious world of arms dealers, I was greeted with a handshake and a simultaneous running of the other hand down my back in a playful, patting manner. This maneuver appeared innocent but was meant as a check for hidden wires. After a meeting, Don and I would play back the tapes. If we discovered technical problems or there was too much background noise, making the conversations inaudible, we immediately wrote a memo for the file outlining the conversation. By the end of Operation Wayward, we had collected hundreds of transcripts of conversations.

Don was the primary undercover in our meetings. He had to focus on what was being said. We didn't want to burden him with also wearing a recording device or running the equipment. Meetings in the MARCOM office could easily last over the one-hour limit on the audiotape. I would participate in the conversations, but simultaneously I would always keep track of the time. When I knew the tape was about to run out, I would make an excuse to leave the meeting and go to my adjoining office and change the tape. Changing the tape in the concealed devices I wore in meetings outside the office was more problematic.

Regardless of our preparation, strange things could happen. Once, Don and I were with Rizzo in a nice Washington-area hotel restaurant and I knew I had to change the tape. I made my excuses and went to the restroom. I had to get partially undressed to retrieve the tape recorder and unhook the wires to put in a fresh tape. The systems available today are different, but back then we primarily used a NAGRA recording device that operated a mini reel-to-reel system. The system was fairly bulky, but we liked it because the recording quality was high. As I was sitting on the toilet taking the tape out of the recording device, the tape slipped out of my hand. It bounced on the floor, rolled under the partition, and headed toward the door. All the while, the precious recording tape was unwinding! I quickly zipped up and ran after the tape, dodging the startled patrons of the restroom and their curious looks. I wound up the tape on the empty spool and made a very ungraceful exit. Things like that never happen in Hollywood cop shows.

Popular media also portrays federal undercover agents as living the good life. In fact, it was essential for the success of Project Wayward and our operational "credibility" to give the impression that MARCOM was successful and that Don Gordon and John Costa were financially well off. The reality was that both Don Bludworth and John Cassara were low-grade civil servants. In the late 1980s, studies showed that journeymen federal law enforcement agents in the Washington, D.C., area earned a smaller salary than unionized grocery clerks. To get around our modest means, Customs let Don borrow a seized Mercedes automobile and a Rolex watch. Of course, since the goodies were government property, as soon as the operation was over they were promptly returned. The more immediate problem we both had was dressing the part. There certainly wasn't any clothing allowance. Don taught me that buying new shirts and ties and interchanging jackets and slacks helps keep a wardrobe looking new at a low cost.

The credibility that we worked so hard to achieve finally bore fruit. Almost five months after Rizzo appeared unannounced at the MARCOM offices, he proposed the type of illegal transaction that we had been waiting for. Rizzo surfaced a scheme to illegally export and divert thirty-eight gyroscopes to South Africa. The gyroscopes were manufactured in the United States by the Northrop Corporation and required an export license. The former SEAL team member said that he had previously tried, without success, to purchase the gyroscopes directly from Northrop. Thinking the deal was suspicious, Northrop would not acquiesce to the sale. Rizzo now proposed that he and the Frenchman establish a front company in Canada for the express purpose of diverting the gyroscopes through Canada to South Africa. He wanted MARCOM to purchase the gyroscopes from Northrop under the pretense that the equipment would only go to Canada. Rizzo added that his South African contacts would produce the needed purchase orders, letter of intent, and all other related documents for the purchase and shipment of the gyroscopes. Particularly important to our investigation, Rizzo acknowledged that both he and the Frenchman had developed the diversion scheme because they were aware that the gyroscopes could not be legally exported to South Africa.

Things started moving quickly. Over the next few days the Frenchman telephoned Don and said that an associate in Canada by the name of Morty Bergman would help structure the transaction. Shortly thereafter, Rizzo and I met in the MARCOM office. I asked him if he thought Morty would travel to Washington, D.C., "so that everybody could meet face to face." Rizzo said that no meetings should be held in the United States because then the job "would be considered a conspiracy." I didn't want there to be any misunderstanding at all on Rizzo's part about what we were about to do so I replied, "What we are doing now is a conspiracy."

The former SEAL team member and self-styled arms broker agreed and the hidden microphone captured every word.

Ten days later Morty traveled to Washington and met with Rizzo, Don Gordon, and John Costa in the MARCOM office. Collectively, we were conspirators in our efforts to circumvent the Arms Export Control Act. Morty was about thirty years old, soft-spoken, slight of build, and quite intelligent. He described himself as a South African national who had been residing in Canada for the last few years. He explained that his principal business was in the diamond industry as neither Canada nor the United States would recognize his South African law degree. Morty said that he came to Washington to meet with us per the request of the Frenchman. He added that the South Africans wanted to be reassured that MARCOM was legitimate and that they would be "comfortable" working with their American contacts.

As the meeting continued, we discussed in detail the scheme to illegally export the gyroscopes to South Africa, including pricing, the legal ramifications, the establishment of a front company, methods of shipping the items, and how to launder the profits. Morty described one of his contacts in Israel as an "intelligence type." He said he would travel to Israel to meet with this individual; determine if there was a violation of Israeli law; set up a front company in Israel to handle the transshipment; and determine if the material could, in fact, just be delivered directly to the South African embassy in Tel Aviv.

Morty was also working on setting up banking arrangements in the Isle of Man. He explained to us that it was just as important to launder the money as it was to transship the goods. Rizzo added that, "The thing that could blow this whole thing apart is to trace the dollars. . . . You want to lay enough traps out there so it is just impossible for these people." He continued, "You make it such a pain in the balls that they're committing suicide. The guys have a heart attack trying to crack it . . . no paper trails. The way you do it is to layer it. And you throw so many layers at them . . . their heads start spinning. They get around one barrier and they hit another." As somebody who subsequently spent a lot of time investigating money laundering, I can attest to the accuracy of Rizzo's statement.

After our Washington, D.C., meeting, Morty traveled to Israel to put in place the infrastructure for the deal. Shortly thereafter, the Frenchman faxed a purchase order for the gyroscopes to MARCOM. The purchase order had originally been forwarded to Kivun Communications and Guidance Systems Ltd. in Jerusalem, the cover company Morty had established in Israel to facilitate the transaction. Later, we also received an end-user certificate listing Kivun Communications as the final destination for the gyroscopes. By this time, from discussions with Morty and Rizzo, it appeared that the actual buyer of the gyroscopes in South Africa appeared to be a subcontractor of the huge South African arms manufacturer, Armaments Corporation of South Africa, or Armscor.

While the undercover operation proceeded, Northrop received an inquiry from Israel Aircraft Industries Ltd. (IAI). The Israeli company requested the same number of gyroscopes with specifications identical to those requested by the South Africans. In fact, Morty had previously identified IAI as a firm that could assist in acquiring the gyroscopes for diversion to South Africa.

Meanwhile, a mysterious South African traveled all the way from South Africa to Washington to meet with us at MARCOM. Customs agents, under the guidance of Case Agent Harold Gay, put the South African under surveillance for his entire visit. Although our visitor was never positively identified, we surmised that he was from a South African intelligence service that had also wanted to "check us out"; apparently, this was an exercise of spy versus undercover law enforcement. We obviously passed his test because in a meeting shortly thereafter, Rizzo told Don and me, "We've got running orders right now to expand our network, to send them potential sources for different types of equipment. . . . The idea is to expand our network. The word I have from the boys overseas is that the government likes what we've done with our channels and they want us to grow and prosper. They [the South African government] are going to have a lot of business flowing our way."

We never learned for certain what the gyroscopes were to be used for. At that time Armscor had known ties with Saddam Hussein's Iraq. One theory was that the gyros were to be part of Armscor-produced antiarmor munitions destined for Iraq's military. We even had one undercover meeting with an Iraqi general. However, later undercover conversations suggested that the U.S.-manufactured equipment was to be used in a South African antiarmor missile designed to defeat the top-of-the-line Soviet T-80 battle tank. The Soviets had supplied the Angolan government, run by the Marxist Popular Movement for the Liberation of

Angola (MPLA), T-80 tanks, and there was apparently concern within the South African military regarding how to defeat the tank if it were confronted on a battlefield. Whatever the end use, signs suggested that Project Wayward had also tapped into the underworld relationship between Israel and the apartheid government of South Africa.

In the mid-1980s Israel lobbied hard for U.S. support for a new jet fighter with technology on par with the U.S.-manufactured F-16. Israel's Ministry of Defense, IAI, and politicians argued that the development of the fighter aircraft, named the Lavi, was a matter of both survival and national pride. However, the plane's prototype was built in large part with American technology and $1.3 billion of American taxpayer funds.[3] As part of the deal, Israel guaranteed that the technology transferred from the United States for the development of the Lavi would stay in Israel. After the prototype was developed, the decision was made to cancel production primarily because of its enormous price tag. The debate was intense and feelings ran high on all sides.

Project Wayward and my personal discussions with U.S. aeronautical industry representatives indicated that the sale and transfer of some U.S. technology that designated Israel as the end user was, in turn, transferred by Israel to South Africa. Personally, I wanted the investigation to pursue this connection. I felt the MARCOM undercover operation had an unprecedented opportunity to get a glimpse into the underworld of personal contacts and wheeling and dealing that has seen U.S.-designed and U.S.-funded technology and weaponry transferred from Israel to third parties in violation of U.S. law. I wanted Don Gordon and John Costa to travel to Israel and South Africa to meet with some of the players and potentially widen the net.

U.S. law enforcement undercover operations overseas are permitted, but only with the full knowledge and participation of the host country. For example, during Project Wayward, Don and I had undercover meetings with Morty in Canada. The meetings were fully coordinated with the Canadian authorities by the U.S. customs attaché assigned to the American embassy in Ottawa. The Royal Canadian Mounted Police did a fantastic job of providing full surveillance and operational support during the meetings. However, U.S. law enforcement undercover agents cannot operate in a foreign country without the host country's permission. I had to remind myself that I was no longer in the CIA, which, as we have seen, routinely conducts operations without the knowledge of the local government. In the case of Israel and South Africa, such cooperation would have been impossible. Moreover, the operation would have been too dangerous. Without diplomatic immunity, Don and I would have been subject to arrest and detention. And the governments involved in the scheme were part of the problem—not the solution. Besides, official Israel is generally considered hands-off in both the U.S. intelligence and law enforcement communities. Despite the restrictions, I informally proposed a possible operational scenario to the AUSA in Washington who was coordinating the investigation. He quickly vetoed it by saying, "What would you like me to do, indict the government of Israel?"

As an interesting postscript, the same U.S. technology that was transferred in the mid-1980s to support development of the Israeli Lavi has recently appeared in a new Chinese warplane. According to an unclassified U.S. Office of Naval Intelligence report entitled *Worldwide Challenges to Naval Strike Warfare*, the design of the new Chinese warplane was "undertaken with direct external assistance, primarily from Israel and Russia, with indirect assistance through access to U.S. technologies." In fact, the potential adversarial fighter is "based heavily on the canceled Israeli Lavi program."[4]

During the plentiful downtime we had in the MARCOM office waiting for the next meeting or phone call, Don gave me a continuing education on the arms business, the Customs Service, and Customs politics and personalities. I had already been struck by some questionable practices and integrity issues in the Customs bureaucracy—which was so much different from what I had previously encountered in the CIA and the Secret Service. Although the overwhelming percentage of Customs employees was competent, honest, and honorable, frankly, I was sometimes appalled by the many scandals and instances of mismanagement that seemed to permeate the organization at all levels. Don educated me on the culture of the Customs bureaucracy and why such behavior was allowed to continue. He summed it up by saying, "Management protects management. If it didn't, the whole system would collapse." Many years later I feel that expression encapsulates much of the failure in leadership and outright moral cowardliness that I saw throughout my career in the government and that was, in my opinion, a contributing factor to the failures surrounding September 11.

Although I had hit the ground running in Project Wayward, the group supervisors involved didn't fully understand undercover operations. They thought that I should spend half of my time away from MARCOM working traditional Customs investigations. Particularly with my Agency background and understanding of the necessity of establishing suitable cover, I was appalled at Customs' operational ignorance. One simply can't be undercover half of the time and official law enforcement the other half of the time. To put it mildly, this is poor tradecraft that can too easily jeopardize an operation and put the agents involved at risk. Don and I had both received some not too subtle threats. Experience has proved that a successful undercover needs to live the life he impersonates. It can't be done part-time.

Management undoubtedly interpreted my hesitation to be both an undercover operative and overt law enforcement agent as arrogance, laziness, or both. An incident in the office only reinforced my views: Another special agent involved in a comparatively small-scale and temporary undercover investigation was ordered by his group supervisor to simultaneously work overt Customs investigations at nearby Washington Dulles airport. By sheer coincidence, the target of his undercover investigation arrived unexpectedly at the airport and saw the agent in his true role. Needless to say, that was the end of the agent's investigation.

Project Wayward, similar to other long-term undercover investigations, took about two years to complete from the first meetings to the arrests. That is a comparatively long time frame for law enforcement management. I found first in Project Wayward, and later in other law enforcement operations, that neither patience nor focus are part of management's virtues. This situation is made worse when the investigation deals with a complex subject that is not readily understood. Moreover, many in management are risk adverse and have little experience with undercover work. Too often, some agents and managers are content to work ho-hum investigations, get their simple stats, and put out the occasional organizational fire. Initiative and imagination are not always encouraged. I found many years later that the same issues continue to haunt us in the stalled War on Terrorist Finance.

Participating in the undercover meetings, I never ceased to be amazed by Don's acting performances. He would have been outstanding on a real stage or screen. Professional actors could have learned lessons from him on how to live a role. He would constantly plot strategy and rehearse possible scenarios and conversations. Prior to one undercover meeting for which he had to engineer "complications" into the deal to slow things down a bit, I saw how Don psyched himself into the role. He morphed before my eyes from Don Bludworth into Don Gordon. During the subsequent meeting, as the very fluid situation demanded, I saw him both shake with rage and deliver impromptu lines of subtlety. Although Don was a great undercover operative because he knew the arms industry so well, I think the success of the operation truly revolved around his ability to act and inspire credibility. He was the best undercover agent I ever saw, either in law enforcement or the intelligence community.

As the deal for the purchase and export of the gyroscopes was finally reaching fruition, Ann Culligan, a broker from New England, contacted MARCOM. Culligan said that she had a business partner in South Africa who had instructed her to contact MARCOM and make arrangements to take delivery of the gyroscopes. Culligan explained that they "do this kind of thing not infrequently," referring to the illegal exportation of controlled commodities. And in a follow-up telephone conversation with Don, Culligan said that she was aware of the restrictions and sanctions currently in force against South Africa but that they only meant more business and profits for her.

Culligan and her husband later drove their van from their New England residence to the MARCOM office in Washington and from there to a local freight forwarder where the gyroscopes were being held. The gyroscopes were turned over to the Culligans, and Ann signed a receipt in alias. Agents from the Reston office surveilled the Culligans all the way back to their residence. The following day customs agents from Reston and Boston executed a search warrant on the residence and seized the wooden crate containing the five gyroscopes. I participated in the search but was also busy working with the AUSA and the case agent, preparing an affidavit for the issuance of arrest warrants.[5] A few days later Morty was lured back to Washington, where he was arrested. The arrest of Frank Rizzo followed. Two South Africans were indicted.

It was a nice case. The story made the *New York Times* and the *Washington Post* and was covered briefly by the national television networks. The defendants were charged with conspiracy, violation of the Arms Export Control Act, and the first prosecution under the Antiapartheid Act in federal court in the District of Columbia. In addition, Bergman, Blanc, and Rizzo were all charged with money laundering. This presents another difference between the intelligence and the law enforcement communities: When I was with the Agency, intelligence failures sometimes made it into the press, but the success stories did not. Recognition was not sought after. In law enforcement, management craves favorable press and publicity. In part this is because of ego but it is also because favorable press is one of the best catalysts and justifications for additional resources.

At the trial, I sat in a witness-prep room with Morty Bergman. It was the first time we had spoken since I had posed as John Costa in the MARCOM office. I had always liked Morty. During the operation, I had gotten to know him very well. Over shared meals, frequent telephone calls, and face-to-face meetings, we discussed our lives and hopes and dreams. He understandably felt betrayed. As part of a plea-bargain agreement, Morty was waiting to testify. He told me that he had major reservations working with Rizzo and that he had also harbored some doubts about Don. Morty said that even though he knew the scheme was illegal, he had decided to participate because I had come across as so sincere and "levelheaded"; he had trusted me. This awkward conversation with Morty in the witness-prep room illustrates the paradox of long-term undercover work: special agents work to establish credibility and a rapport with their targets only to betray them in the end. When a police officer witnesses a crime and then arrests somebody on the street, two lives intersect for a brief period of time. There is a clear "good guy" and a "bad guy." If the police officer ever has to testify at trial, he or she can do so with a clear conscience. The morality of undercover work is not so clear cut. The "target" and the "undercover" enter into a long-term relationship that is intertwined between the professional and personal. It's very hard.

During Project Wayward, I followed Don's lead and began to recruit my own assets and reporting sources, primarily industry representatives and those involved in the arms business. I found it was much easier to get Americans to agree to cooperate with U.S. law enforcement than it was to convince foreign nationals to commit treason and work for the CIA. In domestic law enforcement, there was also the added bonus of being able to speak English! In addition, documenting sources in Customs was child's play compared to the oversight in the Agency. But what I found in law enforcement supported the views I had had earlier, in the intelligence community, that there is no substitute for human assets on the inside to provide information that allows the mission to go forward. For example, during Project Wayward, information I obtained from sources and documented by way of Customs reports of investigation resulted in the seizure of a C-130 transport aircraft that had illegally been flying into Angola and insight into attempts by Libya to manufacture a poison gas complex.

At the end of Project Wayward, Don was transferred to another Customs office. I was happy to see him transferred, as he had wanted, and also get a well-deserved promotion. In one of our many talks, Don told me, "Ten percent of the agents make 90 percent of the cases." I wanted to be included in that 10 percent. And, thanks in large part to Don's tutelage, I felt I was ready for my own undercover operation. I believed I identified some promising targets and an area of inquiry that had previously been largely ignored.

In the 1980s Saddam Hussein was gassing Kurds in Iraq, and so, at that time, I was very concerned about the proliferation and potential threat of biological and chemical weapons of mass destruction, "the poor man's nuclear bomb." An industry source of mine agreed to give me an education into foreign purchasing agents' attempts to procure biological and chemical agents and their countermeasures. I also began to visit the Chemical Research, Development, and Engineering Center at the Aberdeen Proving Ground, the Armed Forces Medical Intelligence Center at Fort Detrick, and other institutions at the forefront of monitoring this type of threatening warfare. Information and contacts that were developed were turned over to Customs headquarters' Strategic Investigations Division.

My source told me that he had received inquiries and requirements from many foreign buyers interested in chemical and biological warfare, including agents from Saddam Hussein's Iraq. We discussed structuring a proposed front company to which the source would direct questionable inquiries. I would work at the front company in an undercover capacity, and the source would stay behind the scenes providing the expertise. It was nothing less than a turnkey undercover operation. Unfortunately, when I proposed the possible new operation to office management, the proposal fell flat. This was long before the threat of chemical and biological weapons were in the news. Management simply was not interested. To borrow the 9/11 Commission phrase, there was a "lack of imagination."

I regret the squandered opportunity. In retrospect, I know 1989 was definitely the right time for such an operation. Just two years later Iraq invaded Kuwait and the United States became involved in the first Gulf War. As far as we know, Saddam never deployed his weapons of mass destruction, but they were feared. His reportedly hidden chemical and biological weapons led us to the current war in Iraq.

Contrary to popular belief and media fiction, most undercover operations are not successful. Too many things can and do go wrong. But I still feel that in the late 1980s casting a MARCOM-like net under the guidance of my source to catch Saddam's agents in their illegal attempts to acquire weapons of mass destruction could have been both illuminating and an interesting law enforcement chase.

At the time, there was a continuing exodus of special agents out of the Reston office because of its poor management. To put it mildly, the work environment at the Reston office was not pleasant. Eventually, I too requested a transfer. I applied for a position with Customs headquarters' Smuggling Division. The division chief, Clark Settles, was a great manager and very supportive, and he was surrounded by a very capable and hardworking staff. He offered me a position in the Money Laundering Section. I didn't know much about money laundering at the time, but I was willing to learn.

I reported to Customs headquarters on Constitution Avenue near 14th Street and immediately immersed myself in helping to develop Customs anti-money-laundering programs. One promising initiative I noticed was a joint U.S. Customs and Italian program called Operation Primo Passo, meaning "Operation First Step." The program was designed to combat Italian-American organized crime—the Mafia—by examining the flow of money between Italy and the United States. At that time it was run by a small pilot task force in the Office of the Customs Attaché Rome, which was attached to the American embassy.

When the United States invaded Manuel Noriega's Panama in December 1989, I was selected to head up a small working group at headquarters to help track down Panamanian drug money hidden in financial institutions. My work in this case came to the attention of the assistant commissioner of enforcement. Shortly thereafter, the Customs Attaché Rome requested that a special agent be sent to direct the Primo Passo task force. Success in government service, in large part, involves being in the right place at the right time. Although I had only been in Customs a few years and did not yet have much experience in its money-laundering programs, I applied for the opening and was backed by the assistant commissioner. So, in 1990 I realized my wish to go back overseas. This time I was going to Rome, a particularly thrilling destination for me as a third-generation Italian American or, more accurately, Sicilian American. I thought this would be a wonderful opportunity to discover my roots.

3

The First Step

The American embassy in Rome is located on the Via Veneto, one of the most famous and fashionable avenues in the world. During the 1950s, the Veneto, with its elegant cafes and shops, was synonymous with the *dolce vita*. The cafes and posh hotels are still there, as is the monumental Aurelian Wall at the upper end of the avenue. In fact, the wall and its Porta Pinciana, which form the entrance to the Veneto, have surrounded Rome for almost eighteen centuries. When the wall was originally constructed, the decline of the Roman Empire was already underway. Emperor Aurelio launched the massive construction of towering walls and fortifications in an unsuccessful attempt to hold off the inevitable sack of Rome by the barbarians. At the other end of the Via Veneto is the ornate Piazza Barberini, named after the wealthy Roman family and patrons of the arts. During the last years of the nineteenth century, the Ludovisi family laid out the Veneto so that it had a wide curve to help the carriage horses make it from the Piazza to the original Villa Ludovisi. The villa is still hidden behind the Palazzo Margarita, which today is the very beautiful American embassy.

Ten years before I landed in Rome I had arrived in another ancient European city. Working under deep cover for the CIA, I was kept far away from the American embassy. In Rome, my family and I were officially accredited with the American embassy. I was part of the Office of the Customs Attaché.

U.S. law enforcement has a network of attaché offices around the world. In the early 1990s Customs had about twenty attaché offices. The Drug Enforcement Administration likewise had representatives overseas, as did the Federal Bureau of Investigation, which calls their overseas offices legal attachés or legatts. Today, the FBI has approximately fifty legatts around the world.

The United States has law enforcement representatives overseas for many reasons. For example, if the FBI is working an investigation in the United States and an investigative lead goes overseas, the Bureau will task the appropriate legatt office or offices to continue to follow the investigative trail. If there isn't an overseas attaché presence, the State Department's regional security officer, part of the Diplomatic Security Service, will support the investigation. Most of the time, requested overseas information is obtained in conjunction with host government counterpart agencies, for example, local police and customs services. Depending on the country involved and America's operational agreements with its counterpart agencies, U.S. law enforcement may also be allowed to conduct limited investigations or interviews. Obviously, U.S. law enforcement has no jurisdiction overseas. The United States also has reciprocal agreements with foreign law enforcement counterparts to try to respond to their requests for information. The U.S. law enforcement presence overseas also sometimes facilitates training and technical assistance of those counterparts. Some of the training is done in the host countries, and sometimes promising foreign colleagues are identified and sent to U.S. law enforcement training academies for instruction. I can attest that personal contacts and relationships developed between international law enforcement professionals are often able to cut through bureaucratic obstacles and facilitate getting a job done. Official—and unofficial—liaison relationships are increasingly important and have paid many dividends in the War on Terrorism.

The United States is fortunate to have a rather large attaché network. In the early 1990s only the United States and a few other major countries had law enforcement representatives posted overseas. Today the concept has been copied around the world, and the growth of law enforcement representatives attached to embassies has been rapid. Of course, there is the International Criminal Police Organization (INTERPOL). Today, INTERPOL is the world's largest international police organization with 184 member countries. It offers secure global police communications, data, and support services. But INTERPOL has its limitations, including a history of outdated technology, a labyrinthine bureaucracy, and unreliable protection of sensitive intelligence information.[1] It has also been victimized by unrealistic expectations generated by pulp novels and James Bond–type fantasies. Simply put, an international police agency that actually investigates across borders, let alone has the power to arrest, does not exist. (Even the European Police Office—EUROPOL—is only a support service for the law enforcement agencies of the European Union member states.) INTERPOL facilitates an international law enforcement information exchange by issuing electronic alerts and requests for information through its in-country representatives and it is currently building and improving databases and the technical means to share information, but INTERPOL will always be hampered by sovereignty concerns and the diverse legal standards and systems of its member countries. Conversely, attaché offices have a history of being able to build effective bilateral relationships.

The Customs Attaché Rome, with six special agents and a small support staff, was one of the largest overseas U.S. Customs offices. In addition to investigations in Italy, the Office of the Customs Attaché Rome was also a regional office, which covered fifty-six countries, including those in the Middle East and much of sub-Saharan Africa. As a result, depending on the office's annual travel budget, its agents were often on the road representing U.S. Customs interests elsewhere. The FBI, DEA, and Secret Service also had representatives at the Rome embassy, and of course, the embassy boasted a rather large and traditional State Department presence, including political, economic, commercial, and consular officers, as well as regional security officers of the Diplomatic Security Service. The embassy also housed a large U.S. military and intelligence presence. But regardless of an officer's or agent's parent agency, the ultimate boss in the embassy working environment was the U.S. ambassador.

In the late 1980s an issue of major concern for both Italy and the United States was the impact and growth of the Mafia. Nobody knows the exact origin of the Mafia, but it seems to have developed in the middle of the nineteenth century in poor Sicilian towns and villages. In Sicilian dialect, "mafia" means "beautiful, proud, and something worthy of respect." Nineteenth-century Sicily had little central government, and Sicilians relied on each other to protect their concerns. Justice had to be obtained directly. A society of common interests developed based on Sicilian family, loyalty, and *omertà*—a code of honor and silence. The strongmen that settled disputes in the absence of government or courts came to be called mafiosi. Folklore depicts the early Mafia as an organized group of Sicilian Robin Hoods, demanding protection money from the rich, nobility, and upper class and giving it to the poor.

The reality, however, is that the Mafia grew in scope and criminal intent and soon permeated into almost all sectors of Sicilian life. Extortion, intimidation, murder, and organized criminal enterprise became the modus operandi. Over the years the Mafia moved from the countryside and into the cities, delivering both protection and votes. The Mafia then infiltrated industries and government bureaucracies and became the de facto power of the entire island. Eventually, the Mafia spread its grasping tentacles to the rest of Italy and beyond. In fact, in Italy, the Mafia is sometimes called the Octopus. Its tentacles found even more riches when, through family ties, intimidation, bribery, and payoffs, it won many government bids for the execution of public works projects. To add insult to injury, often these projects were never completed or were of very poor quality. Later, the Mafia tried to integrate some of its profits back into the very economy it looted by investing in legitimate business, including financial institutions.

Italian organized crime grew in fertile ground, in part because of the corruption endemic in Italian society. To be fair, corruption makes some sense in the Italian context. Over thousands of years the Italian peninsula has endured wars, invasions, and the rise and fall of various city-states and republics. Distrust of the government at all levels was, and still is, the norm. Today's massive underground economy and widespread tax evasion are symptoms of the historical Italian disdain for government. Italians are survivors.

During the 1970s and '80s, the Sicilian Mafia dislodged the French underworld in Marseille, which was famous for the French Connection. The Sicilians took control of heroin smuggling operations from the Middle East to the United States and established illegal laboratories for conversion of morphine base.[2] New connections and more sinister ties developed between the Italian and American mafias. Their relationship was exposed in the early 1980s, during the Pizza Connection investigation, in which New York pizza parlors were uncovered as the fronts for an Italian-American operation that smuggled heroin into the United States and laundered the resulting proceeds.

Further investigations in the United States revealed that organized criminal groups of southern Italian origin, working for different narcotics smuggling organizations, had begun to cooperate with each other. Mafialike organizations such as the 'Ndrangeta, based in Calabria, and the Camorra, from the province of Campania, exercised increasing power. Soon enough, these groups were moving into the even more lucrative trade of cocaine. In fact, the Mafia attempted to garner a monopoly on the cocaine trade in Europe. U.S. and Italian officials became increasingly concerned as they watched a new transnational Mafia forge criminal, business, and financial ties around the world.

Combating the Mafia became another focus of America's War on Narcotics. In the United States, federal law enforcement found that its greatest successes in combating organized crime came from aggressive use of domestic task forces, a multiagency approach that brings together different areas of jurisdiction and expertise. The Department of the Treasury, specifically the Internal Revenue Service and Customs Office of Enforcement, also realized early on that the most effective law enforcement weapon directed against organized crime targeted the Mafia's most vulnerable point—the international movement of funds.[3] In a natural union of the two concepts, during an Italian-American Working Group meeting in 1988, the Customs Attaché Rome proposed an international task force designed to combat Italian-American organized crime, specifically the laundering of narcotics proceeds, through examination of suspicious money flows between Italy and the United States. The idea became Operation Primo Passo. It was the first truly international money-laundering task force.

The Primo Passo group was physically located in the office space of the Customs Attaché. When I arrived in August 1990, three law enforcement officers from the Italian Guardia di Finanza, or fiscal police, were assigned to the task force. They were joined by a U.S. Customs intelligence analyst and an Italian foreign service national (FSN) criminal investigator. (An FSN is a local national that works at an American embassy.) There had been two previous temporary-duty Customs special agents assigned to Primo Passo; I was selected to be the first permanent director. Though my language skills were limited, the common language for the task force was Italian. And despite my comparative inexperience with money laundering, my mandate was to give Primo Passo direction, all the while balancing the interests and personalities of both the Italians and Americans.

❉

Money laundering can be made a complicated topic, but simply, it is the disguising or concealing of criminally derived income to make it appear legitimate.

In 1986 the United States became the first country in the world to make money laundering a crime and enacted a law that is still one of the most powerful in the world (Title 18, U.S. Code Section 1956). Over the years, the broad law has become a favorite of federal prosecutors because of its substantial penalties and broad reach. The law also has an extraterritorial reach if at least part of the offense takes place in the United States. The law also authorizes civil penalty lawsuits by the government.

During the early and mid-1990s, there was a sometimes heated debate between the DEA and Customs that centered around the "predicate offense" for money laundering. Because at the time the War on Narcotics was focused on the estimated hundreds of billions of dollars of narcotics-related money laundered every year, DEA insisted that the battle against money laundering was synonymous to the battle against narcotics trafficking. Criminal investigators at Treasury felt strongly, on the other hand, that concealing the proceeds from almost all forms of serious criminal activity should be considered money laundering. Meanwhile the Italians, at the time of Primo Passo, only recognized five "specified unlawful activities," or predicate offenses, that could be charged as money laundering, including kidnapping, which was rampant in Italy during the 1980s. Over the last fifteen years the United States and the rest of the world have adopted Treasury's original and more inclusive version of money laundering. Today, at the federal level, the United States recognizes approximately two hundred predicate offenses for money laundering, including terrorist finance.

With the exception of crimes of passion, most criminal behavior is motivated by greed and thus begets illegally gotten money that must be introduced into legitimate financial channels via seemingly legitimate sources. Dirty money is laundered in three recognizable stages: placement, layering, and integration. In the placement stage, illicit cash must somehow be deposited into financial institutions. Because large amounts of cash are involved, law enforcement feels that criminals are at their most vulnerable when they try, for example, to purchase monetary instruments with dirty money or deposit illegal funds directly into an account. Layering is the attempt to further separate the source of the funds from illegal activity by way of complex transactions such as wiring funds to multiple accounts in multiple jurisdictions. Integration is the final stage of money laundering in which criminal organizations try to create the appearance of legitimacy by, for example, investing the laundered funds in tangible goods such as a business or property.

No one is certain how much money is laundered every year. In 1989, when I was in the Money Laundering Section at Customs headquarters, I was asked to confirm a CIA estimate that approximately $300 billion dollars was laundered every year, with about one-third of that originating in the United States. In typical bureaucratic fashion, I pulled out a simple desktop calculator and tried to crunch some law enforcement data. My bottom-line numbers, such as they were, did not contradict the Agency's estimate and interagency consensus was achieved. As a result, the $300 billion estimate was used around the world for years. Later, the U.S. Treasury working with the Financial Action Task Force tried unsuccessfully to estimate the magnitude of global money laundering. The absence of uniform data and definitions made this an exercise doomed to failure. Nevertheless, today the International Monetary Fund estimates that globally between $600 billion to $1.5 trillion are laundered every year. It is also guesstimated by observers that about one-half originates from criminal proceeds and the other half from the tax-evading components.[4]

Although money laundering has existed for a long time, the U.S. Congress did not pass legislation to address money-laundering concerns until 1970. The legislation, together with follow-up rules and regulations, is collectively known as the Bank Secrecy Act (BSA). However, "bank *secrecy*" is actually a misnomer. The objective of the law was to promote financial *transparency*. Among the several financial reports the BSA required was, for example, the currency transaction report (CTR), with which banks reported to Treasury currency transactions today exceeding $10,000. The level of compliance with the law by banks in the 1970s and early 1980s was very low. Likewise, the level of scrutiny by federal regulatory agencies overseeing the reporting requirements was minimal.

Not until 1985, the year of a watershed case involving noncompliance by the Bank of Boston, did things start to change. The Bank of Boston pled guilty to violating currency reporting requirements and was fined $500,000.[5] The resultant negative publicity for the bank caused thousands of other banks to begin to comply with the BSA. Congressional hearings were held, and the law was changed to impose harsher penalties and fines for noncompliance. Today, with a few exceptions, the U.S. banking industry provides excellent cooperation. Approximately 12 million CTRs are filed with the Department of the Treasury every year.

Another key BSA reporting requirement covers the transportation of $10,000 in currency or monetary instruments into or out of the United States. Customs Form 4790 (today FinCEN Form 150) must be filed, which is also known as a Report of International Transaction of Currency or Monetary Instruments, commonly known as a CMIR. Still more BSA reporting requirements have been added over the years. But in today's discussion of terrorist finance, it is important to note that the financial intelligence used to combat the War on Terrorism was originally constructed and put in place to help fight money laundering, primarily related to the War on Narcotics.

In the 1980s and 1990s BSA forms belonged to the Department of the Treasury and Customs had direct, computerized, online access to much of the data. The BSA data immediately proved its worth to law enforcement thanks to the tremendous amount of identifying information the forms contained. For example, a CTR contains approximately 150 separate data fields and a CMIR has approximately 70 possible data fields. This means that information such as a complete name, passport number, date of birth, address, account numbers, etc., can often be found on a BSA form. This type of information can prove vital to a successful investigation.

Generally speaking, there are two major categories of financial crimes investigations: reactive and proactive. In a reactive case, a crime has occurred and a criminal investigator is assigned to solve the crime through a variety of investigative techniques, including interviews, developing informants, surveillance, or following a paper trail. BSA filings can provide excellent information in constructing a paper trail, although an individual BSA filing itself is generally not the key to constructing a criminal investigation. The other general, albeit much smaller, category of investigation is proactive. In proactive cases, a criminal violation has not yet occurred. Instead law enforcement examines BSA data for suspect trends and patterns and uses this information to intercept criminal activity in progress and take appropriate countermeasures.

❋

Operation Primo Passo helped pioneer the concept of international proactive financial analysis. Suspect financial intelligence, often that originated in CMIR forms to or from Italy and the United States, was analyzed for suspicious anomalies. The corresponding identifying data for persons and organizations engaged in suspicious financial activities would subsequently be run through other U.S. and Italian financial and law enforcement databases. Sometimes, the identified suspects were found to be associated with the Mafia. In these cases, the Primo Passo task force would write reports outlining findings and send investigative leads to their respective counterparts in both Italy and the United States.

When I arrived in Rome, the Primo Passo task force was concluding its investigation of a subject I will call Alberto Genovese. Our Italian colleagues had uncovered Genovese's name while assisting in the review of suspect financial data. Alberto's brother, Carmo, had been involved in laundering the ransom of a kidnapping by the Camorra organized crime family in Napoli. Moreover, Italian authorities had previously investigated Carmo for illegally exporting capital from Italy, for laundering the proceeds of tobacco smuggling, and for his financial connections with a Sicilian Mafia family. The French authorities had also investigated Carmo Genovese for illegalities surrounding his ownership and operation of a casino in Nice. Indications of U.S. financial ties made the Genovese brothers good targets for further investigation by the Primo Passo team.

As a result, U.S. Customs started an investigation of the suspects' financial holdings in the United States. Several U.S. bank accounts were identified. Acting in response to a request for assistance from Primo Passo, the Customs office in New York worked with an assistant U.S. attorney (AUSA). A grand jury subpoena was obtained, and account records were reviewed. As a result, a "floater" or "feeder" account, which was tied into further suspect bank accounts, was identified. An audit team analyzed this voluminous and complex financial data on the brothers. Financial flow charts were prepared. Further analysis revealed that the Genovese brothers' suspect bank account was part of a multi-hundred million dollar financial operation, and some, if not all, of the funds were part of an international narcotics-trafficking money-laundering operation linked to Colombia.

In the United States, $1.2 million found in Alberto Genovese's New York account was seized. The AUSA in New York assigned to the case made it very clear that additional enforcement action would be bolstered by promised strong and concurrent Italian action. Italian law at the time required the prosecutor to establish the "social dangerousness" of the individual charged. The Guardia di Finanza identified approximately $5 million of Genovese property and assets in Italy, but despite the Genovese links to organized crime, prior criminal background, and known ties to narcotics trafficking, these assets were not seized and all charges were dropped. The Primo Passo group was, needless to say, disappointed and suspected outside political influence and pressure. But corruption, politics, and judicial growing pains were part of the battle we faced in working to develop an effective anti-money-laundering program in Italy. I later saw the same type of pressures and influences while helping construct anti-money-laundering programs in other countries. After the disappointing decision on the Genovese brothers case, it was important to hold the group together and identify other potential targets for joint investigation.

Months later I was invited to address a law enforcement conference in Bologna. Using my broken Italian, I delivered a pointed summary of the Genovese case. I expressed Primo Passo's disappointment in the outcome of the investigation, as well as America's determination to continue to work together with its Italian colleagues.[6] After my remarks, I was approached by the famed Mafia fighter, Judge Giovanni Falcone, who was sympathetic to my frustrations. Italy and the United States both owe much to Falcone for his efforts in the 1980s, which finally began to break down the myths and aura surrounding the culture of the Mafia. Judge Falcone used innovative tactics to persuade several notable mafiosi to break their code of silence and talk about their activities.[7] Some of the information he generated proved useful to the FBI in its Pizza Connection investigation. In 1986 and 1987 Falcone helped preside over the famed Maxi Trial of almost five hundred alleged mafiosi in Palermo. Unfortunately, most of those convicted served little more than token sentences before being released under Italy's then-lax penal code. It was the same high burden of proof that proved so frustrating in Primo Passo's investigation of the Genovese brothers.

Unfortunately, Falcone's success also caused many influential Italian politicians and government officials to take offense. His information and public shaming hit too close to home. He became a crusader against the political establishment. Falcone angered the Mafia *capi*, or bosses, even

more with his relentless pursuit of the Mafia's lucrative international narcotics trade. On May 23, 1992, as Judge Falcone was driving home from
the Palermo airport, a roadside bomb was detonated, killing him, his
wife, and four others. The murders shocked the world. I will not forget
my discussion with Judge Falcone about our common Sicilian heritage
and the importance of continued official collaboration in the fight against
Italian-American organized crime.

The Mafia-ordered murder of Judge Falcone and the follow-up assassination of Judge Paolo Borsellino unleashed a wave of additional Mafia
bombings and attacks, including hits on cities to the north such as Flo-
rence and Milan. On July 27 and 28, 1993, two bombs were detonated in
Rome, one not too far from my family's apartment. But at the same time
the murders of Judges Falcone and Borsellino horrified the Italian people
and seemingly galvanized Italian law enforcement and judicial authorities
to finally take effective and coordinated action. I had the honor and pleasure of working with dedicated and courageous Italian law enforcement
officials in the Polizia, particularly the elite Servizio Centrale Operativo,
as well as the newly formed Dipartimento Investigativa Antimafia. We
worked together on dozens of cases. The FBI legatt office in Rome offered continuing and crucial support to the Italian efforts. Although the
FBI has endured criticism for its work in the War on Terror, I am a witness
to some of the great work the Bureau did to help combat Italian-American organized crime. At the same time, I'm sure the FBI would agree that
the Mafia was finally put on the defensive primarily because of the skill,
dedication, and courage of Italian law enforcement.

In many ways, the Operation Primo Passo concept was ahead of its
time. In the late 1980s and early 1990s, the Italians didn't have an infrastructure fully in place to take advantage of the task force. Perhaps, the
chief success of Primo Passo was that, by education, persuasion, and example, my Italian colleagues learned the value of financial intelligence and
soon adopted legislation to recognize money laundering as a separate criminal offense and to create financial-reporting requirements. Having subsequently spent much time helping countries develop anti-money-laundering regimes, I have learned that first a country must establish an anti-
money-laundering law and then it must create financial intelligence to
assist in the requisite enforcement of the law. Everything else follows from
these two steps. And each country must create an infrastructure and pro-

gram that works well in its own national context. Italy did this and today has one of the very best anti-money-laundering programs in the world.

Operation Primo Passo also demonstrated some difficulties U.S. law enforcement encounters while operating overseas. For example, turf wars among domestic American law enforcement agencies are well known: For years, the DEA insisted that money laundering equated to narcotics investigations. The FBI has always been the proverbial eight-hundred-pound gorilla that muscles into investigations initiated by others and is the first to call a press conference. Customs was sometimes not taken seriously by other law enforcement agencies simply because of its name. The same turf wars occur overseas. During Primo Passo there was intense competition among the three Italian law enforcement agencies, and their resultant reluctance to cooperate with one another hindered some of our efforts. When Customs invited the Guardia di Finanza into the office of the Customs Attaché Rome, both the rival Polizia di Stato and the Carabinieri refused to work with Primo Passo. The Polizia and Carabinieri believed that the Guardia was getting all of the Americans' attention and information. This was simply not true. We had very good bilateral investigations with all three Italian police agencies. We also tried to rectify the situation by opening up the task force to all participants, but the Guardia didn't support the new direction and eventually withdrew its personnel and support. When the Carabinieri (a quasi-military organization with police powers) provided some potential money-laundering information to Primo Passo, we soon realized that the rank-and-file Carabinieri did not possess a sufficient knowledge base to conduct a money-laundering investigation.

U.S. Customs personnel, however, could not conduct the required financial checks in Italy; we were dependent on the various Italian law enforcement agencies to follow through on the information provided to them from Primo Passo. Moreover, law enforcement agencies around the world generally recognize a "third-agency rule," which prohibits the sharing of information with a third party without the originating agency approving the passage of information. Information exchange was further complicated by the Guardia di Finanza, which wanted to use some of the data we had available to pursue revenue cases. Some observers think soccer is Italy's national sport. It isn't. Tax cheating is the national pastime. But Customs felt that cracking down on tax violators was not part of the mission of Primo Passo so we vetoed this direction. However, over the years I have come to believe the Italians were probably right. As we will see, it is increasingly difficult to separate money laundering from tax evasion; they can be two sides of the same coin.

U.S. Customs also contributed to the difficulties. For example, when Primo Passo identified investigative leads and reported them to our domestic offices for assistance and investigation, it was occasionally very difficult to get a response. In particular, the large offices in Miami, New York, and Los Angeles that were swamped with their own work were reluctant to devote the necessary resources to help Primo Passo. Although this is understandable from a domestic management perspective, I had a very awkward time trying to explain to my Italian colleagues why many of the very good leads that we sent to the States for follow-up were not worked, particularly when we expected the Italians to act promptly on our requests for information. Overseas, a one-way information exchange is equated with both incompetence and arrogance, and it will not last long. Years later, in numerous discussions with my counterparts in the Middle East about the exchange of financial intelligence in the War on Terrorism, the same problem repeatedly surfaced. Information flow must be two-way.

✳

The largest, most complex case worked by Operation Primo Passo had little to do on the surface with the Mafia. It began as a spin-off of the largest money-laundering investigation in history, Operation Polar Cap.[8] The original Polar Cap investigation, which concluded in 1989, and subsequent follow-up inquiries uncovered many schemes, which primarily revolved around the buying and selling of real and fictitious gold to mask the laundering of over $1.2 billion in currency generated by the sale of cocaine in the United States. The earliest phase of the operation witnessed bulk cash from cocaine sales delivered to collaborating gold dealers and jewelry makers in New York, Houston, and Los Angeles. Fake gold bars were shipped from Uruguay (even though Uruguay does not produce gold) to gold manufacturers in the United States, giving the appearance of legitimate import businesses. In addition, drug money was packed in boxes purporting to contain gold and then shipped to cooperating jewelry retailers. The principal suspect jewelry retailer in Los Angeles was called Ropex.

A network of primarily immigrant Armenians in the Los Angeles jewelry district manufactured gold chains and jewelry for wholesale distribution and retail sale. Gold is a high value item, and so it was the perfect cover to mask deposits of large sums of money (placement) and to wire large sums out of the country (layering) for gold purchases (integration). The money behind the transactions was actually the proceeds of the sales of narcotics controlled by the narcotic cartels. Gold-purchasing schemes to launder the money became increasingly sophisticated. A variety of schemes were introduced, including paper purchases and sales via fictitious invoicing, which replaced the purchase and sale of real physical gold. I was able to track down much of the fictitious invoicing to its origins in the Middle East.

Even though it is highly unusual for legitimate jewelry transactions in the United States to deal in the large volume of cash generated by Ropex gold "sales," no bank in the Los Angeles jewelry district, save Wells Fargo, was concerned about the origin of the funds. It was a form of "willful blindness" by the financial institutions. Hundreds of millions of dollars were going through Ropex-controlled bank accounts, and the banks involved with the transactions were obviously making hefty profits. Although the banks did fill out the mandated BSA CTRs, they never reported the transactions as suspicious and the money-laundering schemes went undetected for about two years. As a postscript, this very failure of banks to report suspicious transactions in part led the Department of the Treasury to propose that financial institutions begin filing suspicious activity reports (SARs). SAR reporting was finally implemented in 1996. In addition, the inability to recognize anomalies in the CTR data caused Customs and the IRS to explore early forms of data mining and contributed to their 1989 proposal to create Treasury's Financial Crimes Enforcement Network (FinCEN). FinCEN was first proposed to support law enforcement agencies by analyzing and disseminating applicable information contained in BSA reporting. There will be a more detailed discussion of FinCEN later in this book.

As part of the multiagency Organized Crime Drug Enforcement Task Force (OCDETF) investigative efforts in Operation Polar Cap, electronic interceptions of conversations at Ropex were authorized by the courts.

The intercepted conversations and hidden cameras established very clearly that the gold transactions covered the laundering of cocaine profits from the United States to accounts controlled by the cocaine cartel in Uruguay, Panama, and Europe. In reviewing the photographs and transcripts of the suspects' conversations in Ropex, a mysterious individual was observed on multiple occasions discussing gold shipments with individuals who appeared to be close friends and business associates. Some of the recorded conversations were in Armenian and others in Arabic. The OCDETF agents could not fully identify this suspect, but from the taped conversations it seemed he was of Armenian origin. He was called "Vinny," and his business was located in Vicenza, Italy. He was treated by the other conspirators as somebody of prominence. At the conclusion of the Polar Cap investigation, search warrants were served on Ropex, and the subsequent searches uncovered many invoices detailing gold sales between Ropex and Vinny. These investigative leads were sent to the Customs Attaché Rome. The Primo Passo task force was asked to fully identify Vinny and determine if he played any role in the laundering of narcotics proceeds via the misuse of the international gold trade.

I devoted a large part of the next two years of my professional life to unravel the mysteries surrounding Vinny and his gold business. Vinny's trail took me to the gold-manufacturing centers of Italy, to multiple countries in the Middle East, and back to the States. I met numerous people in the gold trade and recruited informants in four countries. Police and customs services in Italy and some Middle Eastern countries proved very helpful.

At the end of the investigation, I was able to present a fairly comprehensive criminal syllabus and affidavit in support of seizure warrants for Vinny's substantial U.S. financial and property holdings. We had to focus on U.S. prosecutorial strategies because U.S. law enforcement cannot prosecute overseas, although at times, an American embassy can successfully request that a criminal of U.S. concern be prosecuted in the country where the criminal is found. I discussed the investigative findings with officials at the Money Laundering Section at the Department of Justice in Washington, D.C. Although the Justice officials were supportive, and despite a wealth of excellent information put together by Primo Passo and additional support provided by many domestic Customs offices, at the end of the day the decision was made not to try to seek the seizure and forfeiture of Vinny's assets: we could not conclusively prove that the assets were a direct result of the proceeds of narcotics sales. In retrospect, this was a wise decision because by the time the Polar Cap investigation was litigated and appealed, out of the approximately 750 accounts identified, subpoenaed, and seized, only two were ever actually forfeited.[9]

Unfortunately, at the time of the Polar Cap investigation, the U.S. government did not yet understand the black-market exchange systems of trade goods that surfaced just a few years later and that will be discussed in later chapters. This is one reason why, after September 11, I am not impressed when governments around the world claim to have successfully blocked millions in terrorist assets. As I learned in Polar Cap and other financial crimes investigations in the War on Narcotics, sometimes the government rushes to freeze assets, but at the end of the day forfeiture is not a foregone conclusion.

Although the Vinny of Vicenza investigation did not result in the arrest and seizure statistics that drive law enforcement management, it was the most worthwhile investigation I ever conducted. As described earlier, the CIA collects "foreign intelligence" as part of the intelligence cycle. In the Vinny of Vicenza investigation, law enforcement collected and reported "investigative intelligence." We obtained much new information about how the misuse of the international gold trade can launder or transfer staggering amounts of value around the world. Unfortunately, despite my repeated attempts to convey these observations over the years, the U.S. and other governments still have not focused on the extent of the problem of trade-based money laundering in its various forms.

✻

Gold is popular with money launderers for many reasons. It has been a haven of wealth since antiquity. It is a readily acceptable medium of exchange from Wall Street to main streets to the back alleys and remote corners of the world. For example, when I was going to be sent into the African bush, I was told to carry gold coins with me in the event that I needed a readily recognized form of value to secure an escape. Gold has both an investment demand and a cultural demand. In South Asia and Arabia, gold plays an intrinsic role in culture and finance. The same is also true in areas as diverse as Latin America and the Far East.[10] Money launderers are also businesspeople. They want certainty in their transactions. If gold is selling for $550 an ounce in Zurich, it will be the same price in London, Tokyo, and Dubai. Precious gems such as emeralds and diamonds are also used in money laundering, but there can be too much subjectivity in the price of rough or unworked stones. Gold is also a unique instrument for money launderers because depending on need, it can act as a commodity or as a de facto bearer instrument, which offers easy anonymity. It can be changed from bar form to gold jewelry or melted and shaped into other forms for transport and smuggling. There is simply nothing else out there like it.

Historically in the War on Narcotics, U.S. law enforcement concentrated on the illegal flow of narcotics from Latin America and resultant money laundering. The United States concentrated on Latin America because it directly affected it; America could literally see the dope and the dollars, the cause and effect. The DEA and European police services have also developed good understanding of the trade in heroin from South Asia to Europe and the United States.

My unique vantage point in Italy, augmented by frequent travels to the Middle East, southern Europe, and Africa, provided a new perspective. Concentrating on what I called "trade-based money-laundering systems," I became increasingly concerned with how suspect finance and trade were intertwined and interrelated. Many trade networks were based on ethnic and family business ties. They surfaced in various forms of alternative remittance systems, also known as parallel banking, underground banking, and more recently, informal value-transfer systems. In contrast to traditional narcotics trafficking along the southwest U.S. border, many times these systems were not visible but opaque. They were highly effective at bypassing, in whole or part, BSA financial transparency reporting requirements. As a result, U.S. law enforcement historically did not see or understand how the systems operated. They were not part of traditional U.S. culture and accepted ways of doing business. And if Western-centric U.S. management did not see the systems, relate to the systems, or understand them, they certainly were not going to devote the necessary resources or develop the tools to combat them.

One such system identified was based on the misuse of the international gold trade. From our Primo Passo vantage point, we identified an international gold and money-laundering cycle that began in Europe and extended to the Americas and the Middle East. No Mafia boss or Dr. Strangelove or Goldfinger was in command of the cycle, like a puppeteer pulling the strings. Rather there was a loose-knit international network of trade and smuggling that was comprised of smaller laundering cycles. Each step in the network played off another and many of the actors didn't know or care how they fit into the overall scheme. The gold cycle fit the pattern of other smuggling networks previously identified by law enforcement and intelligence agencies. For example, many organized criminal groups from the Mediterranean to Latin America got their start in the lucrative business of avoiding high government taxation by smuggling cigarettes. Often the same routes and contacts were later employed to smuggle weapons, narcotics, and even consumer goods. In the early 1990s the gold cycle began and ended with the Switzerland-Italy gold exchange. Although London is historically an important gold center and the trade has somewhat diffused over the years, Switzerland is still considered the world's gold-trading center. Switzerland was attractive to the gold trade because of its longtime policies of financial secrecy and neutrality. Obviously, Switzerland does not produce raw gold itself. Gold is mined in Russia, South Africa, the United States, Australia, and other countries, but large quantities of gold bars are manufactured in Switzerland. The solid gold bars are 99.99 (or four nine) percent pure. Depending on the market, the so-called good-delivery bars are formed into 35.27-ounce kilo bars, about the size of a small brick, which are particularly popular in Western countries and the Middle East. Ten-tola bars weigh 3.75 ounces and are approximately the size of a candy bar; they are popular in South Asia (tola is an Indian unit of weight). Wafer-thin tael bars are primarily found in the Far East. The tael is an ancient Chinese weight, approximately equal to 1.2 ounces. Tael bars are manufactured in various shapes and sizes.

The enormous quantities of gold exported (and smuggled) to Italy, which feed the multibillion dollar gold industry centered in Vicenza and Arezzo, clued Primo Passo in to the Swiss connection. Gold is one of Italy's most important industries. Italy is the largest exporter of worked gold in the world. There is constant demand for high-quality, eighteen-carat Italian gold jewelry. Primo Passo originally believed that organized crime might influence some facets of the Italian gold trade. However, we were never able to discover a direct correlation.

Once the Swiss gold arrives in Italy, it is turned into mass-produced jewelry such as gold rope and chain. Italy has excelled in inventing manufacturing procedures and the requisite machinery to produce hundreds of tons of gold chain a year. Thus the gold in this part of the cycle is not the designer jewelry that Italy is justifiably famous for, but rather mass-produced gold products that require little labor or workmanship. There is little added value or cost in the production of gold rope or chain. The sales price is based on weight. This mass-produced jewelry is exported from Italy to jewelry companies and brokers in the United States and Latin America. Trade data confirms that Italy is, by far, the largest exporter of gold jewelry to the United States. During our investigation, Primo Passo identified a number of suspect U.S. importers.

When I was in Italy in the early 1990s, I attempted to have both the Italian and U.S. customs services give closer scrutiny to suspect gold couriers. Two separate operational proposals prepared by Primo Passo, encouraging a systematic examination of the courier network and the study of a gold financial database, were vetoed by neglect in Customs headquarters. One difficulty in scrutinizing gold transactions was that on the surface targeted suspect gold shipments appeared legitimate and shippers export documents (SEDs) seemed to be in order. It is important to remember, however, that the shipments appeared in order because almost always they contained *real* gold. What was not apparent was that these "legitimate" shipments could also be subject to false invoicing or over- or undervaluation. These were classic trade-based money-laundering techniques often used to provide countervaluation in a process of value transfer.

In another possible scenario, a gold courier might enter the United States carrying a satchel filled with gold rope and chain and declare it as eighteen-carat gold with a value of $300,000. Customs is hard-pressed to give a thorough examination to each and every shipment. For example, is the value of the gold shipment truly $300,000? Perhaps it is twelve-carat gold or maybe it is twenty-two-carat gold. Are the couriers transporting solid golden objects or are the objects simply covered with gold? Declared weight can be different from the actual weight. Value can fluctuate wildly. At busy ports of entry, Customs inspectors are sometimes told not to spend more than a minute on their examinations to prevent backups that impede the flow of people and commerce. It is very difficult for overworked and harried inspectors to detect discrepancies. Without a doubt, the gold industry is comprised of honorable people, and there is little fraud in the overall gold trade. But sometimes the difference between what is real and what is declared is the transfer of value; this is often a sign of customs fraud, tax evasion, or criminal money laundering. And because of gold's value and unique characteristics, a little fudging on declarations goes a long way.

Once the gold reaches the United States, there are many different scenarios for the laundering of funds. For example, street drug sales can be routed to cash clearing houses. Once cash is used to purchase the gold, the money is effectively laundered. In Operation Polar Cap, law enforcement literally witnessed narcotics proceeds taken in the back door of the Ropex jewelry retailer. The books reflected fictitious sales, and the money was subsequently deposited, or "placed," into financial institutions. Another technique was to import both real, and by way of false documentation, fictitious gold from Italy, Latin America, and the Middle East. The books were debited to legitimize the gold purchases. Drug money deposited into financial institutions was wired abroad for "payment" to complete the wash cycle. In some cases of money laundering the gold imports and payments are legitimate, but the importer has a compensation agreement with the exporter (often a member of the same extended family), which requires that it sell or recycle imported goods back to the original exporter. In all of these cases, the importer is able to move large sums of money (either cash or wire transactions) as payment to a foreign "supplier." The same techniques can be used with almost any type of commodity. However, because of gold's unique characteristics and high value, it is much easier for money launderers to justify large payments for shipments of gold than it is to send repeated small payments for shipments of, for example, apples.

A variety of law enforcement investigations over the years have identified gold brokers and retailers acting as fronts for the shipment of gold to Latin America in exchange for tainted funds. It is also known that gold, just like cash, is occasionally simply smuggled across borders. In certain areas of the world, smugglers use gold smuggling vests lined with pockets to hold gold bars. The vests will allow smugglers to conceal the equivalent of $500,000 on their persons. Smuggling $500,000 in currency on a person is impossible. (It has been reported that some gold manufacturers also knowingly assist smugglers by producing small gold bars with rounded edges. The rounded edges do not rip canvas courier bags or sensitive body cavities.) And just like cash, gold can be smuggled via container, vehicle, or vessel.

Suspect gold is also exported directly from Italy to Latin America. Much of it goes to Colombia via Panama's Colon free trade zone. (Some of these gold shipments are part of the Colombian Black-Market Peso Exchange, which will be discussed more fully in chapter 6.) Once in Latin America, the gold can be recycled using many methods, including melting. The cost of melting or smelting gold is relatively low, simply the cost of doing business. When the gold is melted, its impurities are removed, and when the gold is returned to bar/ingot form, it can be deposited/ credited with gold brokers and financial institutions. To further confuse the trail for criminal investigators, value can be transferred or layered between gold accounts, silver accounts, dollar accounts, and local-currency accounts. Once the proceeds from the narcotics-gold exchange are on deposit in a financial institution, funds can be wired to secret offshore accounts; exported or recycled back into the United States to suspect gold brokers/importers in the form of payments; or physically transported back to Switzerland or Italy for more gold purchases, beginning the cycle anew.

In 1991 I originally deciphered the cycle from my vantage point in Italy and my work in the Vinny of Vicenza investigation. The following illustration summarizes the cycle in accordance with my personal views and observations, not those of the U.S. government. The cycle can vary case by case, and many different scenarios are addressed later in this book, when gold's link to other alternative remittance systems is discussed. The underground gold trade can be very complex, particularly to outsiders trying to understand the close-knit ethnic communities involved. This book will also give examples of the misuse of free trade zones, invoice manipulation, and other fraudulent trading practices that are intertwined with the underground gold trade. When trying to simplify the cycle, I sometimes use an article from Panama's *La Prensa*, which discusses a gold seizure in the Colon free trade zone in 2000 that mirrors the gold-laundering cycle originally identified above almost ten years before: "The investigation revealed that the gold comes from Switzerland. It is then sold to jewelers in Italy. The Italian pieces are sent to the United States and Panama. Some of the gold arrives in the Colon Free Trade Zone and

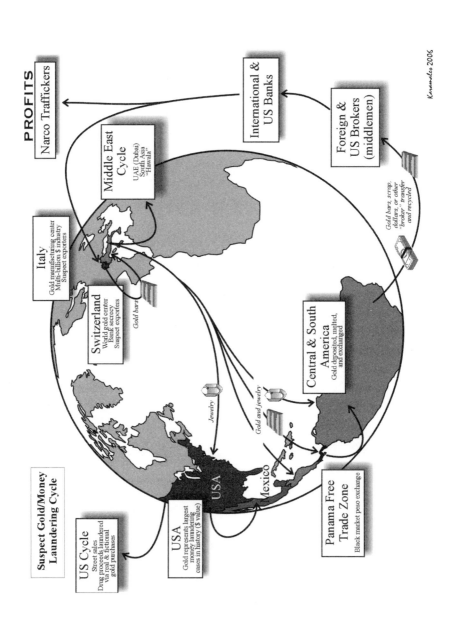

Suspect Gold/Money Laundering Cycle

PROFITS
Narco Traffickers

International & US Banks

Foreign & US Brokers (middlemen)

Gold bars, scrap, dollars, or other "broker", transfer and recycled

Middle East Cycle
UAE (Dubai)
South Asia
"Hawala"

Italy
Gold manufacturing center
Multi-billion $ industry
Suspect exporters

Switzerland
World gold center
Bank secrecy
Suspect exporters

Gold bars

Central & South America
Gold deposited, melted, and exchanged

Jewelry

Gold and jewelry

USA

Mexico

Panama Free Trade Zone
Black market peso exchange

US Cycle
Street sales
Drug proceeds laundered
via real & fictional
gold purchases

USA
Gold represents largest
money laundering
cases in history ($ value)

Kinsales 2006

is sold to middlemen. The merchandise moves on to Colombia where it is used to finance drug operations or it is resold in the United States and Switzerland."[11] As a postscript, because of successful investigations and heightened awareness, there are indications that the amount of suspect Italian gold sent to the Colon Free Trade Zone and Columbia has diminished the last few years.

The "unsuccessful" Vinny of Vicenza investigation proved its worth not in the traditional law enforcement bureaucracy sense of statistics but because it provided an introduction into informal and indigenous alternative methods of transferring value in the Middle East and South Asia. Without fully realizing it at the time, I was collecting useful information in the manner I had as an intelligence officer in the CIA. I found that just as there is a "system" and a cycle involving Europe and the Americas, there are also systems involving the Middle East and South Asia. A very few tried to call attention to these systems early on; they only surfaced in the public arena after September 11. These underground systems can facilitate international money laundering and value transfer. I am convinced they are also an overlooked component of terrorist financing. I found the clues to some of these underground systems by following the trail of investigations to the Middle East.

4

We Are All Susceptible

I sat cross-legged on a plush, ornately decorated pillow, which was in turn placed on an array of brightly colored carpets and prayer rugs. Abdulrahman pulled a delicacy from the whole roasted lamb that was laid out before me and expertly used his fingers to scoop up a mouth-watering ball of *mansaf* rice. Since he was the host and I was the honored guest, he personally fed me the delicious morsel. He delighted in making sure that I had my fill of the platters of wonderful food that kept appearing. This was Iftar, the first meal that breaks the daylong fast during the Islamic holy month of Ramadan, the ninth month of the Islamic lunar calendar. Muslims believe that during this month the Prophet Muhammad received his first revelations from the Archangel Gabriel. During Ramadan, Muslims around the world unite in a period of fasting and reflection, community and family. The Arabs circled around me had just broken their fast. I was pleased and honored to be in their company.

Abdulrahman and his family were only a generation removed from desert Bedouin. Even though massive oil wealth has caused the modernization of Arabian Gulf cities to rise Phoenix-like from the desert, the culture of the nomad has remained in the people. Arab hospitality, the art of welcoming a traveler into the home, is the same now as it was a millennium ago, even though Abdulrahman and his family no longer lived in tents, but rather in a large apartmentlike building. Spread with carpets, the roof of the building was the scene of our feast. We stayed at our simulated rooftop oasis all night, until the shimmering reflection of the half moon off the distant sea in the west gave way to the faint stirrings of sun over the desert in the east. The local mosque and the *muezzin*'s melodic call to the day's first prayer, or *azan*, ended our nightlong discussion of religion and politics abruptly. After *azan*, Abdulrahman and his brethren retired to their respective homes for a long nap, which would help relieve the physical pangs of hunger and thirst of another day of sacrifice. I bid my gracious hosts leave and then proceeded back to the hotel for a shower and a fresh suit. I had lots of work to do during my short visit to the Kingdom of Saudi Arabia. Much of that work entailed trying to begin to process information gleaned from Abdulrahman and others regarding modern Arabian tales of money laundering, fraud, and methods of doing business, which were as foreign to me as the Arabian Desert.

Although my primary duty my first few years in Italy was with Operation Primo Passo, I also traveled frequently to other countries for which Customs Attaché Rome had regional responsibility. At that time neither Customs nor any other U.S. law enforcement agency had a full-time presence anywhere in the Middle East. In 1991 I began to travel to countries in the Arabian Gulf. My journeys to the region would continue for the next thirteen years.

Because I had spent a year at Customs headquarters' Money Laundering Section and had worked with Primo Passo, I naturally wanted to heighten the awareness of what I believed was the global threat of money laundering. I was probably the first American official to raise the subject in many countries in the Middle East. With few exceptions, I found an almost total lack of understanding and a corresponding lack of concern in that region. A police official I met with on one of my first trips to Saudi Arabia expressed a typical view: He told me that there were "few drugs" in the Kingdom of Saudi Arabia. He continued, saying that because narcotics were not officially a problem, then logically money laundering did not exist in his country. It was that simple. He inferred that I was wasting my time bringing up the issue and that I should just go home. He acknowledged that Saudi Arabia did have some petty crime and that customs and police occasionally intercepted a South Asian drug courier. In those cases, the official boasted, criminals were handed the severe punishment mandated under Islamic law—the sharia. He bragged that severe punishment worked as a deterrent to others and suggested that the West copy the Saudi model. In fact, he invited me to attend a public beheading the following Friday in the old clock-tower square in central Riyadh. I declined the invitation.

In large part I shared the official's view about the absence of crime in Saudi Arabia. I felt perfectly safe in Saudi Arabia and all of the countries I visited in the Middle East. As I traveled to the region more frequently

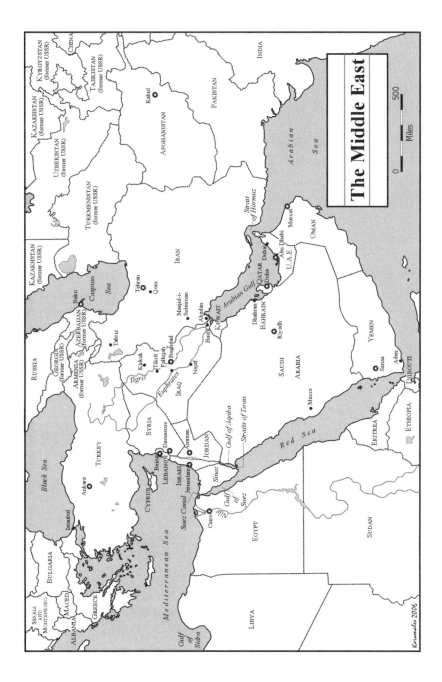

over the years, my family and friends, fearful of the alarmist images they saw on their televisions and influenced by commentators' one-sided views, always cautioned me to be careful. When I expressed to them the peaceful realities that I encountered, they were incredulous. I found civility and kindness in the Middle East. It was a part of the culture. It was a way of life. But while I certainly appreciated the Saudi official's views, I also realized that under the surface lurked another reality. As Abdulrahman told me after Iftar, "Every vice is available here. You just have to know who to talk to and where to look. Every kind of crime is committed. No country or religion has a monopoly on sin or virtue. As human beings, we are all susceptible to the same temptations."

In fact, on my very first trip to Saudi Arabia, I had a quick introduction to the kind of underworld Abdulrahman described. I had met a wealthy businessman who told me that a Pakistani organization had approached him for help in laundering tens of millions of dollars of bulk U.S. currency that would be physically shipped from the United States to Saudi Arabia every month. Once in Saudi Arabia, the cash would be transshipped to Switzerland for deposit. The Pakistani conspirators were prepared to pay the businessman a 4–5 percent commission for constructing a cover story that would disguise the Saudi origin of the funds for the Swiss bankers. The most plausible cover scenario he came up with: the funds were the result of oil business deals transacted and carried out in Saudi Arabia and controlled by an extended member of the very large Saudi royal family (which included more than six thousand princes who had settled with their families all over the country). The businessman told me that he had asked the Pakistani group how and where the cash originated in the United States. Reportedly, he was told that the money was from an "irregular" source but that the offer of a sizeable commission should mitigate any further questions.

This initial conversation escalated into a series of meetings whereby I obtained the informant's consent to participate in a U.S. Customs undercover operation. I even arranged the possible use of a Customs undercover aircraft to pick up the funds in the United States. Legally, upon arrival in Saudi Arabia, the bulk currency would be reported and inspected to make sure it was genuine and not counterfeit. According to the source, we could also import the funds by payoff.

While arranging the many details of the proposed operation, which was coordinated with the U.S. embassy and Saudi officialdom, I checked all relevant U.S. law enforcement databases and made formal and informal inquiries of U.S. federal law enforcement agencies to make sure this was not part of another agency's operation. When everything checked out, I called the informant and gave him the go-ahead to contact the Pakistani conspirators and put the operation in motion. However, at the very last moment I received an urgent notification from the Drug Enforcement Administration that we had inadvertently penetrated part of a domestic U.S. undercover operation. DEA requested the assistance of my informant but asked me to stand down. I immediately called the informant, told him the news, and let him know the proposed Customs operation was over. However, the Saudi businessman insisted that he was still going to the United States. He was determined to meet the alleged criminal money-laundering network face to face. He said he could work just as well for the DEA, and the DEA welcomed his participation. I cautioned him to be careful but wished him well. I then wrote memos to the file outlining what had happened.

Months later, when I was back in Saudi Arabia on other business, I met with my Saudi friend to find out what happened. He explained to me that he had gone to the United States as planned and had met with the DEA. But, according to the Saudi, instead of treating him with respect, the DEA agents treated him like he was nothing more than a cheap snitch. He was outraged, and upon his return he personally reported his complaints to the American ambassador. More than anything else, I could tell his pride had been hurt. I arranged to give him a token amount of money that at least covered his airfare to the States. Over the years we remained friends.

Other indicators of funny money arose while I worked in the Middle East. During one of my early visits to Saudi Arabia, I met informally with a group of Western bankers to candidly discuss concerns about money laundering. According to the bankers, it was not uncommon during those years for large trucks filled with cash, U.S. dollars and Saudi riyals, to pull up to bank branches. The banks would welcome and deposit the cash, no questions asked, because it purportedly belonged to a member of the extended royal family.

Concerned about the indicators of money laundering I had discussed with the bankers, I approached the American embassy in Riyadh, the

Saudi Arabian Monetary Authority, and the Gulf Cooperation Council (GCC) about holding a regional money-laundering conference. Once the idea surfaced, the Financial Action Task Force and the U.S. State Department combined to usurp the conference and promote it for their own purposes; I didn't care. The objective of the conference was to get people together to discuss the problem of money laundering, a good first step in building consensus. It was the same type of catalyst that led to the creation of Primo Passo in Italy.

The conference took place in Riyadh on October 10–14, 1993, almost two years after its initial proposal. Over three hundred delegates from all of the countries in the Arabian Gulf attended. The majority of the delegates were bankers; however, law enforcement and customs personnel were also in attendance. I delivered separate presentations on various aspects of money laundering. Papers from the conference were translated into Arabic.

I mention this effort only because it was the first money-laundering conference of many to follow, both in Saudi Arabia and the region. It was necessary to heighten public awareness of the problem so that we could start talking about appropriate countermeasures. We had to find common ground. Since September 11 there has been a lot of commentary about how the Arab states were remiss or slow to put in place adequate financial safeguards. Many were. But we must keep in mind that the United States passed the Bank Secrecy Act in 1970, about the same time that some countries in the Gulf obtained their independence. It was presumptuous of the West to demand that these countries face up to money laundering, when they were still literally building their own institutions.

Moreover, I was pointedly told by a Gulf Central Bank governor that, "Although the West does not think of the countries of the Middle East as democracies, in fact we have to operate on the basis of consensus. There is a process of deliberation and consultation before a decision can be made to go forward. It is not necessarily your democratic system, but we also have our internal system of reviews, checks, and balances." Over the next decade I traveled many times to all of the countries in the Gulf preaching the anti-money-laundering gospel to a wide variety of audiences. Watching the various countries and the GCC struggle to achieve "consensus" and political will was at times frustrating. But so is watching the American political process.

Culturally, many of the business practices that are deemed suspect in the West are perfectly acceptable in the Middle East. For example, it is quite common for Middle Easterners to use cash for large purchases such as cars. In the United States, we think that using cash for large purchases is suspicious, and our financial transparency reporting requirements reflect this. Moreover, until a few years ago it was quite common for wealthy Arabs to take suitcases full of U.S. dollars with them when they traveled to the United States to go, for example, to the Mayo Clinic for surgery or on vacation to Las Vegas. They would report the cash on the appropriate cross-border currency form, but Customs inspectors would still understandably question why the visitors needed so much. Some of the Arabs felt insulted and reported the perceived ill treatment to the American embassies when they returned from their trip to the States. It was simply a clash of cultures and differing ways of doing business. Sometimes the embassies would get concerned and appeal to me for help. In turn, I would send requests to Customs' offices of inspection and control asking for a little more sensitivity. Nevertheless, only the events surrounding September 11 could persuade the Gulf countries, individually and collectively, that they had to begin to change some of their traditional ways of doing business and adopt world standard anti-money-laundering and counter-terrorist-finance policies and procedures. As I later argue, the next challenge for the region will be to develop the political consensus and will to actually use their new anti-money-laundering infrastructure to go after their own criminals and politically protected elites.

✳

My education in suspect ways of doing business in the Middle East did not originate solely from dirty money inquiries. It was a cumulative process that was built on a variety of investigations into different violations, or predicate offenses. Sometimes the investigations were significant and other times, routine. Over time, I accumulated insight and developed contacts and sources. This is typical in law enforcement around the world. For example, the Office of the Customs Attaché Rome received requests for investigative assistance from domestic offices. In the early 1990s one of the requests was from a Customs office in California. During the course of the California investigation, a search warrant was served on the residence of a recent immigrant from the Middle East. Documents were recovered that showed the suspect was involved with an organized network to steal cars from the United States and export them back home. In fact, the documents outlined that of thirty-seven vehicles that had been shipped from southern California to Jeddah, Saudi Arabia, twenty-six were stolen. Some of them were found on transport ships currently on the high seas. Turn-back orders were issued too late by U.S. Customs. The California office requested Rome's assistance to track down the stolen cars in Jeddah. Since I was going to Saudi Arabia to pursue money-laundering issues, I was assigned the stolen-car case, the first one I ever worked. The subsequent investigation uncovered additional clues to the underworld of financial crime in the region.

While doing some research on the export of stolen cars from the United States, I learned that the problem was serious. At that time it was estimated that at least 1.5 million cars were stolen every year in the United States. Perhaps two hundred thousand of those cars were shipped to foreign locations, but the U.S. Customs Service only intercepted about twelve hundred a year. Southern California led the nation in reported stolen cars, many of which are sent across the border into Mexico.[1] But during a conversation with a Customs special agent in the port of Wilmington, Delaware, who was also looking into the issue of stolen cars, I was told that perhaps as many as ten thousand stolen vehicles were exported every year from that port alone. Many were destined for the Middle East.

A number of scams were involved in shipping stolen cars overseas. Some of the vehicles were stolen for the collection of insurance monies. Many of the stolen vehicles were broken down, or "chopped," and their parts were exported. There were also reports that contraband, narcotics, and even cash were secreted in the vehicles themselves. One would think it would be a relatively simple matter for Customs to conduct routine inspections at ports of departure to identify stolen vehicles. Unfortunately, it was not that easy. Even if vehicle identification numbers (VINs) were checked as required, only a very small percentage of vehicles ever received a physical inspection to verify that the VIN recorded on documents was correct and that the VIN on the vehicle was unaltered. Moreover, as in the case in the California investigation, many cars were often exported before they were even reported as being stolen. Further compounding the problem was the wide variety of documentation that is allowed to prove ownership of a vehicle in the United States, including titles and bills of sales from all fifty states.

Obviously, the principal solutions to America's stolen car problem were to be found in the United States. To this end, Customs, the Federal Bureau of Investigation, state and local police agencies, and the auto industry were increasing their cooperation, coordinating efforts, sharing data, and working to tighten export controls for stolen vehicles. However, I discovered a backdoor approach to the problem: gather intelligence and "mess with" the organized stolen-car rings from overseas. To my knowledge, this had never been done before, and I wanted to give it a try.

While pursuing the investigative leads from the California office, I met an import-export dealer in Jeddah named Omar. He was very knowledgeable about the automobile business and in a short time began to educate me on the underworld of the trade, including the importation of stolen cars from the United States. Omar told me how much he enjoyed doing business with America. He added that it pained him to see how some in the Arab world both broke man's law and sinned against Allah by dealing and profiting from the sale of stolen vehicles. Omar offered to cooperate with my investigation. I took the necessary precautions but was certainly aware that Omar could have been using me, for example, to possibly weaken his competitors.

Omar knew some of the consignees for the stolen cars from California. He quickly identified additional members of the stolen-car network, both in Jeddah and the United States. He fed me information about the suspects, which I in turn relayed to the special agent conducting the parent investigation in California. Omar also volunteered to travel to California and work with the case agent to further penetrate the group of immigrant Arabs that was involved with a wide variety of scams, including the use of stolen credit cards and false identification to obtain vehicles from car leasing companies. Using this ploy, they exported, delivered, and sold the cars in the Middle East before the leasing companies were even aware of what had happened.

I worked with the Customs office in California to help structure an undercover operation that used Omar as the inside informant. Remembering the debacle of the Saudi businessman and his experience with the DEA, I wanted to accompany Omar to the States to ensure everything went well and to hand off Omar to the California case agent, but Customs headquarters, trying to do things on the cheap, refused to pay for our travel. Money could be frittered away on frivolous boondoggle travel by bureaucrats, but it was very difficult to get Customs to approve the kind of operational travel that makes cases. This example also demonstrates the headquarters staff's lack of understanding about what is required to professionally handle a human source. Most of the headquarters staffers had probably never had an informant in their careers. Perhaps it was my background with the CIA that made me appreciate good tradecraft, but I found that many in Customs were amateurish when it came to the handling of human sources of information. At the end of the day headquarters rejected my appeals, so Omar volunteered to pay for his trip to California. Despite the bureaucratic obstacles, he worked successfully with the California case agent and together they helped dismantle the stolen-car network.

On the side, Omar and I also conducted our own little operation in Jeddah, which began with a trip to what I can only describe as a car swap meet. I had never seen anything like it. The swap meet was located outside Jeddah on what I estimated was over a one square kilometer tract of land. There, thousands of cars were being bought, sold, and traded. There were also stalls upon stalls of car parts, car accessories, money exchangers, and people who would handle documentation. There were no Westerners in sight. As Omar and I cruised the car bazaar, he regaled me with stories of why American cars were still popular in Saudi Arabia and throughout the Gulf States. In particular, he raved about the Chevy Caprice, which he said was nicknamed the "Camel of the Desert" because of its reputation for being able to go on seemingly forever without maintenance. He said the demand for the Caprice in the Middle East explained why so few could be found in the States. Any used Caprices that were available for sale were purchased by Arab buying agents and exported to the Gulf. Or they were stolen.

I asked him to explain to me how a buyer of a stolen car imported into Saudi Arabia could document and prove ownership. Omar laughed at my naïveté. He said the official Saudi customs documentation could be obtained via corrupt officials and was available on the streets. In fact, he said he would prove how the system worked and provide me with an example. It was part of my continuing education into the underworld of crime, finance, and trade that dovetailed with my pursuit of money laundering and, later, terrorist finance. At our next meeting, Omar gave me a genuine Saudi customs certificate, written in Arabic with the requisite seal, which could be filled in to prove ownership of any vehicle. It was, in effect, a free pass that could be used to legitimize any stolen car. Omar said he paid 5,000 Saudi riyals for the document, approximately $1,300. He said it was his gift to me. Together we discussed how it could be put to good use.

I made an appointment to see a Saudi customs official I knew in Riyadh. I had previously tried to enlist his help on the stolen-car issue, but as was typical with most of Saudi officialdom I encountered, he had denied that there was a significant crime problem. This time I presented a flip-chart overview on U.S. Customs' stolen-car investigations that impacted Saudi Arabia. The official nodded stoically throughout.

At the end of my presentation, I handed over to him the Saudi customs document that Omar had purchased on the street. The customs official's face whitened. He asked where I had gotten it, and I explained truthfully that it had been purchased on the street. I told him I knew that customs services around the world suffered with the same issues. In fact, the U.S. Customs Service was not immune to this type of activity. He promised me he would correct the situation.

The official was as good as his word. Months later, when I returned to Jeddah, I met again with Omar. He told me that there had been a massive purging of Saudi customs officials in the port of Jeddah and a corresponding crackdown on corruption. Omar and I were both confident that our little operation had been the catalyst for the change. Of course, none of this was written up in a U.S. Customs report of investigation because exposing overseas corruption in this manner was not part of what agents did. There were no arrests or seizures. No statistics were generated. But there are other ways to make an impact. And Omar and I had our quiet satisfaction.

This was not the end of the stolen-car issue for me. Shortly after Omar helped dismantle the stolen-car network in California, I had discussions with a U.S. insurance industry investigator who was visiting Saudi Arabia. He was impressed with the work Omar and I had done. I expressed to him my frustration at not being able to pursue things further because of a lack of funding and interest from headquarters. The insurance representative told me that he was confident he could obtain industry support and funding to assist us. This was the type of government-industry partnership that is often given lip service in Washington. I relayed the offer to headquarters and proposed a possible undercover operation from overseas that would seek to expose criminal networks involved with stolen American cars that had been exported to the Middle East. The answer from headquarters' Foreign Operations Desk was, "We're not interested. They're only stolen cars." Granted, stolen cars were not a high priority for Customs at the time, but I was convinced that by investigating stolen-car networks, we would also uncover many other criminal offenses, including other U.S. Customs violations. In addition, I felt strongly that stolen cars were an issue that all U.S. taxpayers could identify with. I thought if Customs could help make progress in curbing the stolen-car epidemic, it would collectively get a lot of credit with the public and Congress. But headquarters still wasn't interested.

✳

While pursuing the Vinny of Vicenza investigation into the misuse of the international gold trade, Primo Passo obtained many real and seemingly fictitious invoices chronicling the purchase of large amounts of gold. Most of the invoices were for amounts in the hundreds of thousands of dollars. Some of the invoices were forwarded to us from the Polar Cap task force in Los Angeles, and some were obtained in Italy from the Italian Guardia di Finanza. The striking thing about the invoices was that, even though they appeared to originate from many different jewelry firms in Saudi Arabia, Kuwait, Italy, and Switzerland, all of them were markedly similar in format, type font, style, etc. Many of the invoices from the different locales also contained the exact same description and phraseology of the merchandise and even the same common misspellings. Many of the invoices listed the owner of the gold as a Kuwaiti gold broker.

Several months after the February 1991 liberation of Kuwait by U.S. and coalition forces, I traveled to Kuwait City to follow the leads generated by the gold invoices. Working with the U.S. embassy there, I was granted an appointment with a Kuwaiti colonel who was attempting to bring normalcy to police operations. The reconstruction of Kuwait was just getting started. War debris was still present. Since Saddam Hussein's Iraqi army had destroyed much of Kuwait's military and police infrastructure, the meeting was held in a tent and I sat on a carpet. It could have been a scene from *Lawrence of Arabia*. Messengers were rushing in and out carrying dispatches. Piles of weapons were stacked around the tent. Arab citizens in flowing robes were also there, petitions ready, waiting for a minute of the colonel's time to make an appeal for justice. The colonel was swamped with pressing concerns, and as such the scene was chaotic.

Nevertheless, I was treated to Arab hospitality and the ever-ready cup of tea. After a short exchange of pleasantries, I was told I could begin my briefing on the suspicious gold invoices. The colonel was initially distracted by the messengers and press of urgent business, but when I presented the invoices themselves and conveyed my concern that could indicate commercial fraud at the least and the laundering of narcotics proceeds at the worst, the colonel devoted his full attention and left me with his promise to furnish information on the suspect Kuwaiti gold dealer. The promised information was eventually provided and routed back to me in Rome via the American embassy in Kuwait. It was very much appreciated, particularly because Kuwaiti law enforcement obviously had more urgent priorities.

Continuing with my investigation into the regional gold network, I was given the name of Khalid, one of the largest gold retailers in the Middle East. Khalid was receptive to my request for a tutorial on the Middle East gold business. He hosted me to a wonderful dinner, and afterward, late at night, he invited me back to his main shop in the old gold souk to continue our discussion. Traditionally, along the Arabian Gulf, wooden dhows arriving from East Africa, Persia, and South Asia discharged their cargo along the docks of port cities. Souks sprang up near the docks and became the center for trade in foodstuffs, spices, silks, and perfumes. Today the old souks have generally sprawled and expanded. The markets offer goods for modern tastes, including textiles, electronics, and the latest consumer goods. Yet the colorful atmosphere of a bustling marketplace, with noisy bargaining, exotic scents, and friendly vendor rivalry, remains.

Every large Arabian souk that I am aware of has a section devoted to gold, the largest of which can stretch for city blocks. Shop windows filled with golden ornaments, jewelry, necklaces, rings, bangles, and brooches line the narrow streets. A large gold souk has tons of gold on display but little visible security. Theft is very rare. Likewise impressive is the sheer scale of the trade and the variety of golden goods for sale. Most of the golden ornaments manufactured for sale to Arab customers are twenty-two-carat gold. Gold for the Indian subcontinent can be as high as twenty-four-carat. Western-style gold jewelry is imported eighteen-carat Italian gold. Primarily because of the absence of tax and retailer markup, Italian gold is much less expensive in the Middle East than it is in Italy.

The shops and narrow alleyways of the souks are packed with customers. Saudis are the world's largest spenders on gold per capita.[2] At a wedding in Saudi Arabia, literally kilos of gold jewelry and ornaments can be found on the bride. In fact, in most Arabian countries, the giving of gold to the bride at her wedding is very popular. In a country where women are not allowed full freedom to express themselves and find cultural restrictions in public arenas, many wealthy Saudi women find a sort of acceptable refuge in buying, selling, and trading the latest in gold ornaments. If a Saudi woman is divorced, her gold ornaments cannot be taken away. Gold becomes one of her primary means of savings. Women, underneath their black *abayas*, can be adorned in gold ornaments.

Most of the Gulf countries are populated by a large percentage of guest workers. Many come from India, Pakistan, Sri Lanka, and Bangladesh. These nationals are also found in the souks, both as customers and shop attendants. Much of their savings are invested in gold. In South Asia, tens of millions of marriages take place every year, and often the status of a family in the community is judged by the gold exchanged in the bride's dowry. Traditionally in the region, gold has filled many roles as jewelry, savings, a type of bearer instrument, a hedge against unexpected currency devaluations, an escape from the tax collector, and overall, a type of insurance. Because there are over one billion Indians, India has the largest consumption of gold in the world.[3] The demand for gold in India is constant because it is part of the country's culture and lifestyle.

Khalid took me to the back room of his central store, which was located right in the middle of the gold souk. He and his family owned many other smaller gold shops scattered around the same souk. Perhaps another dozen or more of his stores were found in modern shopping malls and hotel lobbies around the city. Sipping the ever-present tea, I sat transfixed as I observed runner after unescorted runner come into the back room carrying sacks or briefcases filled with gold and cash. Before putting the treasure away in his large wall safe, Khalid unceremoniously dumped mounds of gold on an old-fashioned balance scale. He kept a running ledger of amounts. Value was calculated in weight, not crafts-manship: a jeweler keeps his books in gold and assesses his worth in kilos. I had never seen such a display of wealth in my life. And neither the gold nor the cash seemed to have any kind of visible Western-style control or audit trail.

Khalid told me that his business was booming. He said that during the 1991 Gulf War the value of gold increased as a result of new demand. Everybody wanted to add to their gold holdings in case it was necessary to flee. I had heard the stories of Kuwaitis trying to escape their country in the hours and days after the Iraq invasion. As history has demonstrated time and time again, gold was a much better insurance policy, bribe fac-tor, and source of transportable wealth than currency. Moreover, as will be discussed later, some Muslims object on religious grounds to interest payments. This has encouraged both the rise in Islamic banking and the investment in gold rather than traditional or Western-style financial insti-tutions in the hope of capital gains. In addition, many wealthy Arabs take some of their "black gold"—i.e., oil—profits and invest them in the real glittering variety.

Khalid and others also explained to me that gold plays a central role in the regional alternative remittance system that émigré guest workers use to send their wages back home to their countries of origin. Sending money home through traditional financial institutions is both costly and time consuming for guest workers, and transferring money through the regulated sector allowed officials in the home country to better track the workers' monetary flow for tax purposes. Moreover, some of the workers are illiterate and thus are intimidated by filling out the requisite forms in financial institutions. As a result, over the years an alternative remittance system in which representatives of various gold brokers in the Gulf bought the guest workers' salaries developed. The workers used agents whom they could trust. Many were members of the same extended family, tribe, village, or clan. The workers' salary was converted to gold and then sent from the Gulf to South Asia, where there was always a ready market. Before some South Asian countries liberalized their gold trade in the mid-1990s, introducing gold into the black market by smuggling could also add to a broker's profit margin. The gold importer then arranged to pay, in a timely fashion, the guest worker's family or beneficiary in rupees or the local currency at the black-market rate. This system was virtually untraceable and under the radar of regulators in all countries concerned, both in government and financial institutions. Only later did I realize that the misuse of the gold trade Khalid described was actually part of the indigenous *hawala* system of value transfer. This system and its link to terrorist finance will be discussed later in this book.

Information on the gold trade obtained from the Middle East helped me better understand various methodologies uncovered during the Vinny of Vicenza investigation back in Italy. Further I determined that before settling down in Italy, Vinny had spent many years in the Middle East. Unfortunately, back in Rome, the Primo Passo team was frustrated, and the investigation into Vinny had stalled. Working with the Guardia di Finanza, we had a good sense of Vinny's business in Italy. The Italian foreign service national (FSN) assigned to our office developed excellent insight into the Italian gold industry. The Primo Passo analyst did a great job of identifying Vinny's U.S. assets. Yet despite tantalizing clues, we could not take the investigation further. We still didn't know the details of Vinny himself. After a year or more of investigation, we considered closing the case.

As the leader of the Primo Passo team, I didn't want to see our hard work go to waste, so I attempted to find out whatever we needed to learn about Vinny. And to give us the best chance of success, I decided that I needed to operate more like my former case officer self by aggressively developing human intelligence. Since I did not have direct access to Vinny and did not want to confront him prematurely because it could jeopardize the investigation, I dusted off an old trick that I had learned in the Agency: I decided I would work through intermediaries, or "access agents" as they are called in the trade. I would find sources who knew Vinny and have them tell me what was going on.

As a result, in a discussion with a Saudi source, I learned about a Palestinian who reportedly was close to Vinny and was familiar with his gold business. The Saudi later introduced me to the Palestinian. The Palestinian told me about a European business associate who knew Vinny very well and harbored a professional grudge against him. The grudge was the classic vulnerability that every intelligence officer attempts to exploit. The business associate actually lived in Italy, but the Palestinian wasn't sure where. I took what information I had and asked a close friend in Italian law enforcement for a favor. Using the right database, the Italian located the associate's whereabouts in Italy. He had his men place the target under surveillance and later provided me with the findings of the watch. I used that information to contact the business associate, whom I eventually recruited. The new source provided invaluable information, allowing us to continue our investigation. This was the best bit of recruiting I ever accomplished because it was done in a relatively short time period and involved diverse nationalities. Although Customs didn't care—for the law enforcement agency, arrests and seizure statistics were the only thing that mattered—my old employer, the CIA, would have been impressed with my little operation. Up to that time, I had minimal contacts with the Agency, but one way or the other, my old employer started to notice what I was doing.

✳

Because of my frequent travel to the Middle East, I was beginning to become fairly well known in some of the American embassies. U.S. law enforcement had no representatives in the region, so my points of contact in the American embassies in the Middle East were usually the State Department regional security officer (RSO) and the economics officer. The RSO's primary responsibility was the overall security of the embassy and its personnel; I found the RSO could always point me in the right direction as far as dealing with host government law enforcement officials and would do everything possible to facilitate my investigations. The State Department's embassy economics officer was very helpful in discussing concerns about money laundering. During my visits to the embassies, I would sometimes also pay a courtesy call to the ambassador and the deputy chief of mission (DCM). If appropriate, I would brief them on my investigations and solicit their insights regarding the situation in the host country.

Typically, my embassy contacts would help arrange necessary appointments. Of course, they were also welcome to attend my meetings with local officials; embassy officials want to know who is meeting with whom and what is being said. I managed to have meetings with law enforcement, customs, central bank authorities, and other ranking officials in various ministries, departments, or the Chamber of Commerce. I would also visit with local police officers or dockworkers. I wanted to meet with whoever could provide key assistance in my various investigations. In short, I often met with local contacts that embassy staffers could not get ready access to.

The reporting problem is compounded for Embassy State Department officers, including RSOs, because they are not allowed to develop clandestine reporting sources. In addition, some embassy officials from various departments and agencies get complacent sitting behind their desks. It is an easy routine to fall into. Embassy staff members can easily stay busy all day attending meetings and working at their computers and phones. They might go to a lunch or reception and obtain information provided to them by their official interlocutors, although that type of information generally contains few insights and usually reports the host country's official line.

In part, in what was probably a carryover from my case officer days, when I traveled to the Middle East, I tried to learn as much as I could in the streets and the market places. Information from official sources is helpful, but real insight only comes from getting out from behind a desk. Today, meaningful official U.S. reporting is lacking in Iraq in part because the security situation inhibits the collection of information at the street level. There are also certainly stars in our embassies. I never ceased to be impressed how State Department officers would often contend with personal hardships while aggressively reporting useful information.

Aside from my work on the street, I gained access to information and officials of interest because I represented the Department of the Treasury and Customs. It was a tremendous advantage. I was not considered a threat by the host country. And I wasn't. I was truly there to help. After all, most of my investigations impacted both the United States and the country I was visiting. The investigations were a two-way street. I would ask for assistance, but I would also give information that might indicate a violation of local laws. Customs was involved in everything from narcotics, money laundering, intellectual property right violations, transshipments of weapons, child pornography, trade fraud and quota violations, and many other transnational offenses. In almost all cases, the countries appreciated U.S. Customs insight and assistance. I also found that, operating overseas, Customs had an advantage over the FBI: Customs was multifaceted and considered nonthreatening by the host government. But in addition to its police functions, the FBI is known for its counterintelligence work. As a result, some countries don't feel entirely comfortable with the Bureau's growing overseas presence—and neither does the CIA.

Operating overseas in an open, overt, and transparent status was the major difference between my previous experience collecting foreign intelligence as a CIA case officer and my new status as an official American criminal investigator. Before, my covert status and my mission were secret. As a Customs special agent assigned to work investigations overseas, I had no secrets. I welcomed cooperation with my law enforcement and customs counterparts. Granted there were occasions when I still needed to use good tradecraft to ensure my informants' safety. But during my investigative travels overseas, I felt that if somebody wanted to follow me, they were welcome to do so. In fact, on a number of occasions, I did "make surveillance" by what I assumed were operatives from the host country's Ministry of Interior. Undoubtedly, some of my telephone conversations and meetings were monitored. But if asked, I would be quite open about what I was doing. After all, it was true: I was from the U.S. government, and I was genuinely there to help.

U.S. law enforcement and foreign intelligence agencies often battle over turf overseas. For example, in the mid-1990s, the CIA let it be known that it felt that it was within its purview to be alerted to all U.S. government sources of information in a given country. Certain chiefs of station felt that if a Customs, DEA, or FBI agent or even the U.S. military met an informant in "their country," they wanted to know about it. The idea was to stop duplication of effort and prevent recruitment efforts against the same target. General knowledge of an operation was one thing, but requiring the registration of another agency's sources was something else all together.

The CIA's edict was not popular with U.S. law enforcement, and I played their game completely only one time. When the policy was announced, I sent a country clearance cable to the American embassy in a Middle Eastern country I was visiting providing details about my trip, the investigations I planned to conduct, and the people with whom I would be meeting. When I arrived in country, I briefed the counsel general, the regional security officer, and a representative of the CIA. At the end of my visit, I gave an "out brief" on my findings. I was transparent in my work and adhered to the Agency's policy of full disclosure. I had no secrets.

However, when I traveled to my next stop in the region, I had a

surprise waiting for me. The Agency apparently was upset about my ability to meet with some local authorities that they could not get in to see. I
don't know whether or not they were embarrassed, but whatever the
cause I was told to report to the DCM to explain my activities. Fortunately, the DCM was a reasonable man and I had documented all of my
activities every step of the way. I had done nothing wrong. The DCM
actually complimented me on my work. Still, that was the first and last
time I fully followed the Agency's edict. Unfortunately, in the War on
Terrorism, the same interagency/departmental source registration issue
has resurfaced.[4]

During this time frame, I viewed with alarm my former colleagues in
the Agency becoming increasingly dependent on "liaison services" for
the collection of intelligence. "Liaison services" was a quaint designation
for a country's internal and/or external intelligence services. Of course,
the Agency should talk to its sister services, but in such conversations
skepticism should be the watchword. This type of incestuous relationship
is ideal for spreading misinformation and the party line. Sometimes, there
is "circular intelligence" reporting, which is when various reports pull
information from the same basic source, skewing analysis. With the end
of the Cold War, there was a downsizing in the Agency's Directorate of
Operations' overseas presence and a corresponding increase in bureaucratic staffing at headquarters. Combined with increased oversight, scrutiny, and operational restrictions, collecting information from foreign liaison services became a dangerous shortcut for the Agency.

A further deterioration of America's overseas collection capability
that I observed firsthand was a drastic falloff in language ability. I found
that at some CIA offices in the Middle East nobody spoke Arabic. Granted
Arabic is considered a difficult language, but that is no excuse. This lack
of language ability hampered the Agency from "getting out in the street"
to independently assess information from the liaison services. It was a
vicious circle. Both the dependence on foreign liaison services and the
lack of language ability were contributing factors to future intelligence
failures and the current difficulties in the War on Terrorism.

In the early and mid-1990s, it was apparent the Agency was adrift
and in search of a mission. For all intents and purposes, the traditional
reason for its existence collapsed in 1989, along with the Berlin Wall. For
a few years there were those who thought the defeat of communism and

the end of the Cold War also signaled the "end of history."[5] According to this reasoning, Western democratic capitalism had proved itself superior to all rivals, and communism was swept into the dustbin of history. Because history had supposedly ended and it was time for a budgetary "peace dividend," some commentators also called for the end of the CIA. Even from Rome, I could tell that the Agency was in a drastic downsizing mode. It was looking for new ways to justify its existence. The intelligence-collection cycle explained in chapter 1 remained the same, but from a bureaucratic point of view, the Agency needed new intelligence taskings. Thus, the Agency looked to employ its intelligence-collecting expertise in confronting new challenges, including supporting law enforcement.

I got along very well with the chief and deputy chief in Rome. One day, aware of my money-laundering investigations, the deputy asked the customs attaché if an Agency staffer could assist me. Wanting to cooperate, the attaché agreed. However, the resulting meeting between the CIA staffer and the Customs staff was both comical and a little sad. The CIA staffer had been so programmed by Cold War procedures and security concerns that when she came to visit us in our office she literally spoke in inaudible whispers, even though everything discussed was quite open and unclassified. The Customs staff could barely control their laughter. The CIA staffer also discovered that our Italian law enforcement colleagues and Italian office FSNs had access to the same case information. Their involvement presented additional "security" problems for the Agency. Simply put, the cultures and perspectives of the U.S. intelligence and law enforcement communities clashed. Having been in both, I thought I had a unique opportunity—at my relatively low level—to be a bridge between them.

Continuing my informal and collegial discussions with Agency representatives, I would occasionally pass along foreign intelligence that I discovered during the course of my law enforcement work. An Agency reports officer was impressed with this new perspective and asked if he could use the information and send it to CIA headquarters in the form of intelligence reports. I didn't have any objections if he thought the information would be useful to the CIA and wanted to get it into intelligence reporting channels. Familiar with procedures in both communities, I knew only too well that law enforcement and intelligence information streams were totally separate, a fact that came back to haunt us in the events surrounding September 11. Remembering how to write the Agency intelligence reports, I actually drafted reports for the interested officer. He and I collaborated to send a number of intelligence reports, primarily based on information developed in my travels, to Washington. However, this innocent example of low-level law enforcement and intelligence cooperation didn't last long. Almost concurrently, both our respective headquarters told us to knock it off.

A few months later bureaucratic shortsightedness and stupidity reached a new low. A source gave me information he obtained directly from a subsource, who was reportedly involved with the shipment of a weapon of mass destruction from a country in the former Soviet Union to a country that the U.S. government was very concerned about. I was not in a position to judge whether the information was true or not, but I was quite confident about the sincerity of my source. I didn't request or "task him" to collect the information; my source had happened upon it and was very concerned. He wanted to report it to the U.S. government. I thanked him profusely and dutifully reported the information to both the Agency for its evaluation and to Customs headquarters. The response that came back from a Customs official at headquarters' Office of Foreign Operations was—and this is an exact quote: "Don't waste your time collecting such information. Where's the U.S. Customs violation?"

During this same time frame, another source of mine in the Middle East proposed a very promising operation. I had been trying to develop this high-level source for a long time. As the reader recalls from the earlier discussion on my career with the CIA, finding someone with access to information of import is the key. Ahmed was potentially the highest caliber source I had ever worked. He seemingly knew everybody, and he had provided me with invaluable insights. He also boasted a shadowy reputation that, at times, worked to his advantage. As such, he told me that he had received a number of diverse inquiries ranging from criminal networks to politically connected people who asked him to assist in laundering their money. Ahmed suggested to me that he could work with them and provide me with the resulting intelligence. This operation would put Customs Attaché Rome in an ideal position to follow the money and better understand—at very high levels—the underworld of crime and finance in the region. The potential of what Ahmed suggested was staggering. Law enforcement has seen time and time again that the only way to make "impact cases" is to have a well-placed and cooperating source. Ahmed was at the top of the food chain. To my knowledge, an investigation of the magnitude I envisioned had never been done before—or since—in the Middle East.

Unfortunately, as they say in law enforcement, "Big cases, big problems." And my largest and most immediate problem was that it is almost impossible to run an undercover operation long distance. As discussed in the example of Project Wayward, the undercover arms investigation, every undercover operation has its many administrative, logistic, operational, policy, personality, and management issues. In this case, I was based in Rome and Ahmed was in the Middle East, where the United States had no permanent law enforcement presence. The Office of the Customs Attaché's travel budget was not large and would certainly not support the kind of frequent travel necessary to work effectively with Ahmed and run the operation. As much as I didn't want to relinquish full control, I wanted to explore the possibility of having the Agency, my old employer, handle Ahmed and assist in the operation.

During the mid-1990s the Agency was caught up in one of its periodic exercises of collective hari-kari. Under the Clinton administration, a new edict was promulgated that effectively prohibited the CIA from recruiting or handling any source with known criminal records. The CIA director announced that the Agency would no longer accept information from "tainted" sources; this turned out to be a real handicap for an organization trying to reinvent itself by supporting law enforcement or trying to penetrate terrorist networks. Colleagues of mine back at the Agency said that lawyers were sprouting like mushrooms in various dark offices and directorates. Instead of looking for ways to conduct operations, CIA staffers were reportedly looking for reasons to avoid going forward. The restriction on dealing with criminals, no doubt made with the best of intentions, was just one in a series of restrictions put on the clandestine service. However, it was laughable on its face. U.S. law enforcement agencies routinely use criminals and those associated with criminals to gain insight into criminal activity so that they can arrest and prosecute others up the criminal ladder. That is the way the game is played. Yes, some of the contacts are unsavory characters, and yes, sometimes deals have to be made with them to obtain their cooperation. But the use of criminals to combat crime is just plain effective.

When I briefed Agency staff on Ahmed's proposal, the initial reaction was very favorable. However, when they ran Ahmed's name in their database, they found a notation that he had been investigated by law enforcement and was considered a "criminal." As a result, they were prohibited from working with him. Knowing Ahmed, I doubted his "criminal" designation. Nothing in the Customs database said he was a convicted criminal. Before giving up, I decided to query all of my other U.S. law enforcement colleagues at the American embassy to see if any of their databases contained additional information on Ahmed. There was and there still is no central U.S. law enforcement database; the checks had to be done agency by agency.

As part of its database search, the FBI legatt in Rome sent a message into FBI headquarters asking for a records check. What came back surprised us. Although never convicted of anything, reportedly, Ahmed's name had surfaced in the Bureau's continuing investigation of the first New York World Trade Center bombing in 1993. Apparently, he wasn't accused of being part of the conspiracy, but they wanted to interview him as someone who might have knowledge of activities or persons of interest. FBI headquarters asked if I would introduce Ahmed to an FBI special agent assigned to the Rome legatt.

Special agents are very protective of their sources, and I was naturally afraid of losing Ahmed to the Bureau. But this was an issue of national security. Customs interests took a backseat. As a result, I spoke to Ahmed over the phone and asked if he would be agreeable to meeting a friend and a colleague of mine from the FBI. I didn't give him any further details. He probably thought it had something to do with the operation we were contemplating. Ahmed agreed to the meeting. An FBI special agent and I traveled to meet him.

I had never previously worked with the Bureau on an actual investigation in the field, but I felt comfortable in this case because I knew the FBI agent well. Although he had no firsthand experience in dealing with Middle East matters, he had much field experience. Personally, he was a great guy. When Ahmed, the FBI agent, and I finally sat down together over coffee for an introduction and our first chat, I resolved to do everything I could to facilitate the introduction and initiate a mutually productive relationship.

However, almost before I finished expressing my warm pleasantries

upon seeing Ahmed again, the FBI agent said to my source, "Y
has surfaced in the FBI's investigation into the World Trade Center terrorist attack. I am here to ask you questions." I could see the blood drain
from Ahmed's face. I had no idea that the FBI agent would use such a
threatening opening line. He did not even make a preliminary attempt to
establish any kind of rapport and trust. I should have known better. It is
part of the FBI's culture to exert control and take charge. Yet the agent
should have realized that, particularly with a source of Ahmed's stature,
developing a certain level of mutual comfort and respect was crucial. As
much as I tried to pick up the pieces of the broken introduction, it was
obvious that Ahmed was frightened. He immediately denied any involvement or knowledge of the World Trade Center bombing. For all intents
and purposes, the meeting was over before it even began. Unfortunately,
the meeting was also the end of Ahmed's offer to help construct a high-
level undercover operation in the Middle East. I will always regret not
opening that potentially significant window to Middle East underground
finance prior to September 11.

5

All Roads Lead to Dubai

Dubai is one of the seven emirates of the United Arab Emirates (UAE). Not many years ago it was nothing more than a small Arabian Gulf Coast fishing and pearling settlement. But because of its magnificent location on the crosswinds and crossroads of the Arabian Peninsula, it became an attractive location for shopping, trading, and finance. Early commercial success, combined with the relatively liberal, open, and laissez-fair attitudes of the ruling Maktum family, attracted even more traders from India, Iran, and other lands. In 1966, while Dubai was still a political protectorate of the United Kingdom, oil was discovered there. An enlightened Sheikh Rashid bin Said al Maktum ensured that, though Dubai did not have as much oil as its neighbors had, the wealth generated from it was plowed back into developing the emirate's infrastructure. Today, modern Dubai rises where the desert meets the sea like an Emirati Emerald City in an Arabian Oz. Yet even with its modern glass towers, twenty-first-century office buildings, and resort amenities, Dubai remains the lively port of yesteryear, complete with wooden dhows of ancient design (but with modern engines) that follow the same trade routes across the Gulf and beyond.

A wide creek, aptly nicknamed "Smugglers Creek," bisects Dubai into two developing commercial and resort sections: Bur Dubai on one side and Deira on the other. Dhows continue to slip out of the creek laden with items for "reexport."[1] Before the Indian subcontinent liberalized its gold import restrictions in the mid-1990s, dhows and other means were used to smuggle large amounts of gold to India. Because Dubai is the regional transportation hub, gold and other items can also be smuggled by planes, couriers, and forty-foot shipping containers. It is reported that police and customs in the subcontinent have found smuggled gold inside fruit, hidden in false-bottomed suitcases, hidden in the frames and tires of bicycles, melted into machine parts that were covered with a layer of grease, concealed in edible goods, and shoved into the private parts of couriers.[2]

The Gulf is filled with brokers and traders, who have refined the art of the deal through the centuries. Some native Arabs who are well connected through tribe and family benefit from the tremendous wealth and largesse generated through the Maktum enterprise of Dubai. The Arabic word *wasta* means clout through influence, connections, and family ties. Wasta is the means through which things get done, particularly in Dubai. Business contracts and control of land development are given through wasta. Tremendous amounts of money flow into the high-rise apartment buildings, shopping centers, hotels, and resorts that seemingly bloom like desert flowers after a rain. It is said that some of the money for these developments has uncertain origin.

Some native Emiratis who are not quite as well connected still benefit from the system. For example, almost 90 percent of Dubai's population consists of expatriate workers, who are needed to build, staff, and even help manage modern Dubai. As in Saudi Arabia and other Gulf countries, a great many Indians, Pakistanis, Iranians, Afghans, Bangladeshis, and many others looking for work and wealth have flooded the UAE. They bring with them both their entrepreneurial spirit and native ways of doing business. But to open a shop or run the ever-present import-export concern, the expatriate must pay a fee to a native sponsor, so that on paper, the local Emirati has majority ownership. In most cases though, the sponsor is no more than an absentee landlord who exercises no real oversight of the business other than collecting the sponsorship fee. The system is easily abused. Into the mix step the professional criminals, particularly those from India, Pakistan, and states of the former Soviet Union, who are attracted to the wealth-creating opportunities in Dubai's liberal trading sector. Even the occasional terrorist will take advantage of Dubai's liberal lifestyle, modern infrastructure, transportation hub, and efficient financial and business services. In ancient times it was said all roads lead to Rome. In modern times coming from Rome, the trails of transnational crime that I followed eventually led to Dubai.

There were a myriad of investigations. Most had to do with Dubai acting as a type of regional transit hub for money, goods, and people. In the mid-1990s the UAE's reexport business, the great majority of which was centered in Dubai, was worth about $10 billion dollars a year.[3] U.S.

Customs believed some of those reexports were trade diversion and transshipments. Many of the investigations, including following the transshipment of embargoed goods to Iran or Saddam Hussein's Iraq, had difficulty getting traction. U.S. embargoes were not recognized in the region. The local businesspeople who forwarded the goods to prohibited end users literally laughed at me and the government I represented, dismissing my efforts by saying, "Those are your embargoes not mine." I tried to impress upon one local trader U.S. concerns about trade-based money laundering. He didn't have a clue what money laundering was, but he was adept at using overinvoicing and underinvoicing to transfer value in various trade transactions. He was quite proficient in avoiding South Asian taxes and government scrutiny. With complete and obviously sincere innocence, he told me, "Mr. John, money laundering? But that's what we do." Precisely. Money laundering as a crime was not even in the frame of reference of the Arab brokers and traders and the expatriate import-export dealers. It was a foreign, Western concept. The locals were simply putting deals together in the most cost-efficient way possible—in part by avoiding taxes and government scrutiny. This was the same commercial concept their ancestors had used in the centuries before banks. Instead of the transfer of money, the transfer of value continues to be found in trade goods. Today's brokers and traders are just refining the art of the deal, using the new tools that modern Dubai has to offer.

One tool of the modern era is the misuse of free trade zones (FTZs). In an effort to spur even greater trade and commerce, Dubai and other emirates created several FTZs. The largest is Jebel Ali, which is the home for thousands of companies. The FTZs permit 100 percent foreign ownership, no taxation, full repatriation of capital and profits, no import duties, and easily obtainable licenses. Companies located in the FTZs are treated as being offshore or outside the UAE for legal purposes.

FTZs are found around the world, including in the United States. They are generally distinct, closed, and segregated facilities located near ports. Imports of raw materials, machinery, and parts necessary to manufacture and add value to goods are allowed to come into FTZs duty free. This reduces costs and gives companies located in FTZs a competitive advantage. In addition to duty-free imports, many FTZs, including Jebel Ali, pride themselves on their rapid turn-around time for transshipments or goods coming in and going out. Consumer goods, electronics, tex-

tiles, foodstuffs, machinery, and every imaginable type of trade good enter the FTZs in Dubai. Because of the race for quick turn-around time
and the lack of local official interest in goods considered in transit, customs authorities, unfortunately, have little inclination to examine many
of the shipments.

Most trading companies engage in legitimate international trade and
financial activities. Unfortunately, there are a few bad apples. Just as bad
money is mixed with good in various money-laundering methodologies,
making it difficult for criminal investigators to follow the money trail,
bad trade goods and practices are mixed with legitimate trade. The sheer
volume of trade in FTZs makes it very difficult to spot the questionable
transactions. Moreover, many suspect financing methodologies are employed in FTZs. For example, suspect foreign exchange dealers from South
Asia deliver hard currency to brokers in Dubai's FTZs to purchase trade
goods for reexport back to South Asia. This can help to provide value
transfer in the alternative remittance system of *hawala*. And, as will be
described in more detail later, the regional shopping center of Dubai is
integrated into the misuse of the Afghan Transit Trade, which I believe is
used to launder narcotics proceeds and perhaps to finance terrorism.

Counterfeit trade goods, particularly consumer products and electronics, can also be found in FTZs. Although these products are generally manufactured in China, South Korea, and India, FTZs facilitate their
entry into the world's commerce. Unfortunately, several companies involved in the illegal but profitable trading of counterfeit goods have in a
few cases transferred funds or value in the support of terrorists.

I also found in my investigations that misinvoicing in trade is common. For example, if an inexpensive item is mislabeled or described in
accompanying documents in a misleading way, it is often difficult for
customs to determine its true value. An inexpensive item becomes an
expensive item on an invoice with the notation of a pen or a click of a
keyboard. The resulting payment gives rationale to the movement of
money; it is a type of transfer payment. Transshipments through multiple
ports and multiple geographic locations can further disguise the origin of
products. Goods can be repackaged and relabeled in various locations.
Time and again law enforcement has found suspect Lebanese and South
Asian traders located in FTZs around the world. They use impenetrable
family ties and connections to engage in fraudulent trade practices. While

investigating the seemingly nonthreatening transshipment of garments into U.S. commerce, I began a new journey into this underworld of illicit trade and discovered more clues on how fraud and value transfer are commingled in the region. The investigation also provided insight into regional illicit finance and uncovered new challenges in trying to take effective enforcement action in the riddle that is the Middle East.

✳

Primarily in response to intense political pressure from congressmen representing states whose textile manufacturing industries were under attack from an invasion of foreign imports of questionable origin, Customs mounted a program to combat foreign textile fraud and illegal transshipments. The centerpiece of the program was sending textile production verification "jump teams" to foreign countries. The teams were composed of Customs import specialists who had expertise in textiles and special agents charged with developing intelligence about transshipments and pursuing possible investigations. Countries would be targeted for a visit primarily by the import specialists' examination of textile import summaries from countries around the world. A review of data and documents could often identify questionable trading practices.

The teams visited the targeted foreign textile factories where goods reportedly manufactured for export to the United States were produced. In many instances, the U.S. Customs teams, acting in concert with their local counterparts, were able to verify production and export. However, in other cases the teams found evidence of fraud and the transshipment of apparel goods that were designed to circumvent U.S. quota laws.

One verification team I was with visited a textile manufacturing concern in the Middle East, which I will call Global Garment Company (GGC). The company's record of imports was suspicious; it did not appear that their production facilities, equipment, and raw materials could match the volume of exports that the paper documents claimed. However, Tawfiq, the owner of the company, forcefully denied wrongdoing and presented the inspection team, which included representatives of the local customs service, documents that seemed to be in order.

On another visit a short time later to Ajman in the UAE, a jump team discovered documents that implicated the very same GGC, and

Tawfiq, in fraudulent invoicing. The inspection team found that the Ajman company had few employees, and similar to GGC, the U.S. import statistics we studied indicated higher production than observed capacity. In the storage area of the company, we found only a little fabric but boxes and boxes of knit shirts complete with "Made in India" and "Made in Kuwait" labels. The team also found bags and bags of "Made in Oman" labels ready to be sewn in. The Indian minority owner–manager denied our concerns of transshipment of Indian-produced garments.

Typically, India would rapidly fulfill its quotas of garments, and unscrupulous brokers would send excess quantity to other countries that had not yet fulfilled their quotas. Workers would sew new "Made in" labels in the garments so the shirt made in India could then enter U.S. commerce as a shirt manufactured in, for example, the UAE. The transshipments violated U.S. law and also cheated the host country.

Months later, during the course of other Customs investigations, I again visited GGC. This time I was by myself but armed with the new information recovered from the jump team's visit to Ajman. I was determined to confront Tawfiq. The Ajman documents were incriminating on their face. However, Tawfiq knew the intricacies of manufacturing garments. He used a false set of books and ledgers and tried to again explain away the discrepancies, suspect data, and documents. I didn't believe him, and he knew it.

Shortly after I returned to Rome from the Middle East, I received a phone call from Tawfiq. His conscience was bothering him. He wanted to fly to Rome to meet me and confess his involvement in the transshipment of garments. I was very anxious to hear what he had to say. Tawfiq admitted that he had lied to me and the previous jump team. He said that for the last five years he had been helping to transship garments made in other countries to the United States and Europe. He implicated Amit Singh, and his Dubai-based company Rapid Freight Forwarders (RFF), as the mastermind behind the diversion scheme. Tawfiq said he provided Singh and RFF documents with his GGC company letterhead, invoices, seals, and bills of lading to effectively disguise shipments of garments originating from China and India. Tawfiq told me that Singh paid him about $2.50 per dozen of garments transshipped using his fictitious documents. The payoffs and fraudulent trade were intermixed with his regular production. Sometimes textiles shipments were disguised to show Tawfiq's country as the country of origin, and sometimes Singh sent garments ready to be transshipped to accommodating FTZs that Tawfiq did business with. By the time the garments reached the United States, everything appeared in order.

Per Tawfiq's invitation, Customs Import Specialist Bob Dorsey and I returned once again to Tawfiq's factory. This time Tawfiq provided us with a genuine set of books and documents, which accurately reflected his business. A later comparison of Tawfiq's true records to customs data in the United States and those of the concerned country in the Middle East showed that over a four-year period, Tawfiq had fraudulently transshipped $18 million of garments with a domestic value of almost $50 million into the United States. In addition, Tawfiq provided additional evidence that RFF of Dubai had further masterminded the transshipment of garments from India and China through other countries such as Oman, the UAE, Kuwait, Jordan, and Tanzania. Import Specialist Bob Dorsey calculated that the domestic value of all of the illegal imports easily exceeded $100 million dollars. Although only one case and "only textiles," $100 million is a lot of money!

As a criminal investigator, I was most excited about the documentation and correspondence I obtained from another industry source who proved Amit Singh of RFF orchestrated the transshipments. Included was an RFF document sent to a garment manufacturer in Hong Kong, which actually listed "reexport charges," "relabeling charges," and fees for "unstuffing and reloading containers." RFF also listed import and export charges for bills of lading, customs duties, port fees, and document handling fees for the Emirati ports of Dubai and Fujarah. Also, a notation on the document stated, "Suggest you send us some blank invoices." The document was the proverbial smoking gun. And such a document is rarely uncovered in the Middle East.

All of the documentation we obtained was turned over to the local customs service for their concurrent investigation. During my previous trips I had spoken to the American embassy, the local Ministry of Economy and Commerce, and representatives of the local textile manufacturer's association, as well as the police and customs services. Before Tawfiq's cooperation, Bob Dorsey and I were considering recommending that quotas on the production of garments be levied on the country. It was a small country, and such quotas would have imposed severe hardships on the manufacturers that played by the rules. Although Tawfiq admittedly engaged in criminal activity, because of his cooperation, I approached the director general of the customs service in the country where Tawfiq lived and expressed my appreciation for Tawfiq's help. Nevertheless, it was rightly judged a very serious matter. Probably because of the mitigating circumstances, Tawfiq later only received a stiff fine and a suspended prison sentence.

Import Specialist Dorsey and I next headed to Dubai to confront Amit Singh and RFF. Because U.S. law enforcement had no enforcement authority overseas, we had to work with an appropriate foreign counterpart agency. We spent more than a week being shuttled from one ministry to another, looking for the appropriate agency, but finally, working with the American consulate in Dubai, we were told that investigators from the UAE Ministry of Economy and Commerce would assist us with our investigation. We briefed the investigators and asked that they obtain the equivalent of a warrant and conduct a search of the premises of RFF so that we could recover additional incriminating documents. Working with a contact, I actually had a sketch of the RFF floor plan and good intelligence where the "real" set of books was located. Unfortunately, the local investigators were not interested in the American way of investigations or conducting searches. As a courtesy, we were told that we could go with them on the "raid," but we had to stay in the background and we were not allowed to participate or even speak.

The next morning the UAE Ministry of Economy and Commerce raided the premises of RFF. From the intelligence we had collected, we knew that the main suspect, Amit Singh, was in Europe on business and was not going to be present. However, we were after documents, so we thought his absence wouldn't really matter. The RFF office was still open and staffed by four female workers. True to our agreement, Dorsey and I stayed in the background and watched the local authorities conduct the raid. Things went from bad to comical. The RFF staff denied all allegations of transshipments to the local investigators and insisted that they would not speak further unless their boss was present. Of course, by that time, all incriminating documents would be destroyed. The local investigators didn't know what to do. Finally, understanding that they were at a stalemate, they let Dorsey and me question the staff. Bob and I split the group in two. Without raising our voices or in any way threatening the staff, in five minutes we had confessions. The only problem was that the RFF staff members all broke down in tears. As soon as the local officials saw the employees cry, the interview and the "raid" were over. We never got our documents.

I tell this story not to embarrass any officials or RFF staff. These incidents happened years ago. But I want to again illustrate the challenges and cultural differences between conducting investigations in the United States and in certain countries overseas. This incident was just one of many frustrations. For example, on many occasions during my investigations in Dubai when I confronted South Asian traders with conclusive facts and documents about transshipments, the suspects would construct lies of such magnitude that I totally dismissed their credibility. If a document said one thing, suspects would say it meant another. On a number of occasions, when I proved to suspects that documents that they originated and that I had in front of us were fraudulent, instead staying quiet or admitting guilt they would offer to get another document within a few hours. The new document would magically have the missing or correct seal, certification, numbers, signature, amount, etc. Bypassing credibility, operating in a foreign cultural environment, it seemed that the suspect was willing to do just about anything to try to please me. Yet from my background and training, the transparent actions and maneuvering only heightened my sense of the suspect's criminal action and intent. As U.S. multinational corporations have also sometimes found overseas, U.S. methods of doing business do not always translate well in different foreign environments. Similarly, it is only natural that U.S. criminal investigators operating abroad transport their investigative techniques and accompanying linear logic and reasoning. Although we all spoke English, culturally we spoke different languages and operated from different frames of reference. Later I found that disconnects between different cultures and respective outlooks and ways of doing business sometimes impeded our efforts in the War on Terrorist Finance.

Working with the very helpful American consulate in Dubai and Emirati authorities, I later met face to face with the manager of RFF, Amit Singh. Despite being confronted with damning documentation and the confessions of his staff, he denied all involvement in the transshipment of garments into the United States. In addition, his Emirati sponsor claimed no knowledge of Singh's activities and professed no responsibility. Despite Singh's denials, the UAE authorities later took punitive action against RFF that resulted in a nonrenewal of its license and a closing down of the freight forwarding operation.

However, by the time the punitive action took place, I had completed my overseas tour in Rome and was back in the United States. Somehow, Singh located me and gave me a call from Dubai. Sobbing on the phone, he told me I had ruined his life and his business. However, he didn't blame me. On the contrary, Singh said he wanted to finger the masterminds behind the transshipments, the textile magnates in India and China. I believed Singh had the access and the motivation necessary to make that happen. He said, if I came back to Dubai, he would provide the paper trail I needed to prove the complicity of India and China in massive conspiracies to transship textiles into the United States in violation of quota laws.

Of course, I jumped at the opportunity. This was potentially the Holy Grail for textile transshipment investigations. But again, contrary to what is portrayed in the popular media, I couldn't just get on an airplane and fly to Dubai from the United States. Because I was no longer posted in Rome, and for Customs purposes Dubai came under the geographic jurisdiction of the attaché Rome, I had to get the new attaché's permission to travel and pursue the investigation. Then I had to find funding.

Working with headquarters, I got around the funding issue by getting myself included on the next textile jump team going out to the UAE. Once there I would be able to debrief Singh. Concurrently, the Federal Bureau of Investigation was pestering me to follow-up the botched interview of my source Ahmed and his alleged knowledge of individuals involved in the first World Trade Center bombing. Since it looked like I was headed back to the Middle East, I explored with Ahmed the possibility of stopping in his country for another meeting.

Everything appeared on track, until I ran into the politics and personality of the new attaché in Rome. From his point of view, my proposed travel back to the Middle East boiled down to an issue of bureaucratic turf. The attaché felt that since the Middle East was now his "territory," he and his office should work the investigations. By extension, that meant that if the investigations were successful the attaché office would get the credit.

Customs Attaché Rome was welcome to any credit; I didn't care. I just wanted to see if we could pursue the textile case to the industry magnates of India and China. And it was apparent that Singh would only work with me. Even though I was the one that "ruined" his business, he knew me and he trusted my word. Getting Singh's cooperation, or "flipping" the suspect, was a common law enforcement investigative technique. This was also one way of developing excellent sources of information. When I tried to explain that to the attaché, his direct quote was, "I don't give a damn about your sources or the investigation. You are not going to encroach upon the territory of the Customs Attaché Rome. You're not going. And if you don't like it, you can take it up with the assistant commissioner for investigations." The assistant commissioner was a personal friend of the attaché, and in effect, I became entangled with the proverbial old boy's network—though in this case the assistant commissioner was a woman. The bottom line was that I didn't go, and Singh wouldn't meet with anybody else. The promising trail leading to India and China was never followed. And Ahmed never did meet again with the FBI.

As I noted above, big cases invariably involve recruiting human sources. The Central Intelligence Agency calls these sources agents. Among other terms, law enforcement calls them informants. This book earlier discussed how sources are recruited, their motivation, and the necessity of sources having access to information of interest. In 1996, by the time I left Rome, I had about ten documented sources. Many others occasionally provided me with information, but I did not consider them documented or "official" sources. Most of my sources were to be found in the Middle East. To put things in perspective, I don't believe any other special agent in my same Rome office had any sources at all. Sources were important because they were generally the key to initiating meaningful cases and getting insight into others. They could also provide unique intelligence, which could also be indexed in the appropriate databases. For example, after September 11 the subject records I created on individuals and companies years before in the Middle East were constantly queried by analysts and investigators.

I like to think that my sources worked with me because they could tell that I respected them as individuals; we developed professional friendships. "Snitch," the derogatory term that is sometimes used in law enforcement circles, has never been in my working vocabulary. With the exception of a one-time payment to the Saudi businessman I mentioned in chapter 4, I never paid a dime of U.S. taxpayers' money to any of my law enforcement sources. In fact, on numerous occasions my sources paid out of their own pocket to further U.S. Customs' investigations. Sources worked with me and the government I represented so that we could disrupt transnational crime. Many times I had sources tell me that they would cooperate to "help make the world safer for our children." This sentiment rang true in every culture and every country I ever worked in.

I only bring this up because at the time of September 11, with the exception of the newly opened FBI legatt office in Riyadh, which was charged to investigate the 1996 Khobar Towers bombing, it is quite probable that I had the only documented U.S. law enforcement human sources of information in the entire Middle East. And I was no longer traveling to the region. Frankly, in the years immediately proceeding September 11, the Customs attaché office in Rome was ineffectual and almost irrelevant in its efforts in the Middle East. Unfortunately, this failure had repercussions. As the 9/11 Commission discovered, the lack of U.S. human intelligence in the Middle East directly contributed to the United States being caught unaware. And this lack of human intelligence occurred in both the intelligence and law enforcement communities. I have tried to demonstrate to the layperson some of the difficulties in obtaining human intelligence. The Rome attaché's refusal to allow the continued pursuit of the textile transshipment investigation and further attempts to work with Ahmed demonstrates that inept management and bureaucratic turf should be included on the list of difficulties.

Before leaving textile transshipments, I would like to make a few other observations. The GGC investigation resulted in various spin-off investigations, including one proving that millions of dollars worth of Chinese-made textiles were transshipped through Hong Kong directly to a retailer in New York who had knowledge of the transshipped goods. When the case was presented to the Office of the U.S. Attorney in the southern district of New York, prosecution was declined because it was "just a textile case." This attitude was similar to the one I had confronted with stolen cars. It is not for me to judge the very real resource constraints of federal prosecutors; obviously, there are competing priorities and prosecutorial thresholds. However, Congress allocated a lot of money to crack down on textile transshipments. It does no good if Customs investigates and presents textile cases for prosecution, while the Department of Justice declines prosecution and the Department of Commerce is not particularly supportive. The U.S. government can more easily accomplish its priorities if the concerned government departments and agencies coordinate their actions and act in a unified fashion. It doesn't make any difference if we are talking textile investigations or terrorist finance.

As a final observation, in the late 1990s I visited some garment manufacturers in North Carolina as I helped train special agents going on future textile jump teams. By visiting U.S. manufacturers, the agents received an introduction to some of the things they might encounter while inspecting factories overseas. What struck me in the North Carolina shops were the American workers assembling garments. Trade "globalization" had hit them hard. Confronted with a flood of cheap foreign imports, they knew they were a vanishing breed. They represented the last remnants of a once-proud American industry. At each workstation flew a little American flag. The workers were thrilled to see U.S. Customs in their shop. They hoped that customs agents would help protect their industry. The workers were proud that they were still sewing tags in their garments that read, "Made in the USA." These American workers were playing by the rules. However, from what I saw in many textile sweat shops overseas and by investigating fraudulent trading practices, I realized the global garment industry was not operating on a level playing field. Playing by rules and regulations that were not adequately enforced, the American workers didn't stand a chance. But then again, "it's just a textile case."

✻

Customs established its overseas attaché offices during the height of the Cold War. As explained in chapter 2, Customs did its part in the struggle against the Soviet Empire primarily by investigating the diversion of weapons and high technology to the Eastern bloc. Thus, Customs put the great majority of its attaché offices in Europe. But frankly, another reason for the locations of the attaché offices was that Customs officials were Eurocentric; they had a hard time relating to other parts of the world. And officials would much prefer to live in Paris or travel to Madrid than to live in or travel to nonglamorous cities in the developing world where, in the post–Cold War era, new threats are found. It was hard for Customs to open an office in the Third World, but it was very easy for the agency to send officials out to questionable European posts for plush retirement tours.

The attaché office in Rome covered fifty-six countries. While working there, I was convinced that Customs needed to "break up the Roman Empire" by establishing attaché offices in regions that were showing signs of increasing importance. The two areas that I identified as good locations for new offices were southern Africa and the Middle East, particularly Dubai.

Efforts to open a Customs attaché office in South Africa proved successful. The catalyst for the initiative was the fall of the former apartheid government. Playing within the system and working with friends and colleagues who helped run Treasury's Asset Forfeiture Fund, I found money and political consensus to support a new office. Once again the groundwork was laid through a very successful U.S. Treasury–sponsored law enforcement conference in Pretoria. The American ambassador in Pretoria fully supported the initiative. The goodwill generated from the conference, assisted by additional funds from Treasury, resulted in opening the Office of the Customs Attaché Pretoria.

As a criminal investigator, beginning in the early 1990s, every time I traveled to Dubai I salivated. It was, as they say in the military, a "target-rich environment." Yet it was as if the intelligence community couldn't see the forest for the trees. Even though the CIA virtually ignored Dubai itself, I found there just about every major type of violation that Customs was concerned with. The growth of the city-state was incredible. Its location, on the crossroads of Europe, South Asia, the Middle East, and East Africa, was unparalleled. The local police and customs service needed training and technical assistance. The anti-money-laundering gospel had to be spread in the region. There was an underworld of trade and finance that I was convinced the United States needed to understand and attempt to monitor. I had started to develop some very good sources and insights. But as explained earlier, working investigations and handling sources long distance is not productive. As a result, I wanted to open a Customs attaché office in Dubai.

In 1993, 1994, 1995, and 1996 I wrote formal proposals to the Customs hierarchy regarding opening an office in the Middle East, specifically singling out Dubai as the best locale. I had discussions with both local officials and American embassies in the Middle East and found Customs would be welcome. On paper, the objections raised within Customs were primarily financial. But cost comparisons and a review of office statistics showed the move would actually be cost effective. I even proposed closing the Customs Attaché Rome's small satellite office in Milan and using the savings to open an office in Dubai. My arguments fell on deaf ears. I believe the real reasons Customs did not support the Dubai office boiled down to turf and myopic vision.

When I could not garner Customs support, I approached the Secret Service attaché at American Embassy Rome and informally discussed whether the Secret Service would be interested in pooling resources to open a joint Treasury enforcement office in the Middle East. The Secret Service had previously supported my initiatives to give joint presentations on financial crimes to audiences in the Middle East, and these presentations were well attended and received. A Secret Service agent would talk primarily about counterfeit currency, while I would try to heighten the awareness of money laundering. Having a Secret Service background, I also occasionally supported Secret Service investigations and even protective details. To me, it seemed very logical that if Customs and the Secret Service, sister Treasury agencies, would share office space, support personnel, and expenses, the cost of putting a Treasury office in the Middle East would be halved for both agencies. Although the Secret Service attaché in Rome supported the idea, it did not get very far in Washington. Again I witnessed the bureaucracies' "lack of imagination." They were wedded to the old way of doing business, and cost and mission efficiency were just not part of the business equation.

Convinced that opening an office in the Middle East was still worth pursuing, I tried again. As discussed, in the mid-1990s there was much soul searching going on within the CIA about its mission and the methods it used to collect intelligence. Intrigued with the possibilities, I proposed for the Agency's consideration a cover scenario that would have focused additional collection in the Middle East on targets of importance to both law enforcement and the Agency.

After September 11 there has been much in the press about the so-called wall between the intelligence and law enforcement communities. Policies, procedures, and bureaucratic cultures prohibited the type of information sharing and cooperation that were necessary to help thwart the terrorist attacks on the United States. For example, during the time I was overseas in Rome, internal Department of the Treasury rules, specifically order 240, effectively discouraged coordination and the type of support I envisioned between Treasury law enforcement and the intelligence community. Treasury order 240 was one of the bricks in the wall.

I was very frustrated with the bureaucratic constraints at the time because I knew each side could further advance their respective missions if they were allowed to better support and utilize the other. There were good people on both sides, but they weren't talking to each other. For example, despite my repeated personal appeals, a visiting Customs headquarters official refused to even meet with the Agency in Rome to discuss possible joint cooperation. This was exactly the type of bureaucratic roadblock subsequently identified in the 9/11 Commission report.

In late 1993 I received an invitation from CIA headquarters to discuss my cover proposal with CIA officials. I knew I was skirting Treasury guidelines, but this was something that I thought was important. I remembered my Customs colleague Don Bludworth's insight on how he would sometimes have to resort to his own devices to get things done in the bureaucracy. Don told me, "Don't ask for permission, ask for forgiveness." Because the customs attaché in Rome was totally unaware of my discussions and, I knew in any event, would never understand the issues or give me permission, I took leave and paid for my trip to Washington myself. It was my first time back inside CIA headquarters since I had been forced to resign from the Agency ten years earlier.

The meeting went well, and the Agency was interested in the scenario I outlined. I flew back to Rome optimistic. However, fate again intervened. A short time after my visit, on February 24, 1994, the FBI arrested CIA operations officer Aldrich Ames for treason. The Agency felt that it was again under assault. They circled their wagons. There was no longer any desire to consider an operational proposal such as mine that was a bit outside the norm. The initiative was over. Despite my best efforts, I could not get the bureaucracies to move forward on my repeated attempts to open an office in Dubai.

Prior to September 11, when I returned from overseas to Washington, D.C., I was called either "Mr. Dubai" or "Mr. Gold" in the corridors of Customs headquarters. I would talk about the importance of those topics to anyone who would listen. In 1996, in my last formal proposal to open a Customs attaché office in Dubai, I prepared a presentation that was given by the chief of foreign operations to the commissioner of Customs. My proposal again laid out the reasons why Dubai was an attractive area for a new Customs office. One of the final slides in the presentation had a picture of a calendar with the year "**2001**" and the caption "**Forward Thinking**" in bold typeface. The slide discussed how a Customs office in Dubai would position the United States well for the new challenges of the next century.

A postmortem investigation of September 11 disclosed that the terrorist attacks cost al Qaeda approximately $300,000–$500,000. It is estimated that most of the funding either originated from or transited Dubai.[4] A few years later there was a watershed investigation into successful efforts by Pakistani nuclear scientist Dr. A. Q. Khan to engineer a nuclear bomb and disperse the technical knowledge to countries the State Department had designated as "state sponsors of terrorism." The investigation disclosed that the same type of Dubai-based trading companies discussed earlier helped procure much of the needed equipment. Moreover, the financial trail in the nuclear scheme led to Dubai[5]; Khan had substantial financial and real estate holdings in Dubai[6]; and reportedly, Khan used Dubai gold dealers to help launder his profits.

Opening a U.S. law enforcement office in Dubai prior to September 11 probably would not have prevented the attacks. However, I am completely convinced that if America had had an office in Dubai, U.S. law enforcement would have been much better positioned to react in the confused days, weeks, and months after the attacks occurred. I am also quite certain that with the right kind of U.S. law enforcement presence in the region, the U.S. government would have had much better understanding and insights into the regional underworld and methods of illicit finance throughout the Arabian Gulf and South Asia. The lack of understanding has impeded American efforts. I sincerely regret that I was not more persuasive in my arguments with the bureaucracies. More than ten years after my original proposals, in 2004 Customs finally opened an office in Dubai. The unwarranted delay further stalled the U.S. War on Terrorist Finance.

✳

During the time I was assigned to Rome, I was classified as a mid-level GS-13 "journeyman" criminal investigator. In one sense, it was the best position I ever had. I was given wide latitude to pursue a variety of criminal investigations. And many times an investigative trail took me to fascinating lands where I met incredibly interesting people. As a GS-13, I was not bogged down with management issues. However, as a journeyman agent, I was also not taken seriously by upper Customs management. Although I tried very hard to make myself heard, the structure of government bureaucratic hierarchy conspires against innovation coming from the bottom up. I also found that sometimes worthwhile ideas are not given a fair hearing or are not implemented because somebody feels threatened, a supervisor's ego gets in the way, or a concerned office feels like the proposal impacts its turf. Poor management compounded the structural impediments. Frankly, I found few who had open minds and were willing to explore imaginative or innovative ways of doing things. Rather, the emphasis was on maintaining the status quo and personal perks. Dialogue and possible cooperation with the intelligence community or pushing for a realignment of overseas offices after the Cold War to help counter new and emerging threats were only two of many examples of what the 9/11 Commission called a "lack of imagination."

Too often in my experience, I encountered managers who spent an inordinate amount of time fighting the bureaucracy for scarce resource dollars. There was nothing wrong with that. But often the battles for dollars were not about advancing the mission; rather they were what the Italians call making a *bella figura* (beautiful image). The mission and office effectiveness were put on the back burner while efforts went into increasing allowances for prestigious European cars, housing, and boondoggle trips. And although I had the pleasure to work with some wonderful colleagues overseas who worked incredibly hard, often under trying circumstances, too often the wrong people were selected to go overseas. And in a small office, one or two nonperformers dramatically impact overall office performance.

At the time it cost Customs, or rather U.S. taxpayers, approximately $450,000 a year, not including salary, to function in an overseas environment. Rome was a very expensive overseas post. Housing, education allowances for dependents, travel, cost of living adjustments, and State Department–required embassy fees are all very expensive. To maximize the return on the investment, more effort should have been put into selecting the right law enforcement candidates to serve in foreign assignments.

The State Department and the CIA have missions that revolve around sending people overseas. They naturally attract personnel with more internationally oriented skill sets and outlooks. Moreover, their bureaucracies are set up for the requisite administrative support. Domestic U.S. law enforcement agencies that send personnel overseas do not enjoy the same advantages. In fact, all too often, an agent in a domestic Customs office who was recognized as a malcontent, slacker, or somebody that had reached his or her level of incompetence was sent overseas. This was the Customs way of "making the problem go away." Yet, if anything, sending domestically "challenged" agents overseas can magnify problems much more, particularly when the agents double as de facto U.S. diplomats. Preferential transfers overseas given to unqualified personnel also contributed to problems.

Another major contributing factor to unsuccessful performance overseas is an agent's spouse and family. Overseas living can be very stressful. It is not for everybody. And if their families are not happy, agents will not be productive in their work. While agents assigned to work in embassies speak English with and enjoy the camaraderie of colleagues and an administrative support network, their spouses sometimes suffer, trying to function in a foreign language, environment, and culture. The resulting difficulties and pressures can be magnified in the fishbowl-like environment of the embassy community. All of these influences and more can combine to retard the effectiveness of an overseas office.

I had no chance for promotion during my service in Rome. While the Clinton administration was busy "reinventing the government," Customs announced an agencywide promotion freeze. As a result, I was locked into being a GS-13 for eight years. If I had made the biggest case in history, I still wouldn't have received a promotion—there was no upward mobility. And chances of recognition were worse for those assigned to overseas attaché offices because they could not add to their bureaucratically desirable arrest and seizure statistics. Only domestic agents have authority to lock somebody up and get the statistics that look good to the promotion review boards. Despite having completely different job performance standards, overseas agents were still measured against their domestic counterparts. Statistically, long-term and complex international money-laundering cases mattered little next to the comparative quick arrests and seizures of agents working dope cases along the southwest U.S. border.

Eventually, even the annual performance evaluations were made meaningless because they were changed from "merit based" to "pass or fail." Without debate, Customs and other civil service agencies started moving away from merit because it was considered too "prejudicial." Nobody was allowed to fail. Yet despite the promotion freeze and the dumbing down of professional standards and accountability under the guise of equality, the troops noted that somehow political favorites still managed to get promoted. And hypocrisy reached a new low when the Customs commissioner who insisted upon a promotion freeze for his troops looked the other way when his wife was promoted within an incredibly short time frame from a low-ranking GS-7 to the top-ranking GS-15 position at a sister Treasury agency. Eventually, personnel quality equates to agency effectiveness.

Despite the frustrations, I probably enjoyed my assignment to Rome more than any other. The scope of Customs investigations was widespread and varied. Special agents were given comparatively wide latitude on how to pursue the leads. In addition to money-laundering investigations, most personnel in the Office of the Customs Attaché Rome did excellent work targeting intellectual property rights violations, general smuggling, narcotics couriers, fraud, diversion of munitions and high technology, child pornography, and other violations. And because of our location in Rome, we enjoyed particular success assisting in the repatriation of stolen artwork and antiquities.

For example, I participated in a quick but effective investigation to recover stolen Italian Renaissance art. The Italian Carabinieri unit charged with protecting Italian *patrimonio artistico* generated the case. Two thieves working around Venice had stolen from private residences paintings, ceramics, and furniture dating as far back as the 1300s. Working with an informant, the Carabinieri discovered that the thieves were trying to fence the stolen objects to interested buyers. The Carabinieri thought that if the informant introduced American buyers to the thieves, they would be less suspicious. They proposed a classic "buy-bust" scenario. Arno Pieratti, my friend and colleague in the Customs office, and I were asked to pose as the undercover buyers. The plan was that we would negotiate with the suspects and Carabinieri would move in and make the arrests.

Arno was a great agent who enjoyed the friendship and respect of all he worked with. He was an Italian American with a beautiful fluency in both languages. He was helpful time and time again in various investigations and in dealing with our official Italian counterparts because he understood the culture and ways of doing business in the host country. On the morning of the operation, the Carabinieri took Arno and me to a village outside of Venice where we met with the informant and the Carabinieri surveillance team. The informant gave us a quick tutorial on how buyers of stolen art would present themselves and the type of questions they would ask. The Carabinieri only wanted us to begin the fictitious negotiations and confirm that the suspects, in fact, had the stolen artwork in their possession. They had surveillance teams stationed around the meeting site.

That afternoon Arno and I, posing as American buyers of Italian artwork, met with the suspects. The informant had arranged the rendezvous in the parking lot of a coffee shop. All smiles, the suspects walked us over to their vehicle. Inside the trunk and strewn over the seats were dozens of Renaissance-era paintings on canvas, gilded wood, and ceramics. It appeared to me as if the suspects had part of a museum in the back of their car. Arno and I worked to develop credibility with the suspects and eventually convinced them that we represented very wealthy private buyers. During the monitored discussions, the Carabinieri took pictures from concealed surveillance posts that ringed the parking lot. After giving the suspects ample opportunity to incriminate themselves, Arno and I told them that we would have to check with a fictitious contact before beginning negotiations on price. We agreed to meet with them again in a few days.

The Carabinieri had told us before the undercover meeting that they were not going to make any arrests at the meeting place in order to protect our identities and the informant's. Instead, the Carabinieri were going to allow the suspects to depart and later engineer a vehicle stop during which they would "discover" the stolen artwork. As planned, the Carabinieri, feigning a routine vehicle-safety inspection, stopped the suspects' vehicle on the road back to Venice. While examining the vehicle, the Carabinieri pretended they had chanced upon the artwork. The suspects were asked to follow the Carabinieri back to their Venice headquarters for questioning. Unfortunately, that's when things started to go wrong. The suspects knew they were going to be asked to explain why they had so much valuable artwork in their car and where they got it, and so, on the highway leading back to Venice, they started to throw the priceless artworks out the windows of the car! As soon as the Carabinieri realized what was happening, they stopped the vehicle and arrested the thieves. Many beautiful pieces were destroyed. However, the operation was considered a big success as millions of dollars worth of stolen art treasures were recovered.

The art case was one of the last investigations Arno and I worked together. Arno's six-year assignment in Rome came to an end, and he was rotated back into a mandatory headquarters tour. In 1996 it was my turn to transfer from Rome. Although Customs gave me much support when they sent me overseas, I had virtually no help when it was time to transfer back to the States. The government agencies that I previously worked for had allowed their employees to submit a list of their top three choices for reassignment. The agency would attempt to accommodate their employees' requests when it was time to transfer. However, with Customs I was left to my own devices; the message I received was, "Find yourself a new office." That is easier said than done, particularly for agents working overseas. Agents assigned to attaché offices are out of the normal domestic-focused loop. So once again I paid for a trip back to the States out of my own pocket to see if I could find a new position.

My trip back to the Washington, D.C., area proved successful. I received a job offer from Treasury's Financial Crimes Enforcement Network (FinCEN). The office was located outside of Washington in northern Virginia. As discussed briefly earlier, FinCEN was charged to support law enforcement by giving federal, state, and local enforcement agencies access to the Bank Secrecy Act (BSA) information also known as "financial intelligence." I was very familiar with the use and the promise of BSA data. Primo Passo's proactive targeting of Italian-American organized crime was due primarily to innovative use of the BSA. Although FinCEN did not enjoy the best reputation within Customs, I was struck both by the hospitality of the FinCEN employees and the potential of the young organization. Customs agreed to assign me to FinCEN as its first liaison officer. I was pleased with the assignment, particularly because it allowed me to pursue my continuing interest in combating international money laundering.

The only thing left to do was to say good-bye. Although I experienced the occasional challenges and frustrations, my life in Rome had been wonderful. After six years my family and I had developed strong bonds to the *città eterna*, or eternal city. Our daughter was born in Rome. Our boys went to the American Overseas School of Rome. We developed close friendships with many of the embassy families, but we also integrated ourselves with the local *Romani*.

The attaché office had a wonderful farewell party for Cristina and me. After the speeches and toasts, it was my turn to say *arrivederci, Roma*. I was quite used to making public presentations on money laundering, but not to giving public good-byes. I used the occasion to thank the staff at the office and the Primo Passo team. But then I turned to my beautiful wife, Cristina. I told her, and the assembled Italian and American guests, that any success I had in my career was the product of her support. She had held down the family while I was away on my many trips, sometimes for weeks at a time. She was the one who sometimes had to answer the phone in the middle of the night from my sources in the Middle East, sometimes while pretending I was somebody else. Cristina thrived in Rome by using the incredible opportunity of six years in a new foreign environment to grow as a person. She immersed herself in the local environment and culture. Using her innate language ability, she became almost fluent in the Italian language. Because she was European, she was able to help acclimate many arriving American embassy wives to their new cultural realities. My wife was also a wonderful hostess and became a great Italian cook. She graciously entertained the many guests I brought home. Her positive attitude was contagious. Somehow she managed to do it all, while having a baby and raising two very lively young boys. Too often we forget to say thank you or *grazie*.

Later, I reflected on how Cristina gave up her family, friends, career, and native country so that she could marry me. As I knew she would, she became the perfect partner to go overseas with. Many remarked that they had never seen anybody adapt so easily and completely to a foreign environment. I could not help but recall how the CIA forced my resignation because I married her.

6

Promise and Potential

Before the current War on Terrorism, the United States was engaged in another war, the War on Narcotics. U.S. efforts against narcotics trafficking somehow do not make as many headlines today, but the war is ongoing and the enemy is also evil. The scourge of narcotics both destroys individual human lives and causes rot in society. A generation ago the government realized that attacking drug-related money laundering is an essential component of our overall efforts to wage war against drug trafficking organizations. By following the money, law enforcement is better able to target the managers and the kingpins in the trafficking networks and simultaneously seek to take away the reason the criminal organizations exist.

In simple terms, narcotics traffickers and their professional money launderers were faced with a tremendous logistics challenge.[1] In the mid-1990s a trafficking organization that sold about twenty pounds of heroin on U.S. streets could generate approximately $1 million worth of illicit proceeds. Normally, the proceeds would take the form of street cash, currency notes in $5, $10, and $20 denominations. One million dollars in street cash weighs approximately 256 pounds, or more than ten times the weight of the drugs sold. If the organization sold cocaine, the cash generated was approximately six times the weight of the drug. Although the narcotics were generally produced outside of the United States, the billions of dollars of illicit proceeds subsequently laundered by the major trafficking organizations originated from inside the United States. For example, if a trafficking organization sold $1 billion worth of cocaine on the streets of Los Angeles, it had to contend with 256,000 pounds of illicit currency. If one uses the mid-90s conservative estimate of $90 billion per year for all drugs sold in the United States, the amount of illicit currency produced weighed more than 20 million pounds. That is a tremendous amount of cash that has to be disposed of or laundered. And the financial crimes that are generated from these incredibly large criminal proceeds are nothing less than a national security threat because they challenge the integrity of the U.S. financial system and fuel other types of criminal activity.

As explained in chapter 3, in 1970 the United States passed the Bank Secrecy Act (BSA), which evolved into a series of succeeding laws and regulations that effectively created financial intelligence, or "footprints." The BSA was meant to create a paper trail to assist Treasury criminal investigators in the War on Narcotics. The primary BSA forms used at the time were currency transaction reports (CTRs) filed by financial institutions and currency and monetary instrument reports (CMIRs) for cross-border currency movements. Treasury investigators, particularly those in Customs and the Internal Revenue Service (IRS), quickly realized the value of the information contained in these forms. Not only was the BSA helpful in narcotics-related money-laundering investigations, but investigators found that the data compiled in CTRs and CMIRs could often provide critical information needed to help solve a wide variety of crimes at the federal, state, and local level. Convinced of the import of the data, Customs and the IRS combined to propose one of the most altruistic ideas in recent federal government history. Dismissing for the moment the bureaucratic dogma of protecting turf, Treasury proposed giving outside law enforcement agencies that had a need for BSA information access to CTR and CMIR data. In 1990 this proposal was the genesis for the creation of Treasury's Financial Crimes Enforcement Network (FinCEN).

As the name implies, FinCEN was a network, a link among the law enforcement, financial, and regulatory communities.[2] Its founding mission was to support law enforcement in its efforts to investigate financial crimes. Over the years, it further evolved into providing three separate but integrated services: analyzing and disseminating financial intelligence, obtaining data via regulatory oversight and control of the BSA, and pioneering new approaches to obtain financial intelligence from overseas. FinCEN was not a law enforcement agency itself. It was not "operational" and did not investigate financial crimes. Rather, it brought together concerned government agencies under one roof and, increasingly, online. In the mid-1990s FinCEN had a permanent workforce of about two hundred people; they were joined by over forty individuals from over twenty different regulatory and law enforcement agencies as long-term detailees.

When I arrived at FinCEN in the summer of 1996 as the U.S. Customs Service liaison, I was immediately struck by the promise of the new organization. Instead of a large bureaucracy, it had an almost campuslike atmosphere. At the time, smart people with diverse experience staffed the network; innovative ideas were encouraged. Unfortunately, I found there was a lot of bad blood between Customs and FinCEN. Customs management still remembered that when FinCEN was created, Customs was forced to give the new sister Treasury organization a substantial portion of its anti-money-laundering budget. Customs personnel, files, databases, and technology were also given to FinCEN, creating a bureaucratic hole within Customs financial-crimes programs that took years to recover from. But despite the politics and the personalities, I understood FinCEN's potential. I bought into the FinCEN promise. I became a public and vocal advocate of its mission to support law enforcement investigative efforts and foster interagency and global cooperation against money laundering and financial crimes.

FinCEN had an array of analytical products, but most typically, it would support law enforcement in the field by providing data in response to a request for information. In a typical but hypothetical case, a Drug Enforcement Administration (DEA) agent in Miami might receive information from an informant that an individual suspect and a front company were involved with the laundering of narcotics proceeds in southern Florida. In initiating the subsequent investigation, one of the first things the DEA case agent would do is check DEA databases to determine if the subject or the front company were already on record with DEA. The DEA agent might then choose to query FinCEN to see if any other records were available. The agent could contact FinCEN directly by faxing in a request for assistance or by contacting the DEA liaison officer who would forward the request to the analytical division at FinCEN. The case would be assigned to a FinCEN analyst who would check appropriate financial, law enforcement, and commercial databases.

FinCEN analysts had access, either directly or indirectly, to all relevant federal law enforcement databases. Checking the financial databases, the FinCEN analyst could determine if the suspect or the front company was on record in the universe of BSA data, which is populated by approximately 13 million new financial forms every year. Finally, the analyst could run the subject names through commercially available databases at FinCEN to find out, for example, its location, if the front company was publicly listed, who was on the board of directors, or the company's declared worth. If there were any "hits" in the law enforcement, financial, and commercial databases, the information was assembled along with a cover summary and sent back to the requester. Generally, that was the extent of the "analysis."

Continuing with the hypothetical example, the DEA agent would receive the information from FinCEN and would also expand his field investigation using traditional law enforcement techniques such as surveillance, developing and debriefing informants, telephone records analysis, and other investigative techniques. After many months of investigation, the agent might discover other business associates related to the original primary suspect. He could also find that the front company sent money out of the United States and had undetermined ties to another company based in France. The DEA agent would assemble the new information and once again send it to FinCEN. This time he would ask FinCEN to run the additional names and, if appropriate, do further analysis to link the associates and identified companies.

In checking the additional names, the FinCEN analyst might determine that the U.S. Customs Service in New York was running a law enforcement investigation on one of the associates. In this case, the FinCEN analyst would contact me, the Customs liaison to FinCEN. The analyst would request my permission to release the fact that Customs was investigating one of the subjects the DEA is interested in. This information could not be automatically disseminated because the law enforcement data did not belong to FinCEN but rather to the agency that originally input the data. In this case, I would contact the Customs case agent in New York and inform him or her that DEA in Florida appeared to be investigating the same criminal network. Generally, the Customs agent would be pleased with this development.

Agents were normally happy to learn that their investigation was broad in scope and that others could be in position to contribute. However, occasionally the Customs agent would be protective of the information and choose not to release it, generally for reasons of personalities, politics, interagency rivalry, or turf. Sometimes, in the interagency wars, the concerns were valid; the competition in the field was often fierce. Continuing with the analysis, the FinCEN analyst might also determine that another suspect's name forwarded by the DEA is on record with the Federal Bureau of Investigation. Perhaps the Bureau's Atlanta office had previously opened and closed an investigation on the suspect. And finally, in checking another database, the FinCEN analyst could discover that the French company also surfaced in a recent request for information forwarded by FinCEN's sister French financial intelligence unit, TRACFIN.

In the late 1990s FinCEN took pride in its use of state-of-the-art information technology to compile, capture, and analyze relevant data. Since FinCEN was so small, technology was considered its force multiplier. Using its data systems and tools, in this hypothetical scenario the FinCEN analyst would write a report and send it to the DEA agent in south Florida. This time the analytical product would provide key information that Customs in New York also had an open investigation into one of the business associates, that the FBI in Atlanta had a closed case on another suspect of interest to the DEA, and that TRACFIN apparently had an open case on the same French company identified by the DEA. Thus, FinCEN could network all the relevant agencies by getting permission from Customs, the FBI, and the French to share their interest in the subjects with the DEA. Points of contact would be provided. And, in addition to a written summary, the FinCEN analyst would provide a link chart or a wiring diagram to show the relationships between suspects, businesses, and financial accounts. The lines on the diagram would connect previously disparate law enforcement efforts by multiple agencies in multiple locales. This type of analytical product proved particularly helpful to case agents presenting complex money-laundering investigations to prosecutors. A picture was truly worth a thousand words, particularly when it helped decipher a complex money-laundering scheme.

FinCEN was overwhelmed with the thousands of individual database queries that it processed. As a result, it engineered systems and programs that allowed the agencies to help themselves. For example, the Platform access program allowed federal agencies to send their representatives to FinCEN to use its databases. And the Gateway program allowed law enforcement agencies in all fifty states and, increasingly, other interested partners to have direct access to all BSA reports under a carefully monitored system that FinCEN controlled and audited. This program proved particularly useful because of its query alert system, which automatically signaled FinCEN when two or more agencies had an interest in the same subject. The alerts were matched with other data so that FinCEN could network the concerned agencies, sometimes greatly enhancing the scope of the investigation.

As the Customs liaison to FinCEN, I enjoyed being able to help my colleagues in the field access FinCEN's data, analysis, and other services. And I learned about the regulatory tools and international initiatives, in addition to direct law enforcement support, that indirectly furthered law enforcement.

In 1995 the secretary of treasury charged FinCEN with administering and regulating the BSA. The most significant development in financial intelligence since the creation of the BSA occurred in 1996 when U.S. financial institutions were obligated to report "suspicious" transactions by filing suspicious activity reports (SARs) with FinCEN. It was believed that bankers were the first line of defense in money laundering through financial institutions. Following internal "know your customer" policy and procedures, bankers are best able to identify atypical or suspicious behavior. A narrative of the suspicious behavior is often included in the SARs; this proved particularly helpful to law enforcement. Previously, finding a useful CTR among the approximately 12 million filed every year was like trying to find the proverbial needle in a haystack. As Stan Morris, the former director of FinCEN used to say, "With SARs, it is now like having a haystack full of needles."

Over the years BSA provisions were extended to cover not only traditional banks and depository institutions, but also what are called nonbank financial institutions such as check cashers and money remitters. Dealing with the new reporting requirements, FinCEN and other concerned government agencies were also fully aware of the continuing need to balance concerns about civil liberties with the need for vigilance in financial transactions. I was impressed with the safeguards and policies put in place to ensure that financial intelligence was not abused.

In 1996 I was also very happy to see FinCEN give key regulatory support to an innovative effort coordinated by a Treasury-led task force targeting New York–area money remitters and their agents who were engaged in schemes to avoid the reporting and record-keeping requirements of the BSA. Treasury enforcement's successful use of a geographic targeting order (GTO) caused a dramatic reduction in the amount of illicit funds sent to Colombia. Instead of using the traditional law enforcement tactics of going after individual "bad guys," agencies worked together to identify and target a financial "system" that was being abused by criminals. A battle in the War on Narcotics was won because the GTO was predicated by regulators, investigators, and prosecutors working together. As the reader will see, later regulatory efforts in the War on Terrorist Finance have proved hollow because of the lack of sufficient coordinated enforcement.

Yet after having spent the previous six years overseas, what most impressed me about the promise of FinCEN was the work it was doing to obtain international financial intelligence, the last of its core services. When I was assigned overseas to Rome, I frequently received requests from my domestic colleagues seeking information from a foreign country. Typically, they would be investigating a narcotics-related money-laundering case with foreign ties. They would identify a country, a bank, and even a bank account where they believed the proceeds of the U.S. criminal activity were laundered. Sometimes suspect money flowed into the United States. The domestic office would ask the attaché office for assistance. For example, in 1993 a Customs office in California asked me to obtain information from the Arabian Gulf country of Bahrain regarding the origin of $500,000 transferred from a Bahrain bank account into a California account controlled by a suspected narcotics trafficker and money launderer. In 1993 the old-fashioned way of obtaining the information was traveling to Bahrain to make an appeal directly to the concerned banking and law enforcement authorities.

As much as the authorities wanted to assist, it was difficult for them to do so because at the time money laundering was not illegal in Bahrain and, in any event, the government did not have an internal infrastructure and procedures to officially pass me the necessary information. In the particular example of the request to Bahrain, because of close working relationships, I was able to obtain the information unofficially, or "under the table." However, the investigating office in California could not use the under-the-table information officially. Other more formal and official methods of obtaining the information could have been explored, such as mutual legal assistance treaties (MLATs) or letters rogatory, but these avenues were time consuming and cumbersome. In the case of an MLAT, for example, a treaty had to be negotiated. In addition, cultural and bureaucratic frictions sometimes had to be overcome.

Thus, when I arrived at FinCEN, I took notice of the pioneering concept of creating an international network of financial intelligence units (FIUs) to exchange financial intelligence in the support of law enforcement. This concept represented the next generation of law enforcement. No longer would a criminal investigator have to travel halfway around the world to appeal to a foreign counterpart for information. Rather, in the foreseeable future, law enforcement officers in the United States following a financial trail would be able to request, through secure and instant communication, assistance from their counterparts in Bahrain, Russia, Mexico, or wherever the trail led. FinCEN was helping to lay the groundwork for such an exchange under the umbrella of what has come to be known as the Egmont Group of Financial Intelligence Units.

The Egmont Group was the brainchild of then–FinCEN Director Stanley Morris and Jean Spreutels, the president of the Belgium FIU, Cellule de Traitement des Informations Financières.[3] The inaugural meeting of the group took place in 1995 in the Egmont Palace outside of Brussels. There the concept of an FIU as a central office that would obtain, analyze, and disseminate financial-disclosure information for appropriate law enforcement authorities was agreed upon. In 1995 only a handful of countries were represented at Egmont. FinCEN, the world's first FIU, played a leading role in expanding the FIU concept around the globe. Today over one hundred countries belong to the Egmont Group. Via a system bolstered with various safeguards, specific financial intelligence is exchanged between countries to support law enforcement in their investigations.[4] In the comparatively few cases when information is needed for judicial proceedings, the financial intelligence is requested officially under, for example, an MLAT, which may be obtained more easily thanks to the information the Egmont Group has already supplied.

When I arrived at FinCEN, I also witnessed the exciting work of the Financial Action Task Force (FATF). Stan Morris headed the U.S. delegations to FATF, and a team of devoted FinCEN civil servants provided tremendous support. The Group of Seven (G-7) industrialized countries created FATF in 1989 to help address the growing global problem of money laundering. Despite its name, the FATF is not a "task force" in the conventional law enforcement sense. It has not made, nor will it ever make, a high-profile money-laundering case. Rather, the FATF is an international policymaking body designed to generate the necessary political will to bring about primarily legislative and regulatory reforms that address money laundering. The cornerstone of the task force's work is its forty recommendations, which have been periodically updated to reflect changing methodologies and concerns. The recommendations are quite comprehensive and cover such areas as criminalizing money laundering, requiring customer identification, establishing minimum standards of record keeping, and reporting suspicious transactions. They have turned into the de facto anti-money-laundering blueprint around the world. After September 11 FATF's mission was expanded to also combat terrorist financing.

In the early 1990s, when I approached countries in the Middle East or Africa requesting assistance in money-laundering investigations, on most occasions I could not get much official help. To put things in perspective, in the early 1990s fewer than two dozen nations had criminalized money laundering. Today, over 150 countries have anti-money-laundering legislation.[5] Moreover, that legislation, the vital first step in assisting law enforcement, is constantly being updated and improved. Today U.S. criminal investigators and assistant U.S. attorneys likely rarely stop to think about how and why foreign countries are cooperating with them by providing requested financial data. In large part, that cooperation is due to FATF policies and pressure. Even countries with traditional bank secrecy laws, such as Switzerland, have changed dramatically over the years and have been increasingly forthcoming in providing vital financial intelligence.

The key mechanism FATF uses to apply pressure to member countries is the concept of "mutual evaluations," or peer review.[6] Not wanting to be embarrassed in the mutual evaluation process, countries time and time again have enacted needed legislative or regulatory changes aimed at bolstering their anti-money-laundering programs. During the periodic mutual evaluations, multinational evaluating teams generally comprised of three subject experts and a representative of the FATF Secretariat will visit the subject country and examine its anti-money-laundering legal framework, financial systems, and law enforcement operations. The examination team generally stays three or four days in country and interviews public and private officials involved in the anti-money-laundering sphere. The team then prepares a detailed report of their findings, which is presented for adoption to the entire FATF plenary.

For example, in 1997 I was selected to be the law enforcement expert for the mutual evaluation of Canada. In this capacity, I did not represent Customs or FinCEN but rather the FATF. This evaluation was particularly important because Canada had dragged its feet on passing needed anti-money-laundering reforms. Responding to intense international pressure applied by the FATF mutual evaluation process, Canada rectified identified deficiencies in its anti-money-laundering programs and adopted legislation that adhered to world standards. Some of the reforms included mandatory suspicious activity reporting by financial institutions, the creation of a Canadian FIU, and cross-border currency reporting. These are all effective anti-money-laundering and anti-terrorist-financing tools.

As the Customs liaison officer to FinCEN, I was a charter member in what was called the Interagency Coordination Group (ICG), which also included principal law enforcement liaisons from the Department of Justice, FBI, DEA, IRS, and Secret Service and a representative from FinCEN. The ICG was, like the FIU, a concept ahead of its time. It consisted of senior journeymen agents who met every week to discuss the concerns of their respective agencies. Although regional task forces exist all over the country, they are limited to a specific geographic jurisdiction and mandate. The ICG, on the other hand, could and did discuss both domestic and international investigations and programs. The members developed trust and a high degree of camaraderie. As a result, the ICG was able to deconflict bureaucratic incidents before they escalated. ICG members also helped share information and coordinate investigations between their respective agencies. And working at FinCEN, the neutral partner, the agency representatives could bring to the table innovative ideas, observations, or requests for mutual support. Intentionally, no senior agency political figures were included in the ICG. As a result, bureaucratic rivalries and turf battles were kept to a minimum. The representatives functioned well together as a somewhat autonomous group. Their only agenda was to maximize the effectiveness of U.S. law enforcement in battling financial crime.

One of the first large projects the ICG was involved in was shedding light on the Colombian Black-Market Peso Exchange (BMPE). The BMPE originated in Colombia years before the War on Narcotics. Just as I had discovered on the other side of the world in Italy and later in South Asia, tax and tariff avoidance was the catalyst for what evolved into the very effective money-laundering methodology of the BMPE. Colombian businesspeople who wanted to import U.S. goods through legitimate commercial banks had to pay a stiff tariff above the official exchange rate. Sales taxes and fees imposed additional costs. By using an underground peso broker, the businesspeople could buy U.S. dollars for less than the official exchange rate and also avoid government scrutiny and taxes. Years after the BMPE was founded, when the flood of Colombian cocaine hit American cities, narcotics traffickers realized the tremendous logistic burden of trying to dispose of a massive amount of drug dollars. At the same time, black-market peso dealers needed more and more American dollars to sell to the Colombian businesspeople for the purchase of consumer goods, electronics, cigarettes, whiskey, machinery, and gold that the Colombian people wanted at the cheapest possible price. Supply met demand.

In the BMPE, as the following illustration indicates, a representative of the narcotics cartel would sell the accumulated dollars of drug proceeds to a peso broker for a large discount. The cash would stay in the United States. The peso broker would then pay the cartel with clean Colombian pesos, often obtained from Colombian businesspeople, taking the narcotics trafficker out of the equation. Representatives of the peso brokers in the United States would then use a variety of techniques to "place" the drug dollars they had just purchased into U.S. financial institutions. Most commonly, they would circumvent the BSA cash-reporting requirements by using a network of runners, or "smurfs," to deposit small amounts of cash in numerous bank accounts. The peso broker in Colombia would then work with a Colombian businessperson. In return for the businessperson's clean pesos, the peso broker would write a check to U.S. manufacturers or distributors from the checking accounts in which the runners deposited the drug dollars. The U.S. manufacturers and distributors, knowingly or unknowingly, would accept payment in drug dollars and export the goods to Colombia.

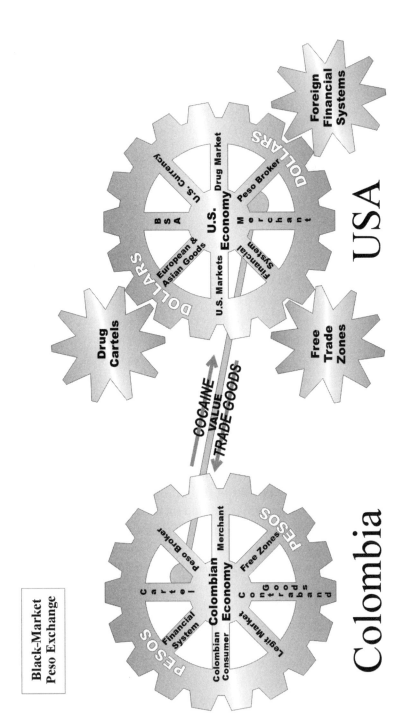

The Black-Market Peso Exchange

1. Drug cartels accumulate dollars from street sales of narcotics in the United States.
2. In Columbia, a cartel representative sells the cash (which stays in the United States) to a peso broker at a discount. The broker repays the narcotics representative with clean Columbian pesos. The narco-trafficker is now out of the picture.
3. In the United States, the peso brokers use various methods to "place" the cash into U.S. financial institutions.
4. Back in Columbia, the peso broker locates businessmen who want to import U.S. trade goods: electronics, apparel, foodstuffs, cigarettes, gold, etc.
5. The broker writes a check from a U.S. account where the narco-funds were deposited, to pay for the trade goods.
6. The BMPE represents a tremendous vulnerability because unlike financial institutions, manufacturers and distributors of trade goods and commodities have no systems in place to detect dirty money.

In the late 1990s the U.S. Treasury Department estimated that peso brokers laundered about $5 billion of drug money annually. The BPME was the largest single money-laundering methodology in the Western Hemisphere. In fact, it was estimated that almost half of all U.S. trade with Colombia was funded by drug money controlled by peso brokers.[7] The ICG, thanks to fieldwork by criminal investigators and insights spotlighted by investigative journalists, brought interagency attention to this pervasive money-laundering technique. Hearings on the BMPE were held on Capitol Hill. FinCEN eventually wrote and distributed an advisory for financial institutions on the Western Hemisphere–based underground finance system.

I was also very happy to meet someone at FinCEN who shared my concern about underground banking in the Middle East and South Asia. Analyst Patrick Jost was one of the most brilliant people at FinCEN. He had a background in anthropology and economics, spoke numerous languages, and was very familiar with the culture and ways of doing business in South Asia. When I arrived at FinCEN, he was desperately trying to bring attention to the ancient underground South Asian system of mov-

ing money or transferring value called *hawala*. He even had a personal-
ized license plate on the car he drove that read "HAWALA."

I had been aware of hawala during my investigations in the Middle
East, particularly those into the underground gold trade, but Patrick was
able to fill in the blanks. Patrick was a government expert on hawala. As
the Customs liaison to FinCEN, I found Patrick to be incredibly helpful
in supporting Customs and other U.S. government investigations into
ethnic-based underground finance methods found in the United States.
Typically, I would get telephone calls from Customs agents investigating
a network of immigrants from East Africa, South Asia, and the Middle
East. The recent immigrants would be involved in various types of crime,
for example, welfare fraud, stolen cars, credit-card fraud, illegal immigrant smuggling, or cigarette smuggling. Using traditional investigating
techniques, the agents would develop evidence of the crime itself, and
then, because Custom agents in particular were trained to do so, they
would also follow the money. The problem was the money trail often
disappeared in a big underground hole. The agents would be convinced
the proceeds of the crime were being sent outside the United States to
the criminals' countries of origin, but they could not figure out how it
was happening. The government's financial-transparency reporting requirements were not working in these cases because the criminals were,
for the most part, bypassing banks and financial institutions governed by
the BSA reporting requirements. The agents would ask me to help in
shedding light on the underground systems.

Hawala is an alternative remittance system that was developed in India centuries ago before the invention of modern finance and communications. The system is based on trust. As I saw in the Middle East, most
hawala networks are based on tribal, clan, and family relationships, making it difficult for U.S. criminal investigators to understand and interdict
the system. Traditional law enforcement investigative techniques such as
undercover approaches do not work in infiltrating such close-knit groups.
Unfortunately, the United States has very few South Asian or Middle Eastern law enforcement agents who are able to approach key hawala opera-
tors. And even if such agents were available or if law enforcement recruited an informant to make the approach, the hawala operator could
well refuse the new business unless he was confident of family or close ties

to the old country. Domestic law enforcement that relies on electronic or telephonic intercepts is equally challenged because the practitioners of hawala generally speak multiple languages and dialects. The United States doesn't employ many agents who can understand, for example, Gujarati.

Patrick Jost explained to me that hawala at its simplest is "money transfer without money movement."[8] For example, Abdul is a Pakistani immigrant driving a taxi in New York City who wants to send part of his wages to his father, Talat, who lives in a village outside of Karachi. If Abdul went to a New York City bank to send the money back home, he would probably have to open an account. Moreover, the bank could only sell him Pakistani rupees at the official exchange rate. In addition he would encounter assorted transfer fees. Because his father, Talat, lives in a remote village, delivery of the funds would present another problem. As a result, Abdul approaches a hawaladar he knows personally in New York who will arrange for the transfer.

The New York hawaladar offers to complete the transaction for a commission much lower than the assorted bank fees. In addition, the hawaladar can offer a much higher rupee-for-dollar exchange rate than the bank offered. Direct delivery of the money to Talat is also included in the price. In fact, in certain areas of the world, hawala is advertised as "door-to-door" money remitting. Abdul thinks this is a much better way to send money home to his father than are "official" bank channels, so he gives the hawaladar the money he wanted transferred to Talat, less the small commission. He does not receive a receipt because the entire relationship is based on trust. As opposed to the often lengthy formal operating requirements of bank-to-bank transfers, this informal transaction takes place in the time it takes to make a few phone calls or send a fax or e-mail. In fact, within twenty-four hours, the money is delivered directly to Talat's home. And the transaction cannot be monitored by U.S. or Pakistani authorities.

Transfers between hawaladars are not settled on a one-to-one basis but are generally bundled over a period of time after a series of transactions. Payment goes in both directions. Remittances flow into South Asia via hawala. But money also goes out of South Asia via hawala. For example, official currency exchange restrictions in South Asian countries often limit the amount of local currency that can be sent out of the country. To get around the restrictions hawaladars are able to provide "hard currency," or dollars, in exchange for rupees.

Hawaladars also profit from exchange-rate speculation or black-market currency dealing.[9] Currency speculation is one of the principal reasons, in addition to low overhead, they can beat the official exchange rates banks offer. In Italy I found tax evasion was the national pastime. The BMPE was originally created to avoid taxes. Likewise in South Asia, the large underground economies and tax evasion help drive hawala. Money remitted through official channels invites possible scrutiny from government tax authorities. The use of hawala avoids government oversight, both in South Asia and the United States.

Eventually accounts have to be balanced between hawaladars. Sometimes direct bank-to-bank wire transfers are involved. Cash couriers also are sometimes used. But most often, and historically, trade is the method employed to provide "countervaluation" or a way of "balancing the books." For example, hawaladars may also operate a side import-export business or have a close relationship with a broker or trading company. The New York–based hawaladar might import compact discs, Bollywood movies, popular clothing, native spices, or gold jewelry from South Asia. All of these products are in demand by the large South Asian expatriate community in the United States. In return, the New York hawaladar might export telecommunications equipment to his counterpart hawala network in Karachi.

If the New York hawaladar owes money to the Karachi hawaladar, he can settle the account by underinvoicing a shipment of telecommunications equipment to reflect the amount owed. To move money the other way, in this case from Karachi to New York, overinvoicing can be used. For example, if a container of electronics is worth $50,000 but is overinvoiced for $100,000, the subsequent payment of $100,000 will pay both for the legitimate cost of the merchandise ($50,000) and also allow an extra $50,000 to be remitted or laundered abroad. The cover of the business transaction and the documentation involved wash the money clean. By way of earlier examples in this book, the reader understands that a customs inspector is hard-pressed to spot moderate discrepancies in invoice pricing and product description. The following illustration describes typical hawala transactions.

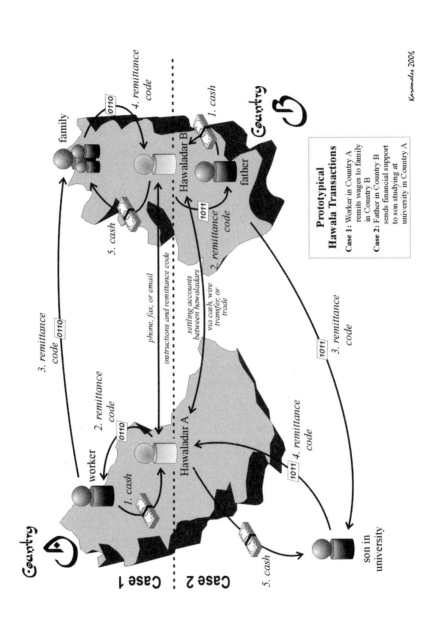

Prototypical
Hawala Transactions

Case 1: Worker in Country A
remits wages to family
in Country B
Case 2: Father in Country B
sends financial support
to son studying at
university in Country A

Karunder 2006

Case 1

Step 1: A person in Country A (sender) wants to send money to a person in Country B (recipient). The sender contacts a hawaladar and provides instructions for delivery of the equivalent amount to the recipient. A small percentage of the amount transferred is the hawaladar's profit.

Step 2: The hawaladar in Country A contacts the counterpart hawaladar in Country B via telephone, e-mail, or fax and communicates the instructions.

Step 3: The hawaladar in Country B contacts the recipient and, generally through the verification of a remittance code previously sent from sender to recipient, arranges for delivery of the equivalent amount in local currency. The hawaladar in Country B charges a small transaction fee.

Step 4: Funds and value move in both directions between hawaladars in Country A and B. Over time, accounts may have to be balanced. Hawaladars use a variety of methods to "settle the books," including the physical transfer of money, bank-to-bank wire transfers, and trade. Historically and culturally, gold is most often used in providing "counter valuation." Methods of value transfer include invoice manipulation.

Case 2

The money transfer is simply reversed, demonstrating that hawala networks are multidirectional.

Hawala is comprised of elements that I observed in my investigations into underground finance and fraud in the Middle East. I was particularly concerned about money laundering, trade fraud, invoice manipulation, fictitious invoicing, and the misuse of the international gold trade. In discussing hawala with Patrick Jost, I found that we shared mutual observations and concerns about Dubai. Once again Dubai surfaced as an integral part of the international hawala equation. As described in chapter 5, Dubai-based trading, import-export, or financial-services companies are part of the Dubai triangle of settling accounts via value transfer. For example, a hawala network between London and Karachi often will clear accounts via Dubai.

In January 2001 I made a trip to the United Arab Emirates (UAE) with ranking officials from the Federal Reserve and the Department of Justice to encourage needed money-laundering reforms. During a meeting with Emirati officials, I brought up the issue of hawala for the first time. Initially, the reaction was combative because, culturally, we were operating from differing points of reference. I was concerned about how hawala could be co-opted by money launderers; months before September 11, I didn't even try to bring up the subject of terrorist financing. But in their discussions of hawala, the Emirati officials thought of the system as nothing more than an informal wage remittance service for their large guest-worker community. Eventually, both sides developed common terminology and our Emirati partners, particularly after September 11, became very progressive in their efforts to regulate this alternative remittance system.

Of course, as our Emirati colleagues told us, the very large percentage of hawala transactions are benign, or "white." As a Somali banker once told me, "Hawala is the poor man's banking system." Simply put, an immigrant or guest worker, whether in New York, London, or Dubai, uses hawala to remit wages back home because it is reliable, inexpensive, and convenient and because it provides door-to-door service. The "poor man" also will use hawala for internal domestic remittances. In a country like Pakistan, where 80 percent of the population is illiterate, there is also a reluctance to use banks because often the customer cannot read, write, or understand the requisite forms. Concerns about corruption and the unscrupulous banker who will take advantage of an illiterate client also drive the use of hawala. In certain areas, women are uncomfortable or not permitted to conduct business. As a result, the "poor" man or woman feels comfortable approaching, for example, the local village gold dealer who also doubles as the village hawaladar for necessary financial services.

Although hawala is officially illegal in India, it is commonplace and an entrenched way of doing business. Yet the root of the problem is not hawala. Rather, hawala thrives in the region because corrupt and often incompetent governments do not adequately regulate their banking systems, while they overregulate everything else. Over the years governments in the region have overtaxed and robbed people of their savings through capital controls, freezing foreign exchange accounts, bank failures, and engaging in currency devaluations. Illiteracy and cultural taboos encourage the people's use of underground hawala networks, while the governments do not provide convenient, inexpensive, reliable, and transparent alternatives. Hawala is not illegal in the United States. U.S. law enforcement authorities have no desire to interfere with an immigrant's wish to remit his hard-earned wages to his home country. The problem the ICG saw at FinCEN long before September 11 was that criminal networks were taking advantage of the same underground and efficient hawala networks to launder criminally derived proceeds. This is sometimes called "black hawala." As we shall see in the next few chapters, policymakers came to understand too late that hawala can also be used by those who finance terrorism.

My discussions with FinCEN colleagues about the BMPE and hawala made me argue even louder that we needed to focus attention on the misuse of the international gold trade. In fact, I argued that gold is an important subset of other ethnic-based alternative remittance systems and should be classified as an alternative remittance system by itself. Although it would be impossible to obtain, I believe an objective evaluation of worldwide law enforcement data would show that, excluding moving money by smuggling, wire, or the misuse of trade in general, money laundering involving gold (including the BMPE, gold-based hawala systems centered in South Asia, and East Asian alternative remittance systems) represents the most significant money-laundering methodology in the world.

Historically, gold is the preferred means to provide countervaluation in hawala transfers. In fact, in 1998 the Commonwealth Secretariat confirmed that "Gold smuggling linked to invoice manipulation plays an important role in the settling of accounts between hawalas." The Commonwealth Secretariat continued that in the mid-1990s, it was believed that if gold (and silver) smuggling were somehow stopped, 80 to 90 percent of hawala transactions would cease.[10]

Gold is also a component of the BMPE. Colombian businesspeople purchase American consumer goods, electronics, machinery, and cigarettes through the drug-dollar exchange. I tried to convince my American law enforcement colleagues to take off their U.S.-only blinders and realize that if Colombian narcotics traffickers used the peso exchange to buy U.S. goods, they would also use the same laundering system to buy goods from other countries. For example, Italy also has a tremendous market for cocaine. The Colombians use the peso exchange system to buy Italian Carara marble for their palatial homes, but more important, they also buy Italian gold. Gold is part of the Latin culture. My argument was a hard sell. But one person who agreed with me was Special Agent Lou Bock of Customs.

Lou Bock was a former DEA inspector who had transferred to Customs. What made him a rare breed was his insight into the overlap of trade fraud and money laundering coupled with his self-taught knowledge of computer programming. He was an incredibly talented agent, and he was very bright. In the early 1990s Lou and a few other agents and analysts tried to examine trade data to more effectively identify potential crimes. With an embarrassingly tiny budget and the help of some computer programmers, Lou was the driving force behind the creation of an innovative program called the Numerically Integrated Profiling System (NIPS). Lou knew the strengths and weaknesses of his fellow agents, and he thus designed his program to be "agent proof." In other words, NIPS provided a technologically challenged investigator with a user-friendly tool to access large amounts of diverse data and point to promising targets for investigation.[11]

The NIPS data sets consisted of U.S. import/export data, trade data provided by foreign governments, BSA databases, and other law enforcement and intelligence information. Much of the export data consisted of information compiled from outbound manifests derived from commercial sources. Import data was compiled primarily from Customs' Automated Commercial System and import entry summary forms. NIPS was a "drill-down" tool that enabled criminal investigators to find discrepancies in trade transactions, such as overvaluation or undervaluation, suspicious quantities, and suspicious countries of origin. Using the drill-down method of analysis, the user could start with a general query and hone in with continuing narrow queries until a likely target was reached. The trade anomalies identified were automatically matched with other databases that tracked the movement of people and money into and out of the United States. Lou built into the program simple queries that every criminal investigator should ask when conducting an investigation: Who, what, when, where? Using the NIPS program, an agent or analyst could do with a mouse and keystrokes what it used to take countless man-hours to do in the field. However, a field investigation was generally still required to answer the most important questions of all: How and why?

Although NIPS could examine all forms of trade goods entering into U.S. commerce, Lou was drawn to gold. Using NIPS, Lou discovered that over the preceding ten years, the United States imported over $13 billion in gold bullion. That does not include gold jewelry, gold scrap, and other categories of gold. This massive importation of gold occurred despite the fact that the United States is one of the largest *exporters* of gold to the world. Using NIPS, Lou and other investigators were able to determine where the gold came from, into what ports in the United States the gold entered, what companies were involved in the transactions, who the couriers were, the unit price for gold in comparison to its market value, etc. For example, Lou determined that some shipments of gold scrap were being sold for three times the average price of gold bullion. As previously discussed, such overvaluation could indicate that value was being transferred or money was being laundered. NIPS also showed that billions of dollars worth of gold were flowing into U.S. ports that do not have significant commercial industries that have a demand for gold.

NIPS also demonstrated that gold exports from Colombia and Peru, the two Latin-American countries chiefly responsible for cocaine production, were mushrooming—almost corresponding with the increase in the cocaine trade. From 1994 to 1997, U.S. imports of Peruvian gold increased from $19 million to $177 million. Gold imports from Colombia also skyrocketed. From 1993 to 1996, gold imports increased from $120,000 to nearly $200 million.[12]

In the mid-1990s, when I first met Lou, he was working on a case targeting the misuse of the international gold trade and money laundering in Venezuela, Guyana, Surinam, and the Netherlands Antilles. Mankind's centuries-long quest for alchemy must have been realized in the Caribbean. Even though gold is not produced or mined in the Caribbean islands, the use of NIPS showed that these countries were shipping massive quantities of the metal into the United States. In Guyana alone, the resulting Customs investigation disclosed that tens of millions of dollars worth of gold was illegally shipped to the United States. Moreover, the resulting loss of tax revenue to Guyana from the undeclared exports was roughly $14 million, and Guyana was one of the poorest countries in the Western Hemisphere.[13]

Lou also used NIPS and subsequent field investigations by U.S. Customs and customs services in other countries to examine suspect cases of gold sent into the United States for "refining." Investigations showed that gold jewelry smuggled into Colombia was sometimes smelted into a form of pigment. The pigment was mixed with a solution of borax and oil to physically alter it from a solid state into a dark liquid or paste. The substance was then sent to the United States for refining. The Colombian government paid approximately a 5 percent export tax credit to the fabricator on the exportation of gold pigment. The pigment or bullion was refined, sold in the United States, and then sent back to South America. In some cases, the gold was actually sold two or three times between Panama, Colombia, and the United States before the cycle operation started again. By all appearances, the same gold was involved in each phase of the cycle. Transactions along the way justified payment and the resulting laundering of dollars. Specialists have confirmed that there is no rationale for transforming gold into pigment other than to defraud governments. The investigation also revealed massive revenue loss to the Colombian government.

NIPS also helped Customs track down a shipment of overvalued gold from Argentina to the United States. From 1992 to 1996 the Argentine government paid $130 million in export rebates on the overvalued gold. This and other examples showed that not only were the criminal networks laundering money via the misuse of trade, but governments were also subsidizing the criminal schemes!

While I became an early disciple of Lou's pioneering work, the Customs management hierarchy paid little attention. These cases and others bore fruit almost solely because of Lou's single-handed perseverance. Constantly fighting the bureaucracy, Lou scrambled for years to keep the NIPS program afloat, but there were always conflicting priorities. The enforcement focus was on dirty money. It took Customs years to accept that the misuse of trade could transfer or launder value as effectively as the laundering of dirty cash.

In November 1997 my constant harping on gold got me an invitation to participate at a FATF money-laundering typologies meeting in Paris. This was an annual event during which law enforcement representatives from around the world met to discuss investigations, money-laundering methodologies, and trends of concern. For the first few days of the conference, I was asked to lead the U.S. delegation, comprised of officials from State, Treasury, and Justice, until the director of FinCEN, Stan Morris, could arrive.

At the meeting I delivered a presentation on the misuse of gold. Although certain countries present in the hall could have been embarrassed by my observations, in fact I found the opposite to be true. The delegates, mostly law enforcement professionals, recognized that gold could be both a commodity and a quasi-monetary instrument. Many of the countries present had their own examples of gold misuse to launder money. After I spoke, I was approached by a Japanese delegate who was also a member of the World Customs Organization (WCO), formerly the Customs Cooperation Council, who asked if I would give the same presentation at the WCO headquarters in Brussels.

After I returned from Paris, I informed Customs headquarters about the invitation to address the WCO. Tammy Smith, chief of operations in the Office of Enforcement, was scheduled to attend the same Brussels conference. I subsequently discovered that Tammy was not a supporter of Lou Bock's work and a naysayer regarding gold as a money-laundering methodology. Nevertheless, she invited me to give her the gold briefing so she could determine if she could give the speech in my stead.

After the briefing, she told me that she would not give the presentation. I asked why not. In an enlightening moment, Tammy succinctly answered, "Because we might get questions from the audience about what U.S. Customs has done in response to the threat we identified. Since we haven't done much, we don't want to be embarrassed. We're not going to talk about it." This comment summarized my frustrations in a nutshell. From Tammy's bureaucratic perspective high up in the Customs hierarchy, she understandably wanted to protect the organization's reputation. From my foot soldier's perspective, I wanted to get the word out to anybody who would listen so the United States and other countries could help take countermeasures to solve the problem.

I was not going to give up. If anything, I was increasingly convinced that alternative remittance systems were causing the West a tremendous problem and that the situation was going to get even worse. A lot of it boiled down to the pressures of changing immigration patterns. A century ago, when my Italian ancestors came to the United States, they brought with them their culture and ways of doing business, including using Western-style banking institutions. Years later, when I went to Rome to help combat Italian-American organized crime, I found the Mafia in large part used the system it was familiar with—banks—to launder money. But over the last generation, large numbers of immigrants from non-Western countries, legally and illegally, are settling in North America and Europe. They too bring with them their culture and ways of doing business, which can include ethnic-based systems of transferring value that do not rely on traditional banking systems monitored by financial-transparency reporting requirements. I am not using the word "ethnic" in a pejorative sense. On the contrary, many of the indigenous methods of doing business have evolved over the centuries and are very sophisticated. Likewise, the cultures they sprang from are very sophisticated.

In January 1999, working with the ICG and FinCEN, I organized a small Washington, D.C., conference to discuss the commonalities of alternative remittance systems. At the beginning of the conference, I asked the audience what the following examples of recent real cases had in common:

1. A network of Somali nationals operating in various areas in the United States is engaged in welfare fraud, as well as smuggling khat and cocaine. The profits from their illegal activities are initially placed in traditional financial institutions. The proceeds are later withdrawn and vanish without a trail for criminal investigators to follow.

2. An undercover operation in the United States is given hundreds of thousands of dollars of narcotics proceeds and is directed by a Colombian money launderer to wire the money to purchase electronics, gold, and securities.

3. An international network of alien smugglers was bringing approximately two hundred aliens a month into the United States from a number of Asian countries. Money to pay for this smuggling operation was collected in the United States and either converted to gold in Dubai or transferred directly to India. Traditional banking channels were not used for any of the transactions.

4. A South Asian gold broker in New York is linked to a heroin-smuggling network. A search warrant executed on the broker's office reveals boxes and boxes of checks from Indian nationals around the

United States. Most of the checks had a Hindu script code written on the lower left-hand corner.

The answer to the question is that all of these real cases used alternative remittance systems to launder the proceeds of various types of crime. The ICG experts then explained how the underground systems involved worked. The ICG tried to get the message out on hawala, BMPE, gold, and the East Asian chit system, respectively. Unfortunately, nothing resulted from the conference.

In November 1999 I tried again. This time the forum was another FATF typologies meeting that met in Washington, D.C. As much as I admired the FATF and its hardworking staff at the FATF Secretariat in Paris, I was becoming increasingly convinced that a glaring weakness in FATF was its Western/Eurocentric views. The West-based FATF drew up its forty recommendations using its background, outlook, and ways of doing business. Alternative systems employed in other cultures were not part of the FATF equation. I felt that there was little understanding and appreciation that these systems could transfer or launder value just as effectively as "traditional" or Western systems.

As a result, I gave a presentation to the assembled delegates entitled, "The Growing Threat of Alternative Remittance Systems." I couldn't have stated it any more clearly. The final slide of the presentation was entitled, "Outlook." I stated point-blank that because of FATF's collective success in regulating currency movement and providing financial transparency, coupled with changing immigration patterns and increasing economic integration, that the years ahead would see an increase in criminals' use of alternative remittance systems. Unfortunately, nothing was done for two more years.

In October 2001 FATF again met in a Washington that had been attacked by terrorists just a few weeks earlier. In an extraordinary plenary on the financing of terrorism, FATF expanded its mission beyond money laundering. Through the issuance of eight special recommendations, the FATF decided to also focus its energy and expertise on the worldwide effort to combat terrorist financing.

FATF's Special Recommendation VI on alternative remittance systems states:

Each country should take measures to ensure that persons or

legal entities, including agents, that provide a service for the transmission of money or value, including transmission through an informal money or value transfer system or network, should be licensed or registered and subject to all the FATF Recommendations that apply to banks and non-bank financial institutions. Each country should ensure that persons or legal entities that carry out this service illegally are subject to administrative, civil or criminal sanctions.[14]

Although it took September 11 to focus FATF and U.S. government attention on the "growing threat of alternative remittance systems," at least the FATF special recommendation was a start. However, although licensing and registration, coupled with new rules and regulations, are part of a necessary process, they will not solve the problem.

7

Cracks in the System

In 1999, after almost three years as the Customs liaison to the Financial Crimes Enforcement Network (FinCEN), I started getting hints about my next transfer. At that time three years was about the norm for a Washington-area assignment. I knew I could be transferred anywhere from New York City to the southwest U.S. border. If it were just up to me, I would have enjoyed going back to the field working investigations again. I really liked Customs. The broad depth of its work, much of it with an international nexus, was both professionally challenging and personally fascinating. However, my family was comfortable in northern Virginia and didn't want to move. As a result, I approached FinCEN about the possibility of joining the young agency. There were only a few special agents on the FinCEN staff. The agents could not investigate; they were there to provide the analysts with some real-world insight. I enjoyed a good reputation with FinCEN management. I convinced the acting director that I wanted to help FinCEN realize its potential. Because Customs and FinCEN were sister Treasury agencies, the transfer was not complicated.

My first assignment at FinCEN was with the International Division, trying to coordinate FinCEN's work with the Egmont Group of Financial Intelligence Units (FIUs). More and more FIUs were joining the Egmont Group every year. For countries building anti-money-laundering programs and infrastructure, FIU development became a cornerstone. The increasing number of FIUs meant more financial intelligence was available to U.S. criminal investigators from countries previously difficult to approach. However, most U.S. law enforcement agencies were still not aware of Egmont or what the member FIUs could do to support their investigations. One of my primary goals was to promote the use of the Egmont Group by U.S. law enforcement. My other major goal was to try to expand FIU development and Egmont membership to countries in the Middle East and Africa. In the mid- to late 1990s, Egmont membership closely mirrored the Western-centric emphasis of the Financial Action Task Force (FATF) because the Western "developed" countries had the prerequisites in place for the creation of FIUs, i.e., anti-money-laundering laws and financial intelligence. A country can't have an FIU unless it has gathered data to analyze and disseminate. The other major prerequisite to Egmont membership was having the political will to exchange information. I was satisfied that Egmont membership ensures appropriate safeguards on financial intelligence exchange. I truly enjoyed going out on the road and promoting the use of FIUs by domestic U.S. law enforcement and the development of FIUs by our foreign friends.

In mid-1999 things began to change administratively at FinCEN. The agency had a new director, whose previous career was primarily with the Secret Service. Although Secret Service agents do not generally have experience with money-laundering investigations, I was initially very impressed with the new director: he was articulate and personable and had a track record as a manager. Shortly after the director was hired, he was joined by FinCEN's first and only senior law enforcement policy adviser, and later one of two deputy directors, Tammy Smith. Tammy had transferred to FinCEN from Customs. I was also happy with this appointment. Both she and the director were agents, and both were from organizations that I was very familiar with. Although FinCEN had promise and potential, it also had a myriad of problems, a situation exacerbated because FinCEN had been adrift for over a year with an acting director. Thus, I was very optimistic when the new management team announced that they wanted to reorganize FinCEN and make it more responsive to the needs of law enforcement. I bought into their agenda completely.

A short time after the new management team was in place, the director called me into his office. Seated next to him was Tammy. They asked if I would reorganize FinCEN's Office of Investigative Support (OIV), the analytical division. I was perfectly happy with my work in the International Division and did not want to leave, but working in the government, one serves as directed. I had previously made known my view that OIV was not adequately serving the needs of law enforcement. The director's and Tammy's own reviews of procedures had confirmed my observation. The director said that he would back me "100 percent" in necessary reforms and intimated that I would soon become the assistant director for OIV. I agreed to give the overhaul my best effort.

FinCEN analysis, the bread and butter of the organization, had some major problems. First, the great majority of the analysis was not analysis but rather data retrieval by a process derisively known among the troops as "checky checky." Analysts would check databases, assemble data, put a cover sheet on the product, and send it back to the requester. The resulting printouts were sometimes very thick and very heavy. The product could better be called "analysis by the pound" or "analysis by hitting the print button." Sometimes the product was adequate, but often the requester in the field ended up disappointed and frustrated. Occasionally, real analysis, involving links and associations among individuals, companies, and bank accounts, took place. Instead of the cursory data checks, the analysts would peel the onion skin away and delve down into the second or third layer to provide real insight for the field. But these instances were comparatively few and far between.

The second problem with OIV was the lack of proactive analysis. Being "proactive" does not mean reacting to a request for support from the field but rather taking the initiative to identify an anomaly in the databases or a noteworthy incident, trend, or pattern of suspicious activity that needs to be brought to the attention of law enforcement. This was the kind of work that the Primo Passo team did in Rome using comparatively rudimentary data and primitive analytical tools. I felt strongly that FinCEN should aggressively exploit the tens of millions of BSA filings in its databases and put to good use its self-vaunted information technology "force-multiplier" capabilities. FinCEN actually did little with the millions of suspicious activity reports (SARs) and other forms of financial intelligence it had at its disposal; this data was stored in a kind of electronic library, without a viable category and retrieval system. Without a specific request from law enforcement, the data was not exploited. Unfortunately, there wasn't even a proactive section at FinCEN. The little proactive work being done was primarily found in the Artificial Intelligence Section (AI) of OIV, an early attempt to data mine the Bank Secrecy Act (BSA). As Customs liaison, I had seen how some of the AI reports could both initiate and support investigations. However, the new FinCEN management team did not support AI, and the system was slowly being allowed to atrophy by neglect.

Third, I was concerned that OIV never missed an opportunity to miss an opportunity. Over the years FinCEN had refused to participate in the largest and most significant money-laundering cases, including, for example, Customs Operation Casablanca. On May 18, 1998, the secretary of treasury and the U.S. attorney general announced Operation Casablanca's culmination as "the largest, most comprehensive, and significant drug money laundering case in the history of U.S. law enforcement."[1] The director of FinCEN should have been on the stage, helping make the press announcement. Instead, there was another egg on the organization's face.

In 1998 approximately 60 percent of the estimated 176 tons of South American cocaine was smuggled into the United States through Mexico.[2] Mexico was also a lead smuggler of heroin, marijuana, and methamphetamine. During that time frame, Mexico's seizures of all of these drugs fell substantially. Its antidrug force, the Center for Antinarcotics Information, was permeated with corruption and often only pretended to cooperate with U.S. law enforcement. Many politicians were in bed with the *narcotrafficantes*. A State Department colleague who specialized in anti–money laundering often quoted in public forums a line from a speech given a few years earlier by a former Customs commissioner saying, "Mexico is a criminal enterprise masquerading as a government."

Operation Casablanca opened a window into this insidious network. Over the course of three years the U.S. Customs–led undercover money-laundering investigation resulted in the arrest of 167 individuals and the seizure of over $103 million in U.S. currency and tons of marijuana and cocaine. Most important, twenty-six Mexican bank officials and three Mexican banks were charged with laundering the drug money. The investigation revealed that officials from twelve of Mexico's largest nineteen banking institutions were involved in money-laundering activities. Bankers from two Venezuelan banks were also charged in the money-laundering scheme. Operation Casablanca was particularly significant because it uncovered a systematic scheme to knowingly launder money via a large number of primarily Mexican institutions. Instead of targeting individual criminals, Operation Casablanca was focused on trying to dismantle a money-laundering *system* or infrastructure exploited by the cartels.

When Operation Casablanca was just getting off the ground, Bill Gately, the assistant special agent in charge of the Financial Investigations Division of the Customs Office of Investigation in Los Angeles, asked me to obtain FinCEN support for the promising investigation. Gately was a dynamic and innovative criminal investigator who had recruited well-placed sources of information who reported on corrupt Mexican financial institutions. He and his team of agents constructed an undercover operation that provided a window into the complicity of banks in the laundering of narcotics proceeds. Trying to build an investigation, he wanted FinCEN's help in analyzing financial data. He also wanted FinCEN to make the appropriate queries in the newly created SARs database.

Despite Gately's briefs at FinCEN and my personal and repeated appeals to management for assistance, FinCEN eventually made the decision not to support Operation Casablanca. At one level, analytical support was vetoed because the operation was erroneously judged as not promising. At another level, FinCEN was simply too structurally focused on processing the never-ending stream of requests for the support of checky-checky cases and didn't want to devote resources to Casablanca. Although I did what I could to provide backchannel support and relevant SARs to the Casablanca Task Force in Los Angeles, my efforts were no substitute for FinCEN's full institutional resources.

During the course of the investigation, I kept warning FinCEN management that they had made the wrong decision. It didn't take a crystal ball to see that this was going to be one of the largest money-laundering cases in history. Sure enough, when Operation Casablanca finally concluded, it generated headlines around the world. Particularly as a young organization with the mandate of supporting law enforcement in efforts to combat financial crime, FinCEN was embarrassed. It held an internal postmortem attended by top FinCEN management. While I was the Customs liaison to FinCEN, I was also asked to participate. The assistant director for OIV made numerous excuses for FinCEN's repeated refusals to participate. I finally stopped him and said, "I have worked in money laundering and undercover operations for many years. Sometimes you win and sometimes you lose. And actually, most times you lose. It is like rolling the dice. But Operation Casablanca was the closest thing to a gimme that I ever saw. FinCEN blew it. Now let's move on."

The fourth problem in OIV was FinCEN staffing. There were far too many high-ranking managers and support staff and not enough workers. Even though FinCEN was a very small agency, its politics worked against intraorganization communication and mutual support. There was layer upon layer of review of analytical products. The backlog of cases fluctuated, but it could often take months and months for an agent in the field to get a response to an inquiry. It was not uncommon for requests originating from foreign FIUs to take over six months to be answered. And well over 90 percent of the investigations being supported were simple first-tier inquiries. Morale was low, cliques were rampant, and most analysts felt like they were assigned to a never-ending case-processing assembly line—consisting of stifling office cubicles. The work could at times be drudgery; all the more reason the analysts deserved a better work environment and support. Previous management had failed them, and I hoped to help make things better.

The easy part was to draw up a reorganization chart. In addition to the mandatory first-tier analysis, I added other sections to fill the recognized gaps in the OIV work product. I dubbed the new sections "proactive," "added-value" for more in-depth analysis, and not wanting a repeat of the Operation Casablanca debacle, "significant-case support." New supervisory personnel were appointed. Lines of communication with FinCEN's other divisions were increased. It was a good plan on paper, but unfortunately, it was never allowed to be implemented as envisioned. A senior FinCEN manager insisted that everything be funneled through her.

The significant case support section was the first casualty of my reorganization. Operation Casablanca had embarrassed FinCEN because the agency had chosen not to support the investigation. The next international headline-making case was the Bank of New York (BONY) investigation, which began in 1998, about the same time Casablanca ended. British and U.S. investigators, primarily from the Federal Bureau of Investigation, discovered that about $7 billion was being moved through a small number of accounts at the New York bank. A BONY executive, Lucy Edwards, helped facilitate capital flight and dirty money from Russia into the United States. Edwards's husband, Peter Berlin, had a front company that controlled the accounts through which most of the money moved.[3]

In the early stages of the investigation, the FBI in New York requested FinCEN's help in analyzing the financial flow. A number of analysts were involved with the project, and Susan Davis, a young analyst at FinCEN, did a terrific job of assembling a link chart tracing the movements of the money involved. When finished, her chart covered almost an entire wall and identified previously unknown financial flows involving about a dozen countries. Susan managed to construct the flowchart in such a way that there were not any overlapping lines but rather direct associations. It was a very professional product.

When Susan and I went to New York to present the findings to the FBI case agent, he and his staff were very impressed. In examining the flowchart and looking at all of the leads going to foreign countries, I thought FinCEN had a unique opportunity to do more. I believed that FinCEN could take advantage of the Egmont Group and enlist appropriate countries' help in determining what happened to the funds. The BONY investigation was generating worldwide press and other countries were independently looking at pieces of the money-laundering puzzle. I proposed to the FBI that FinCEN not only use Egmont channels to request international financial intelligence, but that appropriate Egmont member analysts later collaborate on a joint analytical product. I envisioned a roomful of American, British, French, German, Belgian, Italian, and other nationalities working together on a common analytical product and creating an even more massive and in-depth financial flowchart. With the help of America's foreign friends, the chart would not only show financial flows but also additional foreign links and possibly the disposition of funds. It would be the first international collaboration on a money-laundering case of this magnitude in history and would enable the analysts and investigators to literally follow the money trail around the world. Susan's wall chart would be expanded to cover an entire room. It would also, in one move, prove the worth of FinCEN and Egmont and make them "relevant."

The FBI loved the idea. I asked them to put a request in writing for FinCEN support, which they did. It was signed by a very high-level FBI official. Using the old-boy network, I informally queried the relevant Egmont members to ask if they would be interested in participating in such a project. Without hesitation, every member country agreed to the proposed joint BONY analytical product. I was very excited at this opportunity to take international money-laundering analysis to a new level. After having gotten my ducks in a row, I next presented the proposal to the senior FinCEN manager.

The manager vetoed it for no reason other than I had not first cleared the idea with her. Later, I found out, as the FinCEN troops used to say, "If it is not [the manager's] idea, it is a bad idea." Regardless of the FBI's written request and Egmont members champing at the bit to get started, she said no to any further FinCEN support.

A few years later, when the BONY case was closed, the director of the FBI sent the director of FinCEN a nice letter thanking FinCEN for its early support in the investigation. Susan's impressive analytical work was recognized. The FinCEN director enjoyed the pat on the back his organization received. Although the letter was a nice gesture, I still regret the wasted opportunity to fully utilize the financial investigative tools that many of us had worked so hard to develop. The Egmont Group has still not fulfilled its potential. And the BONY investigation was not an example of FinCEN "significant-case support" but was rather just another missed opportunity in a continuing series of missed opportunities. And the worst was yet to come.

My deepest frustrations occurred in proactive case development. In my mind, identifying and disseminating key "information that law enforcement doesn't already know," the common request and refrain from law enforcement to FinCEN, was the reason FinCEN was created. However, proactive case development had never previously been emphasized or systematically approached. Such case development should have attracted the very best of FinCEN's talents, energy, and resources. However, we were hard-pressed to assemble three good analysts to proactively examine the 13 million annual BSA filings, including the hundreds of thousands of SARs, filed every year.

The senior manager and I clashed immediately on proactive work. The manager insisted that analysts only look for the "gems." While I concurred with that philosophy, BSA data didn't have the word "gem" imprinted on the filings. I felt that in trying to identify the gems, if an analyst discovered something of potential interest to law enforcement, FinCEN had the obligation to bring it to their attention, particularly because representatives from all the federal law enforcement agencies were physically located at FinCEN. I polled the law enforcement representatives and without exception, they told me that they wanted to determine what was important to their respective agencies; they didn't want to defer the determination to FinCEN. Unfortunately, the manager vetoed that concept as well. Instead of listening to law enforcement's wants and needs, FinCEN was going to dictate to law enforcement what they were going to get—or not get.

Things deteriorated still further when we received a proactive-reactive request from a Drug Enforcement Administration (DEA) office in

Florida for help in developing targets of interest. A new DEA group supervisor had been assigned to a new office. Wanting to make a good impression with his troops, he approached FinCEN and asked for assistance in identifying potential targets for investigation. Obviously he wanted leads that had a nexus to narcotics and that could be developed in the area of his office's jurisdiction. The new proactive section "reacted" to the request and developed five excellent potential leads that fell within the parameters of the request. The target packages were readied for review. We addressed them to the DEA requestor.

However, the senior manager decided that the five individual target packages would not only be sent to the DEA office in Florida, but also to the FBI in Florida, Customs in Florida, the IRS in Florida, and the local multiagency task force. The thought was that since FinCEN was a "neutral broker," lead information should be shared with everybody. While that sounds fine in theory, the reality for investigators in the field is that if everybody gets it, nobody will work it. Why should the DEA spend resources to develop a case if all of the DEA's sister enforcement agencies have access to the same information and may also end up working the same case?

I was forced to telephone the DEA requester and tell him that FinCEN would be sending the information that he had specifically requested to all of his competitor agencies. Of course, he refused to work the referrals. FinCEN's credibility was destroyed with that agent. The DEA liaison at FinCEN was also extremely upset. Agents talked. Their discontent spread rapidly. Making matters even worse, the senior manager later decreed that FinCEN would no longer entertain any such proactive-reactive requests for assistance. In other words, when requests to FinCEN came from law enforcement for the development of target packages, FinCEN would no longer identify potential leads. FinCEN was supposed to be a service agency. It was created to help others. But again, instead of listening to what customers wanted, FinCEN dictated.

Although this example of bureaucratic tug-of-war may seem petty to outsiders, it had serious consequences. Both before and after September 11 limited attempts by FinCEN to match classified information with BSA reporting[4] for the most part proved ineffective because of FinCEN's continued insistence on giving multiple agencies access to the same investigative lead information. In addition, FinCEN would not divulge to its law enforcement colleagues what specific part of a report needed to be closely examined. While again, in theory, this timid approach can be argued at a policy level, the reality was that time after time FinCEN-generated leads were not worked in the field. Criminal investigators have lots of leads in their in-boxes. When they pick up a FinCEN report and either determine that other agencies have been given the same information or cannot readily determine what part of the sometimes-lengthy narrative is important, then often they will discard the entire report. FinCEN could have easily remedied this situation but management refused. Even with the recent specter of terrorist attacks FinCEN did not listen to what its customers wanted.

I had severe philosophical and stylistic differences with the senior manager. It soon became apparent that I was not the yes-man she envisioned. I was advised by a close associate, who on the surface managed to get along with the manager, that to survive I would have to learn to "kiss her ass" like the rest of the organization's staff. I had never done that in my career, and I wasn't about to start. So, the senior manager succeeded in appointing a very weak individual, who had failed at every previous managerial assignment he had been given in FinCEN, to the position of assistant director, OIV. The new deputy assistant director was likewise very weak. The two new managers were also close personal friends of each other. This transparent maneuvering gave the senior FinCEN manager free reign to impose her will on OIV, completely controlling the people and the process. Despite her title, in my opinion, the senior manager became the de facto assistant director of OIV and later, the de facto director of FinCEN.

Things continued to deteriorate from there. The paper flow and review process were based on the senior manager's constantly changing edicts, which completely constipated the analytical pipeline. These delays and frustrations only caused increased criticism of the analysts and their products. Analysts came into my office beaten down and distraught, questioning their work and their worth. Some were in tears. They voiced their frustrations about the senior manager's biting sarcasm and constant interference. Most of the principal proactive analysts left. One very talented young analyst actually quit the government in frustration. This became the culture of the FinCEN bureaucracy. Meanwhile, FinCEN's senior management team, knowingly or unknowingly, misled officials in the Department of the Treasury and congressional oversight staff with so-called FinCEN success stories, which were few and far between.

FinCEN's hyped information technology solutions were also becoming perilously nonfunctional. The reasons were many, but primary among them was failed management. In the spring of 2000, looking for yet another solution, the senior manager became the driving force behind a new analytical tool, which I will call the Anomaly Analytical System (AAS). In theory, the system was ideal. It supposedly was engineered to discover common components, anomalies, or links in the financial database that human analysts or other analytical programs and tools were unable to associate. It was hoped that AAS could evolve into the chief targeting tool for proactive work. I too was initially hopeful. We desperately needed such a tool.

However, I became concerned when I learned respected analysts privately viewed the prototype system as a joke. They identified fundamental flaws in AAS. Moreover, AAS was based on very old FORTRAN software. The program was user-unfriendly and delivered a very difficult to decipher final analytical product. Nevertheless, often using canned data, AAS was taken on the road and demonstrated to the field. The senior manager promised her law enforcement colleagues that AAS would be the type of analytical financial tool that could proactively identify quality leads for investigation. Despite most of the professional analysts' quiet reservations, we were told by the manager that it was our "responsibility to make it work."

Try as we might we could not. As the senior manager and the developer kept pushing and pushing, the flaws in the system became more and more apparent. Still, we were directed to put together a small team to study AAS and see if we could make it function as advertised. We were not allowed to discuss our reservations with the system so, trying to get the word out, in weekly memos and management briefs to the director, which were forwarded to the Department of the Treasury, we referred to the team's efforts as the Component Research Analytical Project. Our team enjoyed quiet chuckles. The project's acronym was never deciphered.

The development of AAS continued eating up hundreds and hundreds of thousands of taxpayer dollars and probably millions more in lost salary and opportunity costs. I became very concerned and wrote a memo to the director. He would not make a decision himself, so he called for a meeting to allow concerned offices and individuals to voice their observations about AAS. I privately warned the director before the meeting that, in my opinion, the senior manager's presence would intimidate anybody from publicly speaking out against the development of AAS. Uniformly, FinCEN staff was afraid of her wrath and retaliation.

Despite what people privately told me about their negative views of AAS, during the very well-attended meeting I was the only person to speak out against further development of the system. I was probably also the least qualified to address the issue because I was simply a criminal investigator with no technical or analytical skills. Some mid-level managers and analysts who had privately derided the system publicly sang its praises. Their blatant attempt to curry favor with senior management was both disgusting and cowardly. Other staff members were simply intimidated into silence. When the director called for a vote, mine was the only hand raised to vote against.

As a result, the sole-source contract—unusual in government procurement—was awarded to the developer. Unfortunately, AAS rapidly turned into yet another example of government waste, fraud, and abuse. As predicted, the AAS system eventually failed for all to see and was abandoned. Through continued neglect, the AI system finally collapsed as well. But when FinCEN management was in need of a high-tech demonstration for high-level delegations, the forsaken systems sometimes were dusted off. Often using canned data, they wowed the unknowing but impressionable audience with their bells and whistles and continued to give the impression that technology is FinCEN's force multiplier. FinCEN did excel in multiplying smoke and mirrors.

These anecdotes are shared to make two points. First, FinCEN was never held accountable. The AAS system failed. There is an audit trail and a record. Management made documented decisions. But nobody was ever asked to own up to the failure of the system or the waste of taxpayer money. Second, at the time of September 11, FinCEN, the government agency mandated to analyze financial intelligence, didn't have adequate data-mining tools to analyze the intelligence it collected. In part this was the product of the wasted time and lost opportunity costs involved in the development of the failed AAS system.

The director and the senior manager also dismissed concerns about the growing threat of alternative remittance systems. They believed that the direction of FinCEN revolved around the BSA. From a narrow management perspective, their focus on the BSA made some sense. They were trying to reorganize and did not want to be pulled in different directions. FinCEN management was fixated on traditional Western-style ways of business and banking. If it did not involve a bank account, wire transfer, check, or use of an automatic teller machine, they were at a loss. The emphasis on the BSA was a logical outgrowth of FinCEN's vested bureaucratic interests to preserve its resources and turf. Slow to grasp new and emerging threats, displaying a disdain for non-Western value transfer, reluctant to entertain imaginative ideas, and bureaucratically wedded to the status quo, FinCEN management could not think of a money-laundering or, later, terrorist-finance threat that did not have as a solution yet one more financial reporting requirement.

I had a fundamental and philosophical disagreement with management's approach. The name of the organization was the Financial Crimes Enforcement Network not the "Financial Crimes Enforcement Network Limited to the Bank Secrecy Act." Colleagues in the field had told me their concerns about alternative remittance systems that were not captured by BSA reporting requirements. There was a governmental void in this area, something that would later be called by our enemies "cracks in the Western financial system," and I felt FinCEN was in a unique position to offer assistance, guidance, advisories, and insight. No other government agency in existence could take on this role. Yet the senior manager repeatedly and publicly would wag her finger in my face and say, "We do not do systems. What don't you understand?" What made this neglect most difficult to swallow was the fact that top management at FinCEN were agents. Yet they refused to listen to what their law enforcement colleagues in the field wanted and would not permit FinCEN's assistance.

To make matters worse, in short order, the hawala expert, Patrick Jost, left FinCEN. With him went the U.S. government's sole expert on a system that later proved to be inextricably linked to terrorist finance. The Interagency Coordination Group (ICG) Black-Market Peso Exchange experts also became disillusioned and left. Other very impressive members of the staff left as well. FinCEN management jettisoned the group of able FinCEN staffers who were the driving force behind U.S. efforts with the FATF. FinCEN's work with Egmont suffered from poor personnel selection. The work environment changed from the earlier college campus atmosphere that encouraged innovation to an oppressive and hostile work environment. FinCEN suffered a brain drain. FinCEN talent immigrated to the Department of the Treasury, the National Security Council (NSC) at the White House, the State Department, the Federal Reserve, Capitol Hill, and prestigious financial institutions. In the government, people are policy. FinCEN lost many of its best people, and much of the staff that remained had neither expertise in money laundering nor experience in the field. Many were promoted for all of the wrong reasons. The agency began to spiral downward in a dive from which, I believe, it has never recovered.

The innovative multiagency ICG that was discussed in chapter 6 also became frustrated. Instead of listening to what the law enforcement representatives wanted, the senior manager told them what they were going to get. In reaction, the ICG dissolved itself. It was a shame, particularly because the ICG worked to achieve the type of interagency coordination and imaginative solutions that the 9/11 Commission identified as lacking.

I tried to continue to help agents out in the field. I still fielded phone calls from Department of Justice and Department of the Treasury investigators around the country trying to help them make sense of the financial links in various criminal scams. These investigators were examining various immigrant groups' criminal activity including the stealing and reselling of baby formula, illegally redeeming large quantities of grocery coupons, collecting fraudulent welfare payments, and credit-card fraud and abuse.[5] The money reaped from these crimes was flowing back to the immigrants' homelands via alternative remittance systems, which I was officially prohibited from discussing. After September 11 it was reported that an unknown portion of the estimated tens of millions of dollars raised annually by these scams was funneled to support radical Islamic terrorist organizations. Participating in both domestic and overseas money-laundering seminars and conferences, I was often asked by the organizers to talk about hawala, gold, and other value-transfer systems. Trying to help my colleagues in the field, I disregarded the senior manager's orders and did so. Responding to a direct personal appeal from Department of Justice prosecutors in preparation for a major prosecution on Italian gold being purchased by Colombian narcotics traffickers via Panama's Colon free trade zone (FTZ), I literally sneaked out of FinCEN to tutor the agents and prosecutors. However, even this backdoor strategy became increasingly difficult.

In August 2001 I received a telephone call from a Customs analyst assigned to the New York High-Risk Money Laundering and Related Financial Crimes Area (HIFCA). She knew of my work with gold and asked if I could assist her and task force personnel with insights into the misuse of the gold trade. The task force was pursuing a major investigation that involved the purchase of gold jewelry from the proceeds of narcotics sales. Although there were variations in the methodology, typically the gold jewelry purchased was smelted and poured into molds for machine parts and tools. The golden items were painted black, covered with a layer of grease, and exported to Colombia. I told the New York analyst about the "FinCEN does not do systems" policy, but responding to her continued appeals I sent the analyst some information on the misuse of the gold trade. I emphasized that the materials were from me and not FinCEN.

A week later the analyst called back and told me she loved the materials and asked if I could travel to New York to brief the investigators. The senior manager had denied all such previous requests. Thinking that this time she might relent, I suggested the analyst put the request in writing. The director of the New York HIFCA soon sent a letter to FinCEN requesting my assistance. True to form, the senior manager would not allow me to talk to the HIFCA about gold but instead directed that FinCEN analysts query the BSA database for information that had to do with gold and New York and forward the materials to the New York HIFCA.

When I later called the New York HIFCA to apologize for FinCEN's lack of support, the Customs analyst said (direct quote), "You people do not get it. If we wanted BSA analysis we could do it up here ourselves. We wanted your expertise. This is so typical of FinCEN." Sadly, I had to agree. It was yet another example of FinCEN not listening to the field.

Even after September 11, with the nation at war, the senior manager refused to acknowledge that gold was a topic of importance. This was increasingly puzzling to me because staffers in the NSC told me that the White House was concerned about repeated reports in the press and elsewhere about the misuse of the gold trade and possible links to terrorist finance. The secretary of the treasury made a trip to the Middle East, including Dubai, and reportedly brought up the topics of gold and hawala. Even in the interagency *National Money Laundering and Terrorist Fi-*

nance Strategy, gold and its links to alternative remittance systems were discussed. Congress also mandated that Treasury/FinCEN examine hawala's link to terrorist finance. Of course, hawala is inextricably linked to the misuse of the international gold trade.

Finally, matters came to a head. In response to growing concerns about gold and hawala, I gave an informal and internal brief at FinCEN. When the senior manager learned of the presentation, she called me into her office. In the presence of others, she stated once and for all that I was not allowed to talk about gold. Period. I was literally given a gag order. In all my years of government service, I had never before heard of such a thing. How can we fight battles, let alone win a war, when facts and ideas are censored?

I saw the earlier promise of FinCEN collapse before my eyes. The optimism and upbeat working environment that was described in the last chapter vanished. The analytical, regulatory, information-technology, and international sections at FinCEN were all becoming nonfunctional. FinCEN was increasingly recognized as irrelevant in the interagency community. Work was not done, and personnel were demoralized. Personnel grievances were rampant. Only one office in FinCEN excelled and that was the Office of Equal Opportunity (EEO).

Following the celebration of diversity politics of the Clinton years, the director of FinCEN appointed a full-time special assistant to the director for equal opportunity and diversity. In my opinion, the position developed into a kind of political commissar that was commonly found in the former Soviet Union. Simply put, FinCEN's diversity policies and programs tried to inculcate politically correct groupthink. The cult of victimology was promoted. Personnel grievances became rampant. Freedom of speech knelt at the altar of political correctness.

The special assistant to the director for equal opportunity and diversity and top FinCEN management mandated a continuing series of "special" days and monthlong office "celebrations" to recognize hyphenated groups. For example, FinCEN celebrated African-American month, Asian-American month, Hispanic-American month, Native-American month, Women-history month, etc. This is commonly done around the government, and in my opinion, nothing is wrong with this type of awareness and recognition, if it is done in moderation. However, these celebrations were not limited to posters, simple information sessions, or events during lunch hours. They became part of the work schedule. Various offices within FinCEN had to sponsor the festivities, which included special presentations, skits, readings, publications, games, displays, contests, handouts, souvenirs, e-mail trivia questions, graphics, and guest speakers. Politically correct groupthink required full participation.

On June 6, 2001, the series of celebrations culminated in FinCEN's first Diversity Day. An incredible amount of manpower and money was expended. Diversity Day alone—through direct expenditures for speakers, special programs, souvenirs, and employee salaries pulled to organize Diversity Day—easily cost taxpayers hundreds and hundreds of thousands of dollars. The indirect and lost opportunity costs—taking FinCEN away from its mission—are incalculable. The EEO bureaucracy became further entrenched within the FinCEN culture and the organization chart with the appointment of special counselors or assistants to the special assistant for EEO and diversity within each office or division in FinCEN. While all of this effort might have been appropriate at the departmental level, FinCEN itself still maintained an authorized full-time staff level of about two hundred employees. I could only contrast the resources poured into these activities with the struggle to make even a few good analysts available for proactive case development. Moreover, in their quest for workforce diversity, management overlooked the diversity of ideas.

FinCEN management also banned any type of analysis that could possibly be interpreted as the politically unacceptable concept of "profiling." In relation to proactive targeting, this had serious consequences. When I was in Italy, the Primo Passo team examined anomalies in financial intelligence, particularly the international transportation of currency, trying to find indicators of suspicious financial behavior. We were concerned about Italian-American organized crime. Focusing on one group like this wasn't called profiling at the time; it was both politically acceptable and an effective law enforcement countermeasure. Our examinations of appropriate databases were always professional and never abusive. Both the Italian and American governments endorsed this type of work.

But, in the two years immediately preceding September 11, FinCEN management did not allow databases to be searched in similar ways because they could possibly be interpreted as politically incorrect profiling. It is no secret that various immigrant groups in America are disproportionately involved in organized crime. However, FinCEN analysts were not allowed to effectively and proactively examine financial intelligence, one of the best law enforcement tools available, to assist law enforcement combat immigrant- or ethnic-related organized crime. Even internal discussions on issuing an advisory on hawala to financial institutions could not gain traction because FinCEN management felt it was too sensitive and could be perceived as singling out peoples from South Asia. Collectively, the country paid for it. The combination of a weak proactive section, the prohibition of any analysis that could possibly be interpreted as politically incorrect profiling, and the lack of effective data-mining tools had disastrous consequences.

✳

My frustrations reached a climax on September 11. For years I had watched as the U.S. intelligence and law enforcement communities made decisions that were at times myopic and often just plain wrong. The Central Intelligence Agency, an agency I served proudly for over five years, was put in place for the primary reason of preventing the recurrence of Pearl Harbor. The CIA failed. For almost twenty years, I also served proudly with U.S. law enforcement. Various law enforcement agencies, particularly the FBI, also failed to defend the homeland. Watching television on the morning of September 11, when I saw the planes strike the World Trade towers and then heard that the Pentagon was also under attack, I personally felt that I had also failed. The American people deserved better from their public servants.

In addition to the failures by the intelligence and law enforcement communities to prevent the terrorist attacks on September 11, the system of financial intelligence, which was put in place to help fight the War on Narcotics, failed to generate data on suspicious financial activity that could have possibly helped prevent the attacks. Investigation showed that the attacks were financed by an estimated $300,000–$500,000. Most of the identified funding was transferred via cash, wire transfers, and travelers' checks. The hijackers also made use of money orders and check-cashing services. When dealing with banks, their transactions were in relatively small amounts. For example, on September 10, Mohammed Atta, the suspected ringleader in Osama bin Laden's terrorist plot, was videotaped at an automatic teller machine outside Portland, Maine. The withdrawal limit on the machine was $300.[6]

As explained earlier, financial intelligence was not designed to detect the small amount of funding used by terrorists compared to the large amounts laundered in the War on Narcotics. It was commonly accepted within both the banking and law enforcement communities that there were virtually no meaningful bits of information on the nineteen hijackers out of the universe of approximately 13 million BSA forms filed every year. Even a staff report to the investigating 9/11 Commission reported that no financial institution filed a SAR on the hijackers and that in hindsight there was no cause to do so.[7] However, I believe that even if a few meaningful investigative leads had been included in the financial databases, FinCEN, the Treasury bureau primarily charged to exploit the BSA, would have failed to find and act on the possible leads prior to September 11 because FinCEN did not have the proper data-mining tools, expertise, personnel, proactive infrastructure, and management systems in place.

Although the financial databases were created primarily to fight the War on Narcotics, not the War on Terrorism, I watched transfixed as Treasury's FinCEN and the Office of Foreign Assets Control (OFAC) tried to use yesterday's weapons and tactics for today's war. In one sense, using the existing financial databases for this purpose was like trying to force a square peg in a round hole. But bureaucratically, it made perfect sense. The first law of any bureaucracy is survival. It was in the bureaucracies' vested interest to immediately promote financial intelligence and asset identification, designations, and the blocking, freezing, and seizing of suspect bank accounts after September 11. In my opinion, the misplaced emphasis cost the American government an enormous amount of time, resources, and international goodwill in its new War on Terrorist Finance.

Well before September 11, I had a discussion with the director of FinCEN about trying to find Osama bin Laden's financial assets. Point-blank, I told him that they would not be found in the proverbial Swiss bank account. After the 1998 U.S. embassy bombings in Tanzania and Kenya, the United States had moved in and coordinated the seizure of identified al Qaeda assets in formal financial institutions. Bin Laden and his sophisticated financial advisers were not going to repeat the same mistake. However, the director was not concerned. The mantra at FinCEN was to focus solely on BSA data. In fact, for a long time after September 11, the director kept asking for proof that al Qaeda even used hawala. Years later the 9/11 Commission's *Monograph on Terrorist Financing* acknowledged al Qaeda's use of hawala and the realization that the terrorist organization's funding stayed outside the U.S. formal financial system in ways that bypassed the BSA reporting requirements.[8]

Another reason for my concern was that long before September 11 caused the West to notice hawala, hawala was involved with the finance of terrorism in South Asia. For example, the long-running dispute over Kashmir has made the rate of terrorist attacks in India one of the highest of any country in the world. In fact, in a conversation I had with top Indian law enforcement officials in New Delhi, I was told that "100 percent" of the terrorist attacks in India were financed by hawala. Undoubtedly, terrorist attacks in neighboring Pakistan are also financed, in large part, by hawala. Apparently, FinCEN management did not understand that the abuse of hawala in places like South Asia and Arabia, the breeding ground for al Qaeda, should be a concern to the United States as well. Waiting for proof in part stalled the U.S. War on Terrorist Finance.

As regards the de facto director's dismissal of gold, after the U.S. invasion of Afghanistan, coalition forces found al Qaeda training manuals on how to smuggle gold on small boats and concealed on the body—just as described in earlier chapters. It was discovered that wealthy Saudi donors gave donations to both the Taliban and al Qaeda in gold. The precious metal acted as a currency to the leadership of both terrorist organizations.[9]

In May 2004, in one of the very few public statements by al Qaeda about financing, Osama bin Laden himself offered a reward for killing Americans and coalition forces. The reward was offered in *gold*.[10] More recently, in February 2006, the Taliban offered 100 kilograms of *gold* to anyone who killed the person responsible for the "blasphemous" cartoons of the prophet Muhammad that were printed in a Danish newspaper.[11] After reading this book, the reader now understands what the de facto director of FinCEN never grasped: bin Laden's and the Taliban's offers were in gold because as part of its diversified financing the terrorist organizations use gold; their members are primarily from countries where gold is an intrinsic part of the culture; the regional audience relates to gold; gold is an informal value-transfer system itself and plays an important role in other systems such as hawala; and finally, gold is an international medium of exchange that for the most part is immune to Western-style financial-transparency reporting requirements and countermeasures such as asset freezing and designations.

The only other quote that I am aware of from bin Laden regarding finance is a response to a question raised shortly after September 11 in a Pakistani press interview: Was al Qaeda worried about further attempts in the West to find and freeze its assets? Bin Laden is quoted as saying that such attempts "will not make any difference to al Qaeda or other jihad groups. Al Qaeda is comprised of modern, educated young people who are as aware of the cracks in the Western financial system as they are of the lines in their own hands. These are the very flaws in the Western financial system which is becoming a noose for it."[12] As I said earlier, our enemies are smart. They have successfully avoided the financial-transparency reporting requirements primarily put into place to fight the War on Narcotics. We need to listen to what our enemies are telling us.

Unfortunately some Washington policymakers have not listened nor could they relate to our new enemies. They were wedded to the old ways of doing business. Bureaucratically, they tried to protect their vested interests. They insisted on trying to fight a new kind of war with tools developed for previous conflicts. They operated with Western blinders and an almost total lack of imagination—nothing less than a form of cultural arrogance or "imperial hubris."

I believed that al Qaeda, similar to other global enterprises, would diversify to minimize risk. Astute investors employ this same tactic when they purchase mutual funds. In their quest for diversification, terrorist organizations use various methods to earn, transport, and store value. Of course, they use banks, wire transfers, credit cards, automatic teller machines, and all of the accoutrements of the West. But we should not be surprised when they use them in ways that do not trigger BSA financial-intelligence reporting requirements. Bin Laden called this technique taking advantage of "cracks in the Western financial system." But it also seemed to me that as part of its financial diversification plan, al Qaeda would use the culturally indigenous, underground, ethnic-based systems that many of its members from Arabia and South Asia were familiar with, particularly cash, hawala, gold, and trade-based value transfer. These systems and methods were not just "cracks in the Western financial system," but rather a Grand Canyon that was easily exploitable.

Before September 11, *if* FinCEN management had made the correct decision to examine troubling financial crimes outside of traditional BSA reporting requirements, then after the terrorist attacks FinCEN would have been well positioned to contribute to, if not lead, the resulting interagency debate. FinCEN would have become relevant again. Instead, terrorist finance was just the latest of the most significant cases in recent history that FinCEN management blew.

After September 11 a buzz developed in the domestic and international press about terrorist finance. The media published stories about al Qaeda's exploitation of gold, diamonds, tanzanite, and even the honey trade. The misuse of charities in the finance of terrorism also became a subject of concern. But in discussions about terrorist finance, the biggest "discovery" for both the media and government agencies was hawala. Talking heads and so-called experts appeared regularly on television and gave interviews in the press discussing hawala and the threat of alternative remittance systems. Although I was happy to see this development, I could only ask myself where these so-called experts had been the past few years when they were needed. It is easy and safe to react to events after the fact.

Congress reacted as well. Briefings and hearings were held. Congress wanted a solution, or at least the appearance of a solution, for an underground system that doesn't have a solution. As explained earlier, hawala is intertwined with issues as diverse as overseas currency-exchange controls, tax avoidance, and illiteracy. New laws, rules, regulations, and reporting requirements in this country will not solve the problem. Nevertheless, Congress mandated that Treasury prepare a written report on hawala, in part, in preparation for new regulations. Treasury delegated the assignment to FinCEN, which had recently succeeded in purging almost all of its in-house expertise on alternative remittance systems. FinCEN had to get an outside contractor to report on hawala. The final report edited by FinCEN was considered within the Department of the Treasury as seriously flawed and a major disappointment. Not coincidentally, the word "gold" did not appear once in the report, even though historically and culturally the international gold trade and hawala are inextricably linked.

After September 11 I became heartsick when FinCEN management tried to keep me away from the War on Terrorism. The U.S. government was starved for insight on underground Middle East financial systems. It lacked quality human reporting sources in the Middle East. Very few Americans had ever worked financial investigations in the region. Nevertheless, the senior manager kept me under her thumb and tried to prevent my involvement and foreign travel. However, I did have a number of friends throughout the law enforcement and intelligence communities who were aware of my work. I approached them about a particular source in the Middle East who was well positioned to possibly assist the U.S. government in tracking Middle Eastern and South Asian trails of illicit finance. A few weeks after September 11 I received a telephone call from the NSC giving me permission to go back to the Middle East. Even FinCEN management dared not say no to the White House.

Via personal relationships, business, and access, my source had a unique ability to simultaneously be part of the Islamic and Western worlds. When I spoke with him, he was visibly shaken over the terrorist attacks on the United States. He was also concerned by the increasingly negative publicity and images generated by the media about Islam. Unfortunately, he politely but firmly refused my inquiries about possible assistance to combat terrorist finance. Although the source said he sympathized with the United States, he would not agree to help the U.S. government be-cause of its policies in support of Israel that resulted in the oppression of the Palestinian people. It was that simple. Over the years I had been confronted with these sentiments time and again throughout the Middle East both in personal conversations and in public forums. It was my ex-perience that even very sophisticated Arab interlocutors could not sepa-rate the United States and Israel. The connection between the two was for them a visceral feeling constantly reinforced by ugly images in the Arab media and by American actions, public pronouncements, and for-eign policy. I did not try to argue or change my source's mind. It would have been useless. I include this anecdote only to let the reader know of yet another very real difficulty in trying to obtain cooperation in the War on Terrorism.

✳

Prior to September 11 the FBI did not have an infrastructure in place to analyze terrorism finance.[13] The Bureau instead reacted to events and examined financial records only as part of subsequent investigations. As a result, in the days immediately following the terrorist attacks, the FBI formed a Financial Review Group (FRG). The FRG later evolved into the Terrorist Financing Operations Section (TFOS) within the FBI's

Counterterrorism Division. Shortly after September 11, along with a handful of other FinCEN special agents, I was detailed for a short time to the FRG located at FBI headquarters. We joined other representatives from the law enforcement and intelligence communities.

I was initially very impressed by the spirit of cooperation and camaraderie on display at the FRG. September 11 was still very fresh in everybody's minds. The old agency rivalries were put aside. Bureaucratic walls were broken down. Information sharing became the norm not the exception. We all agreed that a common enemy directly threatened the homeland, and thus, disparate U.S. government agencies were united in their efforts to defeat the enemy.

The interagency goodwill lasted about six weeks. Unfortunately, the traditional Department of Justice versus Department of the Treasury rivalry over which department had preeminence over financial crimes investigations resurfaced. The new twist was terrorist finance, and the arguments evolved into direct disputes between the FBI and Customs. Since I was no longer part of Customs, I looked on with a kind of detached but sad amusement as old political, bureaucratic, and personal rivalries resumed. Most of the issues involved information sharing and what agency had the lead on investigations. The FBI felt strongly that if there were any possible nexus to terrorism or terrorist financing, it should have the lead.

The Bureau is populated with skilled and dedicated criminal investigators who do excellent work in some kinds of financial crimes, for example, white-collar crime and bank robberies. However, the FBI's failure in helping prevent the September 11 attacks and its then almost complete lack of understanding of terrorist finance has been well documented. Treasury, on the other hand, almost by definition, specializes in things involving money and value. As described earlier, value transfer is an often overlooked but key component in terrorist-finance investigations. Customs, then part of Treasury, also by definition, deals with value transfer and trade. Though this is not the FBI's fault, its agents just don't have that kind of mandate, experience, or training. History shows that time and time again Treasury investigators, primarily Customs agents, have initiated innovative and complex financial crimes investigations.

Initiate is the key word. The Bureau is infamous within law enforcement circles of later muscling in and publicly taking credit for investigations that other federal, state, and local law enforcement agencies had started. Customs, exemplified by the creation of FinCEN, when possible makes information available to others. The Bureau, on the other hand, was known for its refusal to share data and case information with outsiders. This is part of its culture. The data situation was further exacerbated by the Bureau's archaic data-retrieval systems. Nevertheless, in law enforcement circles, the FBI is the eight-hundred-pound gorilla. When it throws its weight around, it generally gets its way. It is part of the Bureau's culture to exert control. It also helps that the FBI has a large group of special agents who very effectively lobby Congress assigned to Capitol Hill.

Perceiving that TFOS was moving in the direction of having the FBI dominate terrorist-finance investigations, Treasury moved to create a rival task force called Operation Green Quest. Just like TFOS, Customs opened its Green Quest task force to appropriate federal agencies. As a FinCEN representative, I was also assigned for a short while to Green Quest. But over the months both TFOS and Green Quest increasingly evolved into rival FBI-focused versus Customs-focused efforts. The two task forces often argued about the same information, the same leads, and the same investigations. It was like watching two children playing in separate sandboxes because they could not play together. The net effect was that the U.S. War on Terrorist Finance became further stalled.

While all the bureaucratic squabbling was going on, I approached a friend on the NSC with an admittedly off-the-wall idea. I suggested a very small cadre of innovative and experienced law enforcement and intelligence community veterans be given the mandate and authority to "mess with" America's enemies in the hope of targeting the financial systems they employed. I identified a kind of over-the-hill-gang cadre of very talented patriots who, at the end of their careers, had little use for bureaucratic walls and labels. The cadre just wanted a quiet blessing from the powers that be and a very small budget to see if they could come up with imaginative solutions to disrupt U.S. adversaries. I proposed enough built-in safeguards to ensure that the small group would not develop into a "rogue elephant" operation but would rather be an attempt to infuse some imagination into America's counterattack. The proposal was modeled, in part, on the old ICG. My NSC contact had actually entertained similar thoughts. Given that traditional interagency squabbling was hindering U.S. efforts, it was time to think outside the box. Perhaps in the fiction of Hollywood, this proposal would have been adopted; however, in Washington, bureaucratic realities quickly damned the idea.

The rivalry between the FBI's TFOS and Custom's Green Quest continued to escalate, even after Customs was absorbed into the new Department of Homeland Security (DHS). History will sort out whether creating DHS during a time of war was a wise move. I believe, however, that forcing Customs into DHS has had very serious repercussions, which are only now starting to be appreciated. At least in the short term, this bureaucratic shuffle further retarded our War on Terrorist Finance. Morale among legacy Customs troops plummeted. Management, communications, logistics, and budget systems that had previously functioned reasonably well soon became almost inoperable when they were forced to adopt or integrate into other questionable systems operated by the old Immigration and Naturalization Service, which had likewise been dragged into DHS. At the time this book is being written, there has been far too little strategic thinking within DHS, and far too many layers of review that have further retarded effective and efficient decision making. The history, legacy, and esprit de corps of very proud Treasury enforcement agencies such as Customs and the Secret Service were jettisoned in the stroke of a pen when the short-tenured but politically attuned secretary of treasury abandoned them. Reportedly, Customs and the Secret Service were allowed to depart for DHS without as much as a whimper of dissent by the secretary of treasury. And while Treasury was, in effect, punished, the federal government agencies most accountable for the failures leading up to September 11 (the FBI and the CIA) largely escaped bureaucratic meltdown and, in fact, were rewarded with ever-increasing budgets and staff.

I have no doubt that years from now, DHS will function much more smoothly. Glaring mistakes will be identified and rectified. Through attrition, the old guard will leave and new employees who know nothing of past legacies will be hired. The new employees will be trained in service academies in the "DHS way," and a new uniform DHS culture will be created. New expertise will be forged, and DHS investigations pursued. But these investigations will not be pursued in the area of terrorist finance.

On May 13, 2003, a memorandum of agreement between the Department of Justice and DHS was signed, giving the FBI unprecedented control of investigations and operations relating to terrorist finance. According to the memorandum, "appropriate DHS leads relating to money laundering and financial crimes will be checked with the FBI. If there is a question about whether the investigation is related to terrorist financing . . . the investigation and operation of the matter shall be led by the FBI."[14] The Department of Justice and the FBI won their long-running battle with Treasury, and they subsequently won another quick skirmish with DHS. A colleague of mine who was intimately aware of the acrimony between the FBI's TFOS and DHS's Green Quest said that finding grounds for compromise proved impossible so the decision was made at the highest levels to give the FBI primacy. The bureaucratic checks and balances have now disappeared. The FBI has what it long wished for. It is now up to the Bureau to deliver.

During this time of upheaval, I was becoming increasingly frustrated at FinCEN. If the decisions and direction introduced by FinCEN management had worked, I would have been the first in line to applaud because I continued to believe in the promise of the agency. However, the record shows that these new initiatives failed. Before and after September 11 FinCEN's management declined opportunity after opportunity to use its resources and authority, get involved, and make itself relevant. Stan Morris, the former director of FinCEN, had called the tiny organization the "Little Engine That Could." It never really was that. But without doubt, FinCEN subsequently became the "Little Engine That Couldn't." Its new mantra seemed to be, "I think I can't, I think I can't, I think I can't." Simply put, in my opinion, FinCEN was a cowardly organization. Management was the problem, not the solution. And there was no accountability. The morale of FinCEN's staff further plummeted. In the interagency and even international anti-money-laundering community, FinCEN's reputation increasingly suffered. The real director of FinCEN and his seeming abdication continued to puzzle me. Either he knew that FinCEN was collapsing and did nothing or didn't know and did nothing. Both questions and either answer are appalling.

Meanwhile, the de facto director of FinCEN continued to prohibit my direct participation in many Middle East anti-money-laundering and anti-terrorist-finance initiatives. Countries in the region and U.S. agencies were asking for me by name, but I was not allowed to help. In addition, despite repeated requests from high-level officials at the Department of the Treasury for my assistance, FinCEN management refused. I was also prohibited from accepting a new high-level law enforcement and intelligence coordinating position that was brokered via the NSC. Having experience in both communities and confident I could offer unique insight, I was heartsick when FinCEN management would not allow my participation. The senior manager once told me she would never let me leave FinCEN. In this she failed as well. I had finally had enough and gave FinCEN's management an offer they couldn't refuse.

8

Pillars in the Sand

Exiling myself from the Financial Crimes Enforcement Network (FinCEN) in June 2002, I secured a long-term detail to the State Department's Bureau of International Narcotics and Law Enforcement Affairs (INL). INL is located at State's Harry S. Truman Building in the section of Washington known as Foggy Bottom. A long time ago the area was the industrial hub of the city. The coal-fired factories had tall smokestacks that billowed large amounts of soot and fumes into the air creating a foggy atmosphere. The factories, dirt, and grime are long gone, having been replaced by upscale neighborhoods, the Kennedy Center, and George Washington University.

INL advises the White House, secretary of state, other bureaus within the Department of State, and other federal agencies on policies and program development to combat international narcotics and other forms of transnational crime. Most of INL's efforts and resources have been devoted to coordinating the development of interagency programs, training, and technical assistance to help counter the proliferation of narcotics in Colombia. Today, increasing resources also are being devoted to keeping Afghanistan from becoming a narco-state. INL delivers very little training and assistance itself. It receives money from Congress to implement programs that it has developed in consultations with other federal agencies such as the Drug Enforcement Administration (DEA) and then disburses funds to the agencies and contractors to carry out and administer antinarcotics programs.

Other impressive anticrime programs administered by INL include those that work to combat international corruption and the trafficking of people. INL also houses a very small office dedicated to developing programs, training, and technical assistance to combat international money laundering and terrorist finance. When I was at FinCEN and assigned to

187

its International Division, I had the good fortune of working directly with INL's Crime Office and money-laundering unit, headed respectively by Steve Peterson and Ed Rindler. As soon as I was able to extricate myself from FinCEN, Peterson and Rindler generously offered me a home. I was still a Treasury employee, but I had been "detailed," or lent, to INL for a two-year period. In addition to being allowed to continue to combat money laundering and terrorist finance, I was thrilled because my new job was a wonderful opportunity to be part of yet another federal government department and experience a new bureaucratic culture.

✳

After September 11 the U.S. government was able to slowly articulate a comprehensive anti-money-laundering/counter-terrorist-finance strategy based on three pillars.[1] The first pillar, and the one with which I had the most direct personal involvement, is based on "capacity building" or providing training and technical assistance programs overseas. This pillar supports U.S. objectives because it helps countries develop the tools to help themselves and, collectively, the international community. Some observers have called capacity building the "linchpin" of counter–terrorism finance because it is forward leaning and may potentially pay the most long-term dividends.

The second pillar is based primarily on specific tactical intelligence and enforcement operations and investigations aimed at terrorist-financing networks. These actions include the use of designations and blocking and freezing orders as well as increased financial regulation and supervision. The tactics were designed to identify, disrupt, and, it was hoped, negate suspect financing. It was assumed that increased success would follow from improved coordination among the intelligence, law enforcement, regulatory, and diplomatic agencies and departments.

The final pillar holding up the overall strategy was spearheading international efforts to deter terrorist financing by publicly naming, shaming, and blocking assets and suspect financial transactions on a global basis. This pillar was dependent on facilitating international information sharing and encouraging the political will to act.

The first pillar—capacity building—was initiated immediately after September 11, at a large interagency meeting called by INL to discuss training and technical assistance for countries around the world that were judged to be high risk for money laundering and terrorist finance. As a result of that meeting, INL and the State Department's Office of the Coordinator for Counterterrorism (S/CT) began cochairing an interagency working group to create a list of "priority countries" to receive U.S. counter-terrorist-financing training and technical assistance.[2] The list was primarily comprised of countries an astute reader of newspapers would also identify.

Congress had given S/CT a special supplemental package of $10 million dedicated to counter-terrorist-finance training and technical assistance. As INL had the experience and expertise in developing anti-money-laundering programs and the internal infrastructure to disperse and account for funding, through much time-consuming bureaucratic wrangling, the $10 million was eventually passed to INL. Unfortunately, by the time that I joined INL, outside of a few "assessment trips" to the prioritized countries of concern, there had not been a systematic attempt to develop an interagency implementation plan. That became my primary responsibility.

I was already convinced of the importance of providing training and technical assistance. Although this work is not considered glamorous or sexy within the interagency community, it is recognized as vital. As mentioned, a strong argument can be made that helping countries learn to help themselves is perhaps the most effective long-term strategy in America's War on Terrorist Finance. It is also important to remember that the United States is not giving these countries training and assistance just to be nice. Rather, it is giving them training also to help itself.

Over the years I had considerable experience in promoting the anti-money-laundering gospel overseas. In the Arabian Gulf area alone, I had initiated and participated in numerous anti-money-laundering training courses. But prior to September 11, in many ways, the Gulf countries were not yet ready to accept the fact that they had a money-laundering problem. If they acknowledged money laundering at all, it generally was in the form of an accusation against the West that its crimes and proceeds of its crimes had been transported to the Gulf. Moreover, institutionally it was necessary to first develop a consensus that something needed to be done. The events surrounding September 11 became the catalyst for the consensus. Countries around the world that before were somewhat reluctant to confront money laundering were now clamoring for training and assistance.

In chapter 3, it was noted that with the exception of crimes of passion, most crime is committed for financial gain. Greed, however, is not the motivation behind terrorist financing. Terrorist groups use terror as a tool to seek political gains, influence, or publicity for their cause. Although the illicit funds involved in money laundering derive from criminal activity such as narcotics trafficking, terrorist financing commonly involves both illicit and licit funds. For example, Osama bin Laden was believed to have used part of his substantial personal fortune to help bankroll his early activities. Business enterprises and charitable funding, sometimes involving both clean and suspect funds, also have added to terrorist groups' coffers.

The operational objectives and techniques also differ between money launderers and those who finance terrorist operations. Generally speaking, money launderers want to launder or disguise large amounts of cash by placing it in financial institutions without detection. Financial-transparency reporting requirements were designed to work against that. The objective of those who finance terror is to gain access to both licit and illicit funds or value in order to finance their terrorist activities and support their infrastructure and organizational costs.

Individual terrorist acts require comparatively little funding and have been immune to financial-transparency reporting requirements in this country and around the world. The financial costs to al Qaeda to mount the September 11 terrorist attacks were in the mid-six-figure range. Other al Qaeda terrorist attacks have been much less costly. Although official estimates vary, according to the UN it is believed that the 1998 simultaneous truck bombings of U.S. embassies in Kenya and Tanzania cost less than $50,000; the October 2000 attack on the USS *Cole* in Aden is estimated to have cost less than $10,000; the Bali bombings in October 2002 cost less than $50,000; the 2003 bombing of the Marriott Hotel in Jakarta cost about $30,000; the attacks in Istanbul in November 2003 cost less than $40,000; and the March 2004 Madrid train attacks cost about $10,000.[3] Likewise, the al Qaeda–inspired individual car bombings and terrorist attacks in Iraq have not required large financial resources.

As described earlier, the generally recognized components of money laundering are placement, layering, and integration. In discussing terrorist finance, law enforcement authorities sometimes use the descriptive terms of "earning," "moving," and "storing" assets, wealth, or value. Generally, both traditional criminal and terrorist organizations diversify their financial methodologies. Because terrorist financing is a kind of inverse partner to money laundering, countermeasures against both money laundering and terrorist financing are very similar. Likewise, the appreciable differences between designing training and technical assistance programs to combat money laundering and terrorist financing are few.

At least initially, one of the most impressive U.S. government responses to September 11 that I witnessed was the good work of the interagency community in putting aside bureaucratic differences and cooperating in delivering needed training and assistance. A dedicated group of public servants from various departments and agencies recognized that training had to be a well-coordinated community effort. One agency could not be allowed to freelance on its own. Obviously, no one agency has a monopoly on anti-money-laundering expertise and also, without coordination, efforts would be duplicated. Because both funding and good trainers were scarce, the agencies realized that they needed to work together. Unfortunately, the last few years have seen traditional departmental rivalries resurface,[4] which have hindered America's ability to provide training and technical assistance.

From personal experience and participation in some interagency assessment trips to countries that were included on the prioritized list, I worked to put together counter-terrorist-finance training modules. The modules overlapped with the identified steps and process of establishing an anti-money-laundering regime. The interagency community identified various federal agencies that would be appropriate for delivering or implementing the requisite training modules. INL would provide the funding. This would not be a cookie-cutter approach to building anti-money-laundering and counter-terrorist-finance regimes. Rather, depending on the assessment of the country, appropriate training modules would be selected from the menu of courses and assistance and then modified to fit that particular country's specific needs. If a country was starting from scratch, and many were, five broad categories of training would be offered.

The first step or module in helping countries establish anti-money-laundering and counter-terrorist-finance regimes is the creation of anti-money-laundering laws that adhere to world standards. That the rule of law is the foundation on which everything else is built is a global truism. Legal standards, however, differ from country to country and constantly evolve. For example, the United States started passing its series of anti-money-laundering laws and implementing rules and regulations over a generation ago. The legal basis for the U.S. anti-money-laundering regime has been continually updated and modified. America struggles with a cumbersome and sometimes unwieldy legal framework. Many countries that only recently have developed anti-money-laundering laws have the luxury of learning from the experiences of others. They can also incorporate specific guidance found in the recommendations by the Financial Action Task Force (FATF), appropriate UN Security Council (UNSC) resolutions, and other anti-money-laundering work done by a variety of nongovernmental organizations. Sometimes countries run into difficulties when trying to create and pass effective legislation, particularly while trying to make the legislation fit within national contexts and restrictions. Every country has special interest groups that have to be placated and political interests that must be balanced. But an effective law is a prerequisite in establishing an anti-money-laundering infrastructure. Law enforcement and judicial authorities must have sufficient power to investigate and prosecute money laundering and terrorist financing. And once the law is in place, many countries need help in training their judges, prosecutors, and law enforcement personnel in the intricacies of the new statutes. Sometimes getting these various groups to communicate and work together is a challenge.

After the enabling legislation is in place, the next step in the process can be loosely described as the creation of financial intelligence and the regulation and supervision of financial institutions. Many different types of financial intelligence can result from financial-transparency reporting requirements. However, the minimum standard directs banks to file reports on suspicious activities or transactions by its customers. Once the reporting standards are in place, examination and compliance guidelines and procedures must be created for the reporting institutions. A further goal is to protect the integrity of the country's banking system.

The creation of a financial intelligence unit (FIU), another step in the process, can be undertaken only when there is financial intelligence to analyze and disseminate. Many countries try to put the cart before the horse, insisting on the establishment of an FIU before the fundamentals have been accomplished. This will not work. An FIU is a centralized receiving and disclosing agency. There are many different types of FIUs, including those that are simply administrative in scope and others that are actually involved with investigations. FIUs can be found within a central bank, a ministry of justice, a ministry of finance, a ministry of interior, law enforcement, or a combination of those just listed. The location doesn't matter. I was occasionally asked to suggest to a country where a newly proposed FIU should be placed within competing ministries. Of course, I would decline to answer and rather emphasize that the important thing is to have the FIU work within the national context of the country. As we have seen, an FIU receives financial intelligence directly or indirectly from the reporting institutions, analyzes the information, and if appropriate, disseminates the information to law enforcement authorities for possible investigation.

Financial crimes often are very complex. Sometimes investigators will follow a paper trail and sometimes they will use various techniques, such as an undercover approach to penetrate a criminal organization. Various enforcement tools, such as financial intelligence, surveillance, the use of informant information, electronic intercepts, telephone records, etc., can be used in these investigations. Different countries allow the use of different tools and enforcement techniques. Many foreign police organizations did not previously have units that specialized in financial crimes, including money laundering and terrorist finance and thus need help in financial crimes enforcement. Skilled investigators from various U.S. law enforcement and regulatory agencies delight in working with their foreign counterparts to help them, often for the first time, initiate financial crimes investigations techniques and procedures.

The last training module that I helped create focused U.S. efforts for the first time on trade-based money laundering because I believed that many of the countries that the United States was concerned about were particularly susceptible to trade-based money laundering and terrorist finance. Trade can effectively mask the transfer of value and be the underpinnings of alternate remittance systems, such as hawala. This training module was given primarily to host countries' customs services, which are on the first line of defense at ports of entry or departure. While always trained in such traditional customs responsibilities as inspection and border control, too often customs inspectors and investigators do not even think about money laundering or terrorist finance when seizing contraband or undeclared currency. Following the money or the value was sometimes a very hard concept to sell overseas because it required a different frame of reference. But I was convinced that the United States had to at least heighten the awareness of this very real problem.

American training teams would stay in country for a period of a few days or a few weeks. Sometimes, when necessary, the agency responsible for the training module would arrange to bring students to the United States for training. If there was a pronounced need, if funding was available, and if teams could obtain concurrence from the appropriate American embassy and host government, the United States sometimes would send long-term resident advisers overseas. If there is a good fit between adviser and the host agency, resident advisers can be extremely effective. There is no substitute for being in country and available to cement knowledge and relationships, "hand hold" if necessary, offer encouragement, and impart expertise.

Although it took far too long, in part because of the reemergence of bureaucratic turf fights, eventually the United States made great progress in sending training teams out. Washington policymakers and bean counters were fixated with keeping track of the numbers of training sessions, the students trained, the type of training, the costs, etc. Matrixes were developed. Training and technical assistance became yet another deliverable item in America's War on Terrorist Finance. However, certain developments began to give me concern.

For example, I found that in the rush to appear as though they had done something, America's foreign friends often emphasized comparatively easy bureaucratic fixes such as new rules and regulations without sufficient and corresponding enforcement. Taking this approach, they made the same mistakes that the U.S. government had. Implementation was always the key. Following the U.S. lead, many countries moved quickly to create an infrastructure and reporting requirements that produced financial intelligence. Often they thought the next step, the creation of an FIU, would be the magic bullet to solve their problems.

Unfortunately, it doesn't work that way. The filing of a suspicious activity report (SAR) by a financial institution rarely is enough to make a money-laundering investigation by itself. To my knowledge, a SAR has *never* been enough in a terrorist-financing case. On the contrary, American law enforcement has found over the years that financial intelligence is only one tool, albeit at times a very important one, in the investigator's toolbox. It becomes part of the paper trail used to buttress an investigation. Although I am a strong advocate of the proactive use of financial intelligence to initiate investigations, again experience has shown that the great majority of financial crimes investigations are initiated in the street. Familiarity with criminal methodologies and networks must be acquired, and human sources of information must be developed. There are no short cuts. Both individual and bureaucratic initiative and imagination should be encouraged. A police or customs official must *think* money laundering and/or terrorist finance during the course of a routine investigation. That will lead to the proverbial next question. Moreover, an investigator needs to learn how to collect financial intelligence and follow the trail—sometimes to the mastermind of the criminal organization. And, as discussed earlier, investigators should be allowed to follow the trail even if it leads to those who are politically protected. Unfortunately, for the most part, though many foreign governments have installed necessary legislation to combat money laundering, they have not yet shifted their emphasis to enforcement and implementation of the legislation. The resultant lack of investigations and successful prosecutions is telling and contributes to the stalled War on Terrorist Finance.

There is an unfortunate parallel between some of the above difficulties found in the foreign context and problems faced in the United States. Although admittedly limited by my background and perspective of collecting and reporting intelligence and as a criminal investigator, I believe there has been an overemphasis on bureaucratic quick fixes, such as new rules, regulations, and designations, without the requisite emphasis on enforcement. Rules are meaningless if they are not implemented and enforced.

The second pillar in the strategy is the tactical use of traditional and nontraditional law enforcement and intelligence techniques and operations including designations. Prior to September 11 U.S. policy toward combating international terrorism focused in large part on identifying state-sponsors of terrorism and using economic sanctions to discourage the harboring of terrorists and terrorist groups. Treasury's Office of Foreign Assets Control (OFAC) sanctioned regimes in Afghanistan, Cuba, Iran, Iraq, Libya, Sudan, and Syria with limited impact.[5] OFAC acts under presidential wartime and national emergency powers, as well as authority granted by specific legislation, to impose controls on financial transactions and freeze foreign assets under U.S. jurisdiction.[6] After September 11 OFAC's abilities to sanction and designate were tools that immediately were available to the bureaucracy. They were tools that had been used during the last two wars—the Cold War and the War on Narcotics. With the new war, entrenched bureaucracies, senior managers, and lawyers acted in the ways they were accustomed to. They also moved to preserve their vested interests, reputations, and budgets. As a result, there was a concerted effort to emphasize and then expand the use of sanctions, designations, and corresponding blocking and seizing of funds in the new War on Terrorist Finance.

Shortly after the terrorist attacks on September 11, President Bush signed Executive Order 13224, which blocked the funds of terrorists and those associated with terrorists or terrorist groups. The result was the creation of a list of possible designees put together by the interagency community. A variety of information sources were used to compile the list; the same process is used today. The final determination on designation is made by a policy coordinating committee (PCC) on terrorist financing, originally chaired by the Treasury Department and now chaired by the National Security Council (NSC). Upon the recommendation of the PCC, the secretary of the treasury, in cooperation with the secretary of state and the attorney general, issues a designation and blocking order. The Treasury Department's OFAC implements this order. Those on the list have their U.S. financial assets blocked, and under appropriate circumstances as discussed below, the entities designated are sent to the UN for worldwide adoption.

As part of the third or global pillar in the anti-terrorist-finance strategy, concurrently on September 28, 2001, the UNSC endorsed Resolution 1373, which broadly required all nations to take concrete steps to deny financial and other forms of support to terrorists. However, the resolution neither defined terrorism nor required sanctions against particular terrorist groups.[7] UNSC Resolution 1390, passed in January 2002, required a monitoring group to report on global progress in implementing sanctions against the Taliban and al Qaeda. For a long time after September 11, the U.S. interagency process was consumed by a desire to take advantage of the international goodwill and momentum and to refer as many terrorist-related names as possible to the UN Sanctions Committee for inclusion on the global blacklist. This was important because the United States and

OFAC did not have extraterritorial jurisdiction and required international support and cooperation to identify, block, and seize foreign assets.

By the end of 2001, $112 million had been blocked or seized around the world. This number primarily reflects "fruit of the low-hanging tree," or comparatively easy pickings. Subsequently, countries around the world made concerted efforts to transmit to their financial institutions the names of suspected terrorists and terrorist organizations listed on the UN 1267 Sanctions Committee's consolidated list and the list of Specially Designated Global Terrorists designated by the United States pursuant to Executive Order 13224. As a result, at the close of 2002, the total number of worldwide terrorist assets *frozen* around the world totaled $137 million; at the end of 2003 the number was $146 million; approximately $150 million was frozen by the end of 2004; and at the end of 2005 the number barely budged to a little more than $150 million. These numbers are not cumulative but total. Moreover, at the end of 2005 the total amount of funds that have actually been *seized* total only $64 million. This number has remained virtually constant since 2002.[8]

Although the U.S. government frequently uses these numbers as a metric of success in the War on Terrorist Finance, I believe that the numbers are an indictment of our efforts and one of the best indicators that the War on Terrorist Finance is stalled. In playing hide and seek, we have been looking in the wrong places.

In addition, by the time all is said, done, litigated, and appealed, a large percentage of the frozen funds can be released—and, in fact, have been. The success of designation efforts is also obviously limited by the extent to which they are supported and implemented overseas. In the context of establishing an anti-money-laundering regime, even if the political will exists to cooperate, countries often lack the infrastructure and the procedures to implement and enforce designations. Moreover, many foreign governments have complained to us that they cannot hold suspect funds forever without proof. Unfortunately, because of its sensitive nature, much of this proof cannot be released. And, in some instances, the reliability of some of this intelligence is open to question because of the decimation of U.S. intelligence services, the fact that some terrorist-finance systems were not priority reporting requirements, and a developing reliance on foreign intelligence services that often had their own agendas. In my opinion, some policymakers have the unfortunate inability to un-

derstand that even America's "friends and allies" sometimes try to ma-
nipulate us to serve their interests and not necessarily ours.

Undoubtedly, differing missions and objectives of the intelligence
and law enforcement communities exacerbated these problems. Intelligence collectors used to the procedures of the Cold War, during which
intelligence could be gathered and analyzed without public action, were
now faced with the demands of policymakers for "actionable intelligence."
Policymakers wanted information that could be used in designations.
Unfortunately, because of the way the intelligence was collected and reported, it often could not withstand either public scrutiny or be exposed
to the rigors of judicial scrutiny. Often the policymakers found that the
"intelligence" was far less reliable than they had assumed. Meanwhile,
traditional law enforcement generally was not in a position, nor did it
have the requisite skills, to collect the type of information required.

After September 11 OFAC was in a state of "chaos."[9] Despite
Herculean efforts by many members of its small staff, OFAC could not
keep up with policymakers' demands for an ever-increasing number of
designations and the resulting "measureables" to give the appearance
that the U.S. government was doing something on the War on Terrorism's
financial front. As a result, some designations and high-profile cases such
as al Barakaat ultimately proved futile.

Al Barakaat was a worldwide money-remitting concern primarily serving the expatriate Somali community. It filled a banking need for those
who had fled Somali, which did not have any viable financial institutions,
during and after the long-running Somali civil war. More than anything
else, it was a useful way for immigrant Somali workers to send money
back home to support their families. However, the intelligence community developed information that Osama bin Laden had contributed money
to al Barakaat and that it was also possibly associated with al Itihaad al
Islamiya (AIAI), Somalia's largest radical Islamic group.[10]

I first heard of al Barakaat in the mid-1990s, when I was the Customs liaison to FinCEN. At that time I received a number of requests
from Customs agents, primarily in Michigan and California, investigating a network of Somali nationals involved with various types of crime,
particularly stolen cars and welfare fraud. The investigators could not
understand how the proceeds of the crimes were being sent out of the
country. At that time, the reporting system of SARs was in its infancy, but

working with a FinCEN analyst, we determined that a substantial percentage of the total number of SARs filed at the time was linked to the suspect Somali network. In addition, the financial trail seemed to lead once again to Dubai. I asked FinCEN to devote the necessary resources to examine the data. FinCEN refused. I next requested analytical support from Customs and personally spoke to the head of the Customs' financial analytical unit. It was the only time in my career I used the word "beg" in a request for assistance. However, Customs also refused because it felt, correctly, that the financial analysis was FinCEN's responsibility.

A short time later the Federal Bureau of Investigation became involved, and in 2000 it opened a criminal case. FinCEN finally agreed to assist with the analysis of financial intelligence. After September 11 al Barakaat's assets were frozen and its worldwide records were seized. In the subsequent investigation, the government of the United Arab Emirates (UAE) provided unprecedented cooperation and access to books and financial records. As the early financial intelligence indicated, most of al Barakaat's funds were transferred via yet another type of "Dubai hub." However, the criminal investigation failed to establish a link between al Barakaat and any terrorist organization. Most of the assets frozen in the United States under executive order and in other countries acting under UN resolution were released.

Although the system of identifying suspect international financial transactions and accounts has improved from the initial interagency confusion after September 11, too often the identifying data presented to foreign governments was spurious. Often the reason for a request to block an account was not forwarded or was slow in coming. Wanting to cooperate, foreign officials sometimes bent their own rules to assist the United States. Yet during my travels to the Middle East after September 11, I was often told, both by the staff of various U.S. embassies and Arab officials, of ham-fisted efforts by OFAC and other U.S. agencies. One central bank official in the Middle East told me that some of the names forwarded by Washington agencies for checking were "the Arab equivalent of Mickey Mouse and Donald Duck." Arab names, in particular, have many variations and different spellings. Understandably, American analysts have difficulty making sense of some of the names and data, and as a result, U.S. credibility suffered.

The political environment after September 11 facilitated the passage of Title III of the USA PATRIOT Act. Previously, the financial services industry had resisted many of the financial provisions of the PATRIOT Act that called for additional rules, regulations, due diligence, and reporting requirements by U.S. financial institutions. After September 11 the financial industry was very cooperative in helping the U.S. government unravel the financial trail left by the hijackers. The three-hundred-page law was enacted in just a few weeks and had overwhelming bipartisan support. Perhaps the centerpiece of the USA PATRIOT Act's anti-money-laundering tools were the "special measures" that allow the U.S. government to restrict or prohibit access to the U.S. financial system by countries and foreign financial institutions that do not have in place adequate anti-money-laundering controls. For example, USA PATRIOT Act Section 311 gives the secretary of the treasury authority to impose financial restrictions on financial institutions in jurisdictions judged to be "primary money-laundering concerns." It also prevents the suspect institutions from accessing the U.S. financial system altogether. Section 311 has been used sparingly, but often just the threat of action has been enough to spur countries and institutions to make needed reforms. In addition, as mentioned in chapter 6, shortly after September 11 the United States working with FATF also leveraged international support for "special recommendations" on terrorist finance, which also were aimed at trying to increase international transparency and impose tighter controls against illicit financial flows. These actions are part of U.S. domestic and global anti-terrorist-finance pillars.

Likewise, strengthening the regulation and supervision of financial institutions became part of U.S. strategy. New emphasis was put on record keeping and reporting requirements for banks and nonbank financial institutions alike. September 11 also spurred Congress to pressure FinCEN to act on the long-delayed expansion of regulation to new sectors of the financial community and to compel the registration of money service businesses (MSBs). Financial products and services outside of traditional banks such as money transmitters, check cashing, currency exchanges, money orders, and stored value are all examples of MSBs. An informal value-transfer dealer such as a hawaladar also is classified as an MSB.

When immigrants in the United States use MSBs to send or remit portions of their wages back to their homeland, these remittances are usually in small amounts. MSBs collect funds and then generally use banks and international wire transfers to settle accounts. To put things in perspective, in 2003 outbound remittances through official channels from the United States totaled approximately $28 billion. Direct foreign investment into the United States totaled $27 billion.[11] Of course, unofficially, financial flows via underground systems and trade-based informal value transfer inflate both outbound and inbound totals significantly. Over the last few years the numbers have further increased. For example, according to statistics released by the Bank of Mexico, in 2005 the value of remittances sent to Mexico by people living in the United States totaled $20 billion, a 17 percent increase over the year before.[12]

Nobody knows for certain how many MSBs there are in the United States. MSBs consist of everything from Western Union–type money remitters, to *casas di cambio* along the southwest border, to various types of mom-and-pop remittance houses. MSBs are legal in the United States if they are licensed in the states they do business in and if they register with FinCEN and comply with the new reporting requirements detailing suspicious transactions. In the mid-1990s FinCEN commissioned a study that concluded that there were approximately 200,000 MSBs in the United States. There was no meaningful follow-up to the study until after September 11. As of the end of 2004 approximately 22,350 MSBs were registered with FinCEN.[13] Where were the rest?

Undoubtedly, many MSBs that are immigrant-oriented do not register with the government because they are not aware of the requirement. FinCEN has done a poor job of community outreach to such MSBs, and language difficulties have compounded the problem. In addition, many of the small companies run by recent immigrants do not trust the government. In many instances, this suspicion is a legacy from the countries from which they came. There is also an understandable, but erroneous, concern that the government will use registration information for tax purposes. Yet MSB registration with the government will not in itself solve the problem of illicit money transfers. To understand one of the primary reasons why, I take the reader back to a favorite place of mine, Dubai.

In May 2002 the UAE Central Bank hosted the first international conference on hawala. (Despite a lot of behind-the-scenes work initiating this ground-breaking conference and despite the wishes of the UAE Central Bank and representatives from the U.S. interagency community,

FinCEN management would not let me attend.) The resulting Abu Dhabi Declaration on Hawala called for countries to put in place "effective but not overly restrictive regulations" on the practice of hawala.[14] As a result, the UAE, like the United States and a few other countries, established a regulatory system, including the licensing and registration of its large community of hawaladars or businesses that are engaged in the practice of hawala.

As a result of these measures, over 160 hawaladars have registered with the UAE Central Bank. While this is progress and the Central Bank should be applauded for its continuing initiatives in this area, there is no way to determine how many informal hawaladars actually operate in the UAE. A private financier in Dubai told me how the system works in practice for many of those that did register. According to the financier, a hawaladar with questionable business practices will have one of its non-native "runners" register with the Central Bank. That way the hawaladar is in compliance with the Central Bank's directives. All benign or "white" hawala transactions are accommodated in this manner, giving the appearance that the new regulations and reporting systems are working. However, the occasional suspect or "black" hawala transaction happens in the old-fashioned way—underground and off the books. Without enforcement, informants, and knowledge of the street, or in this case the souk, there is not a realistic method for combating this practice. I offer this example because it succinctly demonstrates what I have seen time and time again in my enforcement career: if a new regulatory obstacle is put in front of a criminal enterprise, they simply go around it.

Undoubtedly, the same thing would happen in the United States; however, the government does not even know with certainty how many hawaladars have registered with FinCEN. The reporting requirements do not call for the designation "hawaladar" itself. Nevertheless, I was told that, in examining the approximately twenty-two thousand MSBs that have registered, it was possible to determine that the number of hawaladars in the United States probably totals in the single digits! My guess is that there are hundreds of hawala-like operations operating in New York City alone.

In both the UAE and the United States, although registration and reporting requirements for hawaladars do not hurt, I feel the measures are simply a feel-good placebo for those who wish for the appearance of progress rather than an effective countermeasure against the misuse of hawala by criminal organizations and terrorists. History has proven that rules, regulations, and reporting requirements are effective only in concert with beefed-up enforcement. But enforcement is time, resource, and labor intensive. Up to now, enforcement has not been the U.S. priority. Increasing the conundrum, if governments crack down too hard, some MSBs above ground simply will go underground. Certain issues don't have an easy answer.

If bankers are the first line of defense against money launderers and they are expected to fulfill the same role in terrorist finance, it would be logical to expect the government to provide guidance and even limited intelligence to the financial industry on how to detect terrorist financing. This hasn't been coming. The government offers precious little insight because, in part, it doesn't know how to detect terrorist financing through financial institutions. (As we have seen, FinCEN has also occasionally declined to send "advisories" to the banking community because of political correctness–related fears.) Likewise, efforts within the financial industry to create internal profiles of terrorist-related entities have thus far proven unsuccessful.

Section 314(a) of the USA PATRIOT Act, however, has proven to be a useful and innovative tool. It requires financial institutions to search their accounts for possible matches on names included on government investigative lists. The procedure is very useful to the criminal investigator who wants to know if subject X has any bank relationships in the United States. FinCEN compiles and disseminates the list of such requests to approximately twenty-four thousand financial institutions. Of course, if there are any "hits," the investigator must still obtain a subpoena to view the records. The 314(a) request program was initiated in November 2002. After some growing pains, the process has proved successful and has resulted in productive leads for both terrorist-financing and money-laundering investigations. As of mid-2005, the 314(a) system has processed over four hundred requests from law enforcement agencies and financial institutions have responded with over twenty thousand subject matches.[15]

Investigation and analysis have shown that prior to September 11 al Qaeda was funded by approximately $30 million per year.[16] The majority of the funding is believed to have originated from diversions of money from charitable organizations and donors. Most of the funding originated in the Arabian Gulf. There is little doubt that al Qaeda considered charities as a major source of its funds. One of the best examples comes directly from a computer that had belonged to al Qaeda and was recovered in Afghanistan by a journalist. On the hard drive were numerous e-mails and other documents detailing the terrorist group's methods of operation. In one e-mail Ayman al-Zawahiri, Osama bin Laden's right-hand man, sent a series of messages to an al Qaeda operative discussing the development of a chemical weapon. In the message traffic, they drew up rudimentary plans for a chemical laboratory and discussed creating a charitable foundation to serve as the front for the operation.[17] And in addition to financial support, some charities have provided cover, logistical, and administrative support for terrorists as well as a medium for the distribution of radical propaganda.

Since September 11 a number of high-profile investigations in the United States and overseas have examined the misuse of charities and fund-raisers. The U.S. government also has designated charities based overseas because of their ties to terrorist finance. However, in the long run, many of the investigations and designations subsequently bear little fruit. As discussed below, the designated Islamic charities also are involved with legitimate charitable and humanitarian works. Although charitable fund-raising provides ready operational cover and a ready means to place, layer, and transfer suspect funds, the government actions sometimes resulted in negative publicity. The subjects of the investigations consistently have denied wrongdoing.

The situation was exacerbated because, until recently, most of the wealthy Gulf countries, where the majority of the funding originates, had no effective financial oversight of their charities. Their investigators and regulatory authorities, such as they were, did not talk to each other. In 2003 I joined a team of U.S. officials on a trip to Riyadh that examined, in part, Saudi charitable procedures. We found that after years of denial, Saudi authorities were beginning to understand they had a problem. Finally, by mid-2004, Saudi Arabia took action and placed all of its overseas charities that had headquarters in the kingdom under a government-controlled umbrella organization. This effectively closed the international branch offices of the Al Haramain Foundation, which had provided support for al Qaeda.[18] Although progress has been made, today Saudi Arabia and other Gulf countries must do more to implement and enforce the reforms and oversight they have announced.

In the majority of cases, the misuse of charities probably occurred without the knowledge of donors and sometimes without the knowledge and consent of the staff of the charity itself. The misuse of charities in the Islamic context, here and abroad, unfortunately takes advantage of the concept of Zakat, one of the five pillars of Islam. Zakat is a form of alms, giving to those who are less fortunate. Zakat is obligatory when a certain amount of wealth—sometimes calculated in gold, called the *nisab,* is reached or exceeded. If the level is reached, all Muslims must give at least 2.5 percent of their wealth and assets each year to the poor. Zakat is considered an act of worship, offering thanks to God for material well-being. Particularly in Saudi Arabia, charitable giving is ingrained in the culture.

A further complicating factor in the misuse of Islamic charities, one that has not received adequate attention, is that many charities apparently are drawn to the use of Islamic banks and their financial services. For many Muslims, Western-style banks are institutions to be avoided. Islamic beliefs keep them from business dealings that involve *riba,* or usury. Yet Muslims need banking services as much as anyone. In fact, Islamic banking is widely regarded as the fastest growing sector in the Middle Eastern financial services market. As of mid-2004 the worldwide Islamic financial market boasted 265 banks with assets of more than $262 billion and investments of over $400 billion. Islamic banking has grown at the rate of 10 to 20 percent for the last ten years. The fastest growth has been in Africa and Asia. Within the next decade, it is estimated that as much as half the savings of the world's 1.3 billion Muslims could be in Islamic banks.[19]

Without charging what the West calls interest, Islamic banks have constructed financial instruments that adhere to the Koran and the Prophet Muhammad's teachings. If Islamic banks cannot charge interest, how do they make a profit?[20] Here again we come back to the importance of trade in the cradle of the Islamic world. This is a complicated subject. In short, Islamic banks can be considered merchants. The banks profit via financial instruments that buy and sell Islamic-approved goods and services. Moreover, using the concept of *murabaha,* often a price that is more than the market value is agreed upon at the outset. For example, a customer can obtain financing for the $10 million purchase price of a commodity such as petroleum or diamonds from an Islamic bank, by agreeing to pay the bank back say $11 million at a later date. The customer can then purchase and sell the commodities at a profit. This way the customer obtains the necessary credit without violating the religious prohibition on interest. Because the bank is actually an investor, the profit for the bank is deemed a just reward for the risk assumed in the business.[21] What is interesting to me is how trade once again manifests itself. This system also has parallels to the overinvoicing schemes related to forms of trade-based value transfer and countervaluation described earlier in this book.

A further vulnerability of the Islamic banking system is that although some of the banks "voluntarily" comply with banking regulations and anti-money-laundering guidelines, in some cases they are under no obligation to do so.[22] Despite often-aggressive anti-money-laundering programs by central banks and other regulatory bodies that cover secular commercial or Western-style banking, Islamic banks often escape regulatory or supervisory scrutiny by bank regulators. Thus far the industry is largely self-regulating, escaping outside examinations and inspections. And all of the new regulations and very real reforms that have been implemented in many countries in the Middle East to help control the misuse of charitable donations via financial institutions are powerless to stop the wealthy donor from writing a personal check from a European account or transferring other types of value such as trade goods, gold, or cash directly into the hands of a suspect acting as a front for a so-called charity.

I don't presume to be an expert on the misuse of charities. I have not had any direct experience in the field. Unfortunately, there are very few such experts; this is part of the problem. For the federal government, the oversight of the charitable sector lies primarily with the Tax Exempt and Government Entities Operating Division (TEGE) of the Internal Revenue Service. The IRS relies heavily on voluntary data compiled and submitted in nonprofits' application forms for tax-exempt status and annual returns. According to the Congressional General Accounting Office in a 2002 study on the oversight of charities,[23] the IRS does not have sufficient information on the extent of the compliance issue and its enforcement resources have not kept up with the growth of the charitable sector. Moreover, the IRS cannot proactively share charitable data with state agencies that oversee charities in part because federal tax laws prohibit certain types of disclosures that state agencies want.

Regarding enforcement, in the last few years the IRS has examined fewer and fewer charities and nonprofit organizations. In the United States there are approximately 1.5 million charities and foundations, and this number is growing every year.[24] The tax-exempt organizations control over $2 trillion in assets. Meanwhile, the number of IRS personnel devoted to the examination of charities number in the few hundreds. To process the ever-increasing application workload, the IRS has been forced to take agents charged with examination to assist in processing. Although there have been recent improvements and revisions in the application form for tax-exempt status for charities (Form 1023), which include more relevant investigative information, and the TEGE is now working more closely with the Criminal Investigative Division (CI) of the IRS on potential cases involving terrorist finance, enforcement resources remain critical.

There is not a single best approach to ensure oversight and transparency of charitable organizations. Each country must structure a system that works in its own national context. However, while the United States is quick to talk about the very real problem of the misuse of charities overseas, in my opinion the government must do a better job here at home of increasing transparency and enhancing oversight and examination of U.S. charities and nonprofit organizations.

As of mid-2005 the United States has designated five U.S.-based charities and thirty-five international charities for terrorist-financing activity and hundreds of individuals or entities as terrorists, financiers, or facilitators.[25] While these seem like impressive numbers, the overall designation concept and the public identification of those who are linked to terrorist finance have had questionable results. As discussed, a designation allows the United States to freeze assets and ask the UN to add the subject to its list of designated individuals and entities, thereby obligating all UN members to take action against the subject's financial assets. But as I argued earlier, U.S. enemies are smart. Few blocked terrorist assets have resulted from the designation process.

In addition, as part of the UN's designation process, member countries are obligated to prohibit designees from international travel. However, terrorist and many criminal organizations are adept at manufacturing and traveling under false documents. In one western European country, a group of terrorists associated with al Qaeda was able to supply passports in almost any nationality for less than $500. As I saw in many of my investigations, the widespread use of fraudulent documents is endemic in certain parts of the world. Many countries of concern do not have the necessary customs, immigration, and law enforcement infrastructure along their sometimes very porous borders. Perhaps as a result, according to a UN study published in 2004, the implementation of the travel ban on designated individuals has had little or no effect on terrorist travel.[26] The whereabouts of the subjects under designations are not known and I do not believe any country has ever reported detecting any designated individual trying to travel.

Policymakers have argued that the amount of funds that are frozen on the day of the designation is not important or completely stopping the international travel of terrorists and their supporters; rather the intent of such efforts is to disrupt and financially isolate those who support terrorist groups. This argument has some merit, and I am not advocating these efforts be completely abandoned. The designation process is an ongoing exercise and there have recently been some promising actions. However, with all due respect to the policymakers, I believe America's overemphasis on designations and the process of designations has been a resource-consuming bureaucratic exercise that has not generated sufficient concrete results.

Probably aware that the metrics on the War on Terrorist Finance are not truly favorable, there have been recent public pronouncements that the "success" of designations, sanctions, freezing, blocking, and seizing assets has prompted al Qaeda to resort to more informal or nontraditional ways of moving and raising money.[27] However, U.S. adversaries have been using cash and alternative, underground, indigenous, ethnic-based, informal value-transfer systems for a long time, certainly before the current round of bureaucratically popular designations and attempts at blocking assets. What is nontraditional for us is very traditional for them.

A few months after September 11 the press and nongovernmental organizations persistently reported that al Qaeda had also been active in the West African illicit diamond trade and the East African trade in tanzanite. Further reports in the press mentioned the misuse of gold and hawala by al Qaeda and their supporters. Such intrepid reporters as Doug Farah of the *Washington Post* and Bobby Block of the *Wall Street Journal* who were based in Africa were able to develop insight and sources into the indigenous and underground trading networks. When high-level government officials read in the press about, for example, diamonds' alleged link to terrorist financing, they immediately ordered their respective agencies to run data to find any official U.S. government reporting. However, not much official information is available regarding the misuse of precious metals and gems by terrorist organizations. Moreover, in some government management circles, if a report is unclassified or "open sourced," it is not given as much credence as classified information. Sometimes the intelligence community reacts poorly to sensitive information that it did not initiate. Probably as a result, the two primary agencies concerned (the FBI and the CIA) discredited the press reports.

During the 1990s, as a result of the peace dividend at the close of the Cold War, we withdrew much of our intelligence collection infrastructure in areas of the world such as Africa where many of today's new threats involving illicit finance are found. The lack of official reporting is sometimes exacerbated in certain areas because it is very difficult and dangerous for official government representatives to physically acquire the information. Moreover, it sometimes takes formal intelligence taskings as part of the intelligence collection cycle to get the process started. To the best of my knowledge, such taskings did not exist prior to September 11. Complicating things still further, the foreign underground financial systems are very complex. Attending interagency meetings, I was extremely frustrated when fresh-faced and freshly minted analysts from the intelligence community would discount something simply because no record of that something could be found in their computers. Most of these analysts had never been out in the field. I spent a career producing both foreign intelligence and law enforcement reporting. I know firsthand that the lack of *official* U.S. government reporting on a subject does not mean that the phenomenon does not exist. It just means that there is no official reporting. Bureaucracies and decision makers sometimes have difficulty grasping this simple concept.

Bureaucratic arrogance, myopia, and the inexplicable lack of enforcement interest in these allegations delayed for almost eighteen months after the initial *Washington Post* stories a serious investigation into the possibility that al Qaeda used the diamond trade for financing. When a few concerned members of Congress finally pressured the FBI to investigate, the trail had understandably grown cold. The FBI agents assigned to the investigation were all undoubtedly very competent, hardworking, and professional. However, even though the allegations involved the misuse of international trade, not one person with a customs, trade background, or even somebody with expertise on diamonds was included in the investigating teams. It was simply not in the Bureau's culture to look outside for help.

While at FinCEN, I had examined diamonds briefly prior to September 11 when an official at the Department of the Treasury asked me to do a quiet study on the gems and any related financial intelligence contained in SARs. The focus at that time was the use of "blood" or "conflict" diamonds, which helped fuel long-running African conflicts like the civil wars in Angola and Sierra Leone. The United States joined other concerned governments around the world and worked to put in place an international regulatory certification scheme known as the Kimberly Process. This regulatory process was developed through a consensus among nongovernmental organizations, industry leaders, and nation-states and helped reduce the trafficking in illicit diamonds by providing a method to verify the origin and movement of diamonds via the issuance of tamperproof "Kimberly certificates of origin." Kimberly, however, was not created to address the issues of money laundering or terrorist financing via illicit diamond trading.

In 2004, because of continuing concerns about diamonds' alleged links to terrorist finance, I once again was asked to examine the misuse of diamonds. After discussions with various nongovernmental organizations and industry and government officials in the United States, Africa, and Dubai, I became increasingly concerned about the striking similarities between the laundering of dirty money and the laundering of illicit diamonds. Because diamonds represent the most compressed form of physical wealth in the world, they have an innate appeal to criminals. The legitimate diamond "pipeline" of mining, trading, cutting and polishing, and retailing can be abused by criminal organizations by placing, layering, and integrating illicit diamonds.

The issue of whether or not diamonds were used by terrorist organizations as part of a diversified attempt to earn, move, and store value was beyond the scope of my inquiry. However, it was apparent that the production of "rough" diamonds, particularly in Africa, is plagued by criminal schemes such as theft, fraud, false invoicing, and corruption. The problem is made worse by the widespread cross-border smuggling in many of the countries of concern.

These are the same types of issues and elements of crime I had seen in other money-laundering methodologies and other regions elsewhere in my career. Although the Kimberly Process was a commendable effort that resulted in meaningful dialogue and reforms, I learned that as a regulatory system it too had been somewhat corrupted and bypassed. One of the primary problems was that criminal organizations pay corrupt diamond diggers and sometimes diamond brokers to combine smuggled or illicit diamonds with officially mined diamonds, just as criminal organizations mix legitimate money with bad to launder funds. The "mixed parcel" of diamonds was then accepted as genuine production and authenticated by Kimberly Process guidelines. In certain areas, the Kimberly certificates themselves are reportedly available for the right price. I also received reports about a network of expatriate Lebanese broker/dealers in Africa similar to those previously discussed in chapter 5. Unfortunately, some of the Lebanese diamond buyers seemed to have ties with radical Islamic groups.

Although a prominent official in the world diamond community described my findings as "spot on," FinCEN never released them. However, in mid-2005 after years of delay, FinCEN did finally issue long-awaited reporting requirements and regulations for dealers in precious metals and stones.[28] The regulations called for under the USA PATRIOT Act, were a tacit admission by the government that diamonds and gold are problems in the War on Terrorist Finance. Although another step in the right direction, I doubt the new "rules" will prove to have any real benefit other than yet one more feel-good reporting requirement. Under the new "rules-based" approach, the onus of constructing an anti-money-laundering plan is on the industry. FinCEN rightfully determined that the industry itself is in the best position to determine what is suspicious. While this sounds fine in theory, if present trends continue, the overwhelmingly honest citizens of the jewelry and precious metals and gems industry who pose no threat to begin with will comply with the new rules and the very small percentage that is involved with suspicious activities will not without adequate oversight, enforcement, and industry dialogue. Moreover, the real threat of terrorist finance related to precious metals and gems is not going to be solved by the issuance of domestic regulations. The primary threat exists overseas along the various "pipelines." Neither the Kimberly Process nor the new FinCEN regulations address those on-going concerns.

✳

As noted, one of the government's pillars in its strategy to combat money laundering and terrorist finance is based on intelligence and enforcement operations and investigations. To be successful, this type of tactical endeavor must be predicated on solid intelligence. Unfortunately, both before and after September 11, I was underwhelmed by both the quantity and quality of human intelligence reporting dealing with terrorist finance. In addition, as explained earlier, we have done a poor job of exploiting the tens of millions of financial intelligence reports on file under the BSA. Moreover, the financial intelligence was designed primarily to combat the War on Narcotics. Financial intelligence was not designed for the new War on Terrorist Finance.

Spending a career in both the intelligence and law enforcement communities leads me to believe that inherent structural difficulties have impeded the kind of intelligence collection and resulting enforcement operations and investigations that the United States needs to combat the War on Terrorist Finance. As the reader has learned in earlier chapters, there are different organizational incentives.[29] Law enforcement wants arrests and convictions, i.e., "statistics," and craves publicity and courts media attention, in part because recognition can indirectly lead to increased budgets. The subtlety of behind-the-scenes but effective intelligence work is often rushed in the effort to produce "measureables." Sometimes, results are not as important as who gets the credit. As confirmed by various commissions and reviews, the law enforcement system that we had at the time of September 11 did not encourage the collection, development, analysis, and sharing of investigative intelligence necessary to initiate and pursue imaginative and effective enforcement operations.

Conversely, intelligence officers do not want publicity. They are very content to work in the shadows. The culture of the intelligence community birthed during the Cold War internally rewards the number of reports produced and the number of operational recruitments and other means that further the production of foreign intelligence reports. Operations designed to collect intelligence are often patient, subtle, and innovative. In fact, after September 11 when the USA PATRIOT Act removed the wall that had previously prevented collaboration between the intelligence and law enforcement communities, law enforcement has increas-

ingly become a consumer in the intelligence cycle. However, in my esti-
mation, the intelligence community has thus far not been able to produce sufficient tactical or strategic intelligence for law enforcement to
advance the stalled War on Terrorist Finance.

Intelligence of whatever origin, however, including financial intelligence, is just a tool in the toolbox. Many tools are required to construct
an investigation and put a case together. We have seen that many of law
enforcement's traditional enforcement tools and techniques, honed against
common criminals and often successfully employed against organized
crime and the War on Narcotics, are not appropriate in the War on Terrorist Finance. Moreover, law enforcement rightfully has to worry about
the rule of law and the protection of civil liberties, the foundation of
America's democratic system of government. Unfortunately, structural
conflicts, bureaucratic cultures, misplaced priorities, and ill-conceived
reorganizations make the foundation of the operational and enforcement
pillar in the U.S. War on Terrorist Finance weak. The result has been a
paucity of successful terrorist-finance investigations, prosecutions, and
convictions.[30]

9

The Back Door

From my new vantage point within the Department of State, I increasingly viewed with concern and frustration many of the government's programs, policies, and priorities in respect to terrorist finance. My feelings crystallized after talking to a South Asian businessman who reportedly had contacts within the South Asian underworld of illicit finance and value transfer. In a damning statement he told me, "Don't you know that the terrorists are moving money and value right under your noses? But the West doesn't see it. Your enemies are laughing at you."

I believe I understood, at least in part, what the South Asian businessman meant. In 2002, as part of an official U.S. delegation, I had traveled for the first time to Pakistan. I visited Islamabad and Karachi and spoke to a large number of Pakistani officials and businesspeople. Although the purpose of the trip was to discuss other topics, I was struck by Pakistanis' repeated description of the regional misuse of the Afghan Transit Trade Agreement (ATTA), which I had never before heard of. Under the ATTA, a 1965 bilateral treaty signed by Pakistan and land-locked Afghanistan, trade goods for import or export into Afghanistan that transit through the Pakistani port of Karachi are exempt from Pakistani duties or customs tariffs. The ATTA was subsequently expanded to include other neighbors of Afghanistan, including a 1974 agreement with Iran that allowed free transit through the Iranian port of Bandar Abbas and a 2003 agreement for transit through Chabahar. Access to the port cities through rail or vehicle provides Afghanistan direct access to the Arabian Sea and the opportunity to transport goods internationally by ship.[1]

The conversations I had as part of the U.S. delegation in Pakistan, later travel to Afghanistan, and my previous experience in the Arabian Gulf, led me to believe that over the years the Afghan Transit Trade (ATT) had been corrupted and an indigenous cycle of trade-based money laundering had developed. The system, which masks money laundering—particularly the enormous sums generated through Afghan opium production—is in an area where many U.S. enemies are found. I believe it also has probably been co-opted in the finance of terrorism. The ATT cycle has elements of other laundering components, for example, tax and tariff evasion, traditional trading networks, indigenous business practices, smuggling, corruption, hawala, foreign-exchange manipulations, etc. The cycle forms a culturally unique South Asian-Arabian mix of business, finance, and crime that is *intertwined* and difficult to unravel. The cycle is also impervious to Western financial-transparency reporting requirements that the United States has heretofore depended on to combat terrorist finance.

Afghanistan accounts for a large majority of the world's opium production. Afghan opium is refined into heroin by production labs, more of which are being established inside Afghanistan's borders. The narcotics are often broken into small shipments, and smuggled across porous borders via truck or mule caravan for resale abroad. The ancient smuggling routes follow mountainous trails out of Afghanistan into Iran, Pakistan, Turkmenistan, Uzbekistan, and other countries. These are the same routes that the Taliban and al Qaeda used to flee Afghanistan after the 2001 U.S.-led invasion. Reportedly, warlords and al Qaeda supporters still earn revenue by placing a tax on each shipment that passes through their territories. Narcotics are smuggled and distributed via caravan and truck. They may also be routed toward port cities. As explained in chapter 5, the dhows still sail the old smuggling routes across the Arabian Sea.

Payment for Afghan narcotics is generated through a variety of means. Perhaps one of the most important methodologies for payment is trade-based money laundering. Hawala is particularly important in areas of Afghanistan where there are still few viable financial institutions, and trade provides countervaluation in hawala transfers. Many known hawaladars in Afghanistan have "import-export" licenses. In certain remote areas, tangible goods are sometimes preferred over currency. There are many techniques to arrange this trade. For example, narcotics in Pakistan and Afghanistan are also thought of as a commodity or trade good. Opium gum is often used as a currency, especially for rural farmers. Stored opium is also used as a bank of value in prime production areas. And the opium poppy is one of the few commodities Afghanistan produces that outsiders value. It is estimated that by mid-2005 well over half of the Afghan economy was based on the production of poppy.[2] Because of this vile form of supply and demand, a barter trade has developed whereby narcotics are exchanged for goods. To put things in perspective, in many areas in the region the going rate for a kilo of heroin is a color television set. The same kilo of heroin smuggled to Europe is worth approximately $13,000 wholesale in Frankfurt and $30,000 in London. How do many of the trade goods that enter the underworld of the economies of Afghanistan and Pakistan—and that are sometimes offered for payment for narcotics—get into the area?

The majority of commodities, such as electronics, foodstuffs, and even gold, that are traded and smuggled in the region originate in Dubai. (Hong Kong, Singapore, and other trading centers also are used but to a much lesser extent.) The ATTA allows shipments of trade goods from Dubai to be off-loaded in Karachi, Bandar Abbas, and other regional ports. Avoiding customs duties or tariffs, the goods are then transported to Afghanistan. Since the various brokers and middlemen involved in this trade operate on very small margins, the avoidance of taxes is very important to ensure profit. Once in Pakistan or Iran, the goods are sent into Afghanistan for sale, barter, or payment for narcotics and/or other goods and services. Many of the trade goods are broken down into smaller shipments and are distributed in Afghanistan or are smuggled back into Pakistan, Iran, and other countries in the region for resale. Pakistani officials said that many times "the only part of the shipments that actually leaves Pakistan for Afghanistan was the paperwork." While on paper the goods appeared destined for Afghanistan via the ATT, sometimes they never actually crossed the border. Officials also related incidents in which the goods were only taken a short distance across the border, literally just out of view. The shipments were then broken apart and transported right back into Pakistan, where they eventually could be found for sale on the streets of Islamabad, Karachi, and other Pakistani cities.

Smuggling is one of the largest industries in Pakistan and represents a major source of income for its people and likewise a major revenue loss for the government of Pakistan. The smuggling of goods is so severe that Pakistan established an antismuggling board and various commissions in an attempt to check the constant growth of the underground economy that has been inflicting billions of rupee losses on the government in revenue collection (or hundreds of millions of dollars of revenue for the cash-strapped government). The smuggling feeds on the rampant corruption at all levels entrenched in the region. Moreover, the tax system in Pakistan is broken. Pakistani tax policy is a major contributing factor to the elements of smuggling, corruption, and the use of hawala—or hundi as it is called in Pakistan. Tax reform is in the works, but until a new system is implemented, many feel that nonpayment of taxes, including the avoidance of trade and customs duties, is the acceptable way of doing business. Undoubtedly, most of the ATT involves legitimate commerce. But the trade goods that help pay for narcotics produced in the region and trafficked by organized crime also enter the subcontinent via the ATT (see the following illustration). There are many methods of payment for these trade goods but in most instances they are purchased in the regional shopping center of Dubai. Sometimes the foreign exchange required to purchase the goods enters Dubai in the form of wage remittances. For example, it is estimated that approximately 5 million Pakistanis work abroad and send money home to support their families. At the time of my visit in 2002, I was told by Pakistani officials that statistics showed approximately $1 billion were remitted every year through the traditional banking system. In comparison, it was estimated that approximately $7 billion a year were remitted through hawala. A few years later, due to increased scrutiny given to hawala, the numbers had improved. Approximately $4 billion a year were remitted through legitimate channels. In addition, the official exchange rate between the dollar and the "kerb rate," or street rate, was marginalized. Nevertheless, it was conservatively estimated that between $2 and $3 billion were still flowing into the country through informal channels and Pakistani expatriates abroad continue to send a substantial amount of hard currency back to Pakistan.[3]

Some of the hawala remittances are sent directly to Pakistan and other remittances go via the "Dubai triangle." Still others are hand-carried back to Pakistan by returning Pakistanis. Both licensed and unlicensed foreign-exchange dealers in Pakistan accumulate dollars, euros, riyals, dirhams, etc., as a result of this cross-border movement of money. Millions of U.S. dollars per day in foreign currency are sent via courier to Dubai. Once in Dubai, the currencies are converted into dollars and wired back in whole or part to Pakistan (which adds to foreign-exchange reserves). In addition, some remittance money remains behind in Dubai

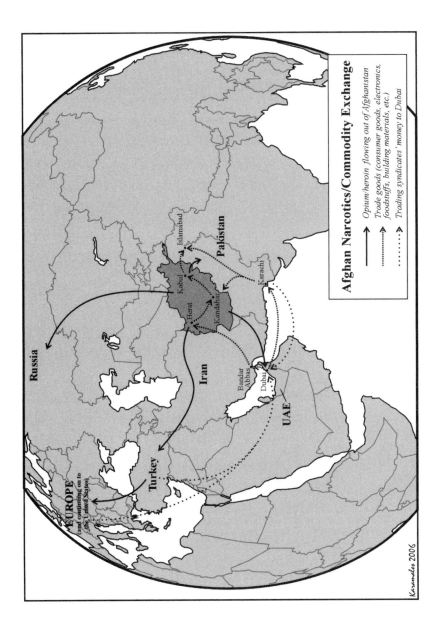

Afghan Narcotics/Commodity Exchange

→ *Opium/heroin flowing out of Afghanistan*

→ *Trade goods (consumer goods, electronics, foodstuffs, building materials, etc.)*

⇢ *Trading syndicates' money to Dubai*

and is combined with funds procured from trading syndicates. Although I do not have specifics, from my past investigative work in the region I suspect that fictitious invoicing again plays a role in this exchange. Traders and brokers in the subcontinent undoubtedly report to exchange control authorities that imports cost more or exports less than the actual price. The difference or credits can be held abroad and used to pay for additional imports. The bottom line is that accumulated foreign exchange, trading credits, and currencies from various sources are used to purchase goods from souks and free trade zones in the thriving regional trade and finance center of Dubai.

Although the mechanics differ, the Afghan trade and money-laundering cycle is somewhat similar to the Colombian Black-Market Peso Exchange (BMPE) discussed in chapter 6. In fact, in comparing the two money laundering "systems," by substituting the words cocaine and opium/heroin, Columbia and Afghanistan, and the United States and Dubai, the similarities between the narcotics exchanges become clear. In the Afghan/Pakistan/Dubai cycle, dollar-based funds are accumulated in Dubai and used to purchase commodities. A massive amount of electronic goods, spices, foodstuffs, gold, etc., are purchased from dealers in Dubai's shops and free trade zones. The companies selling the goods probably do not know or care where the purchase money originates. Throughout the years I found that officials in the UAE have a difficult time accepting that a portion of Dubai trade is used to launder funds. From their perspective, this belief is understandable because on its surface the trade is a legitimate and acceptable way of doing business in the region. The same belief is true of the BMPE in the Western Hemisphere. The ATT and BMPE demonstrate how similar trade-based money-laundering systems have been employed on opposite sides of the world by criminal organizations to launder narcotics proceeds.

Likewise, just as the BMPE in this hemisphere penalizes legitimate Colombian importers because they cannot compete with the cheap prices of goods found on the black market, the domestic Pakistani manufacturing sector has also been severely harmed by the smuggling of competing goods brought into Pakistan by the ATT.[4] As a result, the manufacturing sector has pressured the government to put items with a high susceptibility to smuggling on a "negative list." The list is constantly changing but has covered goods such as tea, tires, television sets, refrigerators, etc., that are imported for delivery to Afghanistan but find their way to the Pakistani black market via the ATT. A few years ago, in some amusing cases, television sets and razor blades were "imported" into Afghanistan via the ATT even though televisions were illegal under the rule of the Taliban and Afghan men were forbidden to shave. As described earlier, the Afghan "imports" were just on paper. The goods themselves, which were routed via the ATT, actually surfaced on the black market in Pakistan.

Organized smuggling groups seem to have found a way around the negative list by increasing their use of Iranian ports of entry. Little data is available on money laundering in Iran, but the underground economy in Iran is enormous, spurred in part by attempts to avoid restrictive taxation. Capital flight is a major problem for the Iranian government and currency-exchange restrictions also encourage the use of hawala. The ATT is a perfect vehicle for Iranian brokers to both circumvent currency controls and export capital by using apparently "legitimate" trade with Dubai. However, the trade is often misused as a method of providing countervaluation in hawala transactions.

Imports under the ATT have sharply increased over the last three years. Afghanistan's improving political situation, economy, and construction projects have combined to increase demand for more and more trade goods. The transit trade is expected to grow even faster in the years ahead. The growth in trade has triggered a logjam of containers in some Pakistani port cities and a shortage of land transport for goods destined to Afghanistan. Partly as a result, Afghan importers are diverting even more imported trade goods to Iran for transit into their country.[5]

Reportedly, the government of Pakistan has a long-standing offer out to harmonize Afghan and Pakistani customs tariffs and facilitate their joint collection. Pakistan would undoubtedly benefit from such an arrangement because harmonization would reduce incentives for smuggling and increase revenues. Afghanistan would likewise gain needed revenue, and adherence to harmonized customs standards would help foster the rule of law. However, both governments are too weak to confront the regional warlords and vested interests that control the smuggling routes and revenue from the misuse of the ATT. A significant share of smuggling revenues is reportedly still controlled by loosely organized special interests that work with corrupt Pakistani and Afghan customs officials to divert duty-free transit trade.

Afghanistan's border tribes, working with their tribal cousins in Pakistan, have also long been engaged in smuggling. During the days of Taliban control of Afghanistan, the transport mafia was reportedly frustrated by the endless series of "toll booths" established by warlords across Afghanistan. The mafia was only too happy to pay the Taliban a single fee to speed them on their way. Al Qaeda operatives in the region reportedly continue to pay top dollar to the truckers for their services. Regarding these overlapping business interests, some regional observers feel that today al Qaeda is probably paying the truckers to haul goods and perhaps people and that the Taliban is still probably collecting from the truckers on any turf over which they still exercise control. Both benefit from the status quo and the continued misuse of the ATT.

The narcotics situation in Afghanistan is deteriorating. In 2002 there were approximately thirty thousand hectares of opium poppy in Afghanistan. By late 2004 opium production had jumped to 206,000 hectares. The numbers are reportedly still climbing. The value of the narcotics is estimated at approximately $7 billion.[6] As is the case with the narcotics business elsewhere in the world, only a tiny fraction of the profits go into the pockets of the farmers. Tremendous amounts of money and value are being produced in a region of the world hostile to us; some of the funds unquestionably are being used to create a lot of mischief. The U.S. government has tried to work with its allies to address narcotics-trafficking in Afghanistan, but the above numbers reflect little progress. A debate rages between those who advocate aggressive aerial spraying and eradication programs and those who are concerned about how that might affect Afghanistan's political stability. However, few attempts have been made to systematically follow the money trail, or in this case "the value trail."

The U.S. government has little leverage or firsthand insight on the misuse of the ATT. Until recently, only one Drug Enforcement Administration operative was assigned to all of Afghanistan and he did not focus on the proceeds of narcotics. Trade-based money laundering is also not addressed by the U.S. military presence. As has been argued elsewhere, both narcotics traffickers and terrorists diversify. Of course, the transit trade is not the only laundering mechanism employed by narcotics traffickers, but as a regional laundering system and methodology, it has been almost completely ignored.

I believed the misuse of the ATT and other forms of trade-based money laundering in the region deserved scrutiny. I tried repeatedly but unsuccessfully to interest American officials in various agencies in my observations. However, once again I found that the system was simply too complicated and not in the Western-oriented comfort zone. Moreover, BSA financial-transparency reporting requirements are ineffectual in addressing this indigenous trade-based system found on the other side of the world. Once again there is little financial intelligence on the misuse of the ATT because there is little nexus to the United States.

In the early 1990s, when I first started investigating the complexities of money laundering in the Middle East and its links to South Asia, my source Ahmed told me, "John, you are in way over your head." He was right. After the better part of a career, I feel I have only been able to scratch the surface. Yet more recently a top Pakistani money-laundering expert told me that the above insight into the intertwined complexities revolving around the misuse of trade in the region is the only example in his experience dealing with American officials of some understanding expressed on how trade overlaps with the issue of money laundering and terrorist finance. He also agreed with the South Asian businessman with underworld ties that up to now America's enemies have been laughing at us. They are aware of the cracks in U.S. financial-transparency requirements. Because of Western blinders, the U.S. government doesn't see what is happening right under its nose.

✳

Increasingly concerned, I feel strongly that new tools for the War on Terrorist Finance are needed. Up to now, America's front-door approach—typified by ever-increasing rules and regulations—has proven, for the most part, ineffectual. The disappointments have been compounded by a corresponding lack of enforcement. Thus, I feel a backdoor approach is required. As the reader has learned, the back door to many forms of alternative remittance and informal value-transfer systems is *trade*.

Experience has shown the best way to analyze and investigate suspect trade-based activity is to have systems in place that can monitor specific imports and exports to and from given countries. As discussed in chapter 6, the U.S. Customs Service pioneered this approach through its creation of the Numerically Integrated Profiling System (NIPS), a computer system that uses U.S. trade data, examines suspect anomalies, and identifies likely targets of investigation. Unfortunately, the opportunities presented by NIPS have never been fully exploited. NIPS, using U.S. data alone, also has limitations, the most important of which is that, to be most effective, NIPS analysts need to compare trade data from other countries. Moreover, following the trade flow when goods are transshipped from country X to Y via Z is difficult, as is monitoring suspect trade that does not enter into U.S. commerce—for example, following suspect trade related to terrorist financing that may move goods from Karachi to Dar es Salaam via Dubai.

If country X exports goods to country Y, in theory country X's export records regarding price, quantity, and general description should match (with some recognized variables) the corresponding import records of country Y. This book has given a few examples of trade fraud found around the world. U.S. Customs has used the technique of identifying trade anomalies to combat the Colombian BMPE, to identify suspect gold shipments from Guyana, and to examine transshipped textiles from the Middle East. In these instances, and many more, Customs was able to match U.S. trade data with cooperating countries' trade data to find suspicious indicators.

Fortunately, the desired trade data is already collected in every country around the world. Creating additional rules, regulations, or databases is unnecessary. All countries have customs services, and all countries impose tariffs and duties for revenue purposes. In fact, most lesser-developed countries are dependent on customs duties to generate revenue. As noted in chapter 2, during the first half of U.S. history, the government was dependent on these same forms of revenue. Many times in my travels, I spoke to officials in lesser-developed countries about the necessity of implementing anti-money-laundering programs. They were not interested. When I demonstrated to them how much revenue they could earn by cracking down on customs fraud and trade-based money laundering, they became all ears. Although there are some differences in the way trade data is gathered and warehoused, today disparate customs services around the world, assisted by various international organizations, are adopting uniform norms, standards, and compatibility.

Over the last generation the United States, the Financial Action Task Force, and other partners have championed an international system of financial transparency. In May 2003 while working at State's Bureau of International Narcotics and Law Enforcement Affairs (INL), I proposed that the United States should actively promote the concept of "trade transparency." Borrowing from the financial intelligence unit (FIU) model, which examines suspect financial transactions, I also suggested that the government examine the feasibility of establishing a prototype trade transparency unit (TTU), which would collect and analyze suspect trade data and then disseminate findings for appropriate enforcement action.

The objective was to establish a new investigative tool for customs and law enforcement that would be better able to combat entrenched trade-based value-transfer systems and customs fraud found around the world.[7] The new tool would help the United States and its partners better combat alternative remittance systems such as hawala, the BMPE, and the misuse of gold, diamonds, and other commodities by criminal and possibly terrorist organizations. I hoped that one day there could be a worldwide TTU network somewhat analogous to the Egmont Group of Financial Intelligence Units. Learning from the administrative mistakes of FinCEN and Egmont, however, the new TTU network would be enforcement oriented and directed.

A TTU would be able either to obtain trade data of interest directly from another TTU or to pull down the data of interest from an administrative gatekeeper. For example, if the U.S. TTU was interested in examining a suspect trade anomaly between India and the United States, the U.S. TTU could contact the Indian TTU and arrange for the exchange of the data. By comparing specific declared imports and exports from both sides, determining indications of possible overinvoicing, underinvoicing, fraudulent trading practices, export incentive fraud, and other illegal techniques, is a relatively simple process. In another example, if the U.S. TTU was concerned with the possibility of terrorist financing via trade that does not enter into U.S. commerce, the global TTU system might facilitate examination of the needed trade data either directly from the concerned countries or through an administrative gatekeeper.

The costs involved with developing a TTU in the United States would be minimal. Customs, now Immigration and Customs Enforcement (ICE) within the Department of Homeland Security (DHS), already has most of the reporting and analytical systems in place. Improved NIPS-like programs have already been shared with other countries, and the technology and software that enables the compatibility of customs data exists. Developing TTUs in other countries will be dependent on many variables, but Treasury and INL have agreed to assist with the initial development of TTUs in some lesser-developed countries. And, in all likelihood, any costs incurred will be more than compensated for by immediate revenue gains.

I am convinced that adopting trade transparency as the next frontier in money laundering and establishing a worldwide network of TTUs could have numerous additional benefits. Besides being an excellent device to better monitor forms of trade-based money laundering such as hawala and black-market exchanges, the international TTU network would also help countries control various types of customs and export incentive fraud. The network would help monitor the worldwide trade in conflict diamonds, conflict timber, and other commodities that sometimes fuel regional conflicts and civil wars in the lesser-developed world. New data would be available to analyze effectively and monitor trade quotas. Forms of smuggling, including narcotics smuggling, could be reduced. For certain countries, increased trade transparency would help reduce multilayered corruption. It would give law enforcement agencies new tools to combat the increasingly troublesome trade in counterfeit goods, and it would provide desperately needed tax and tariff revenues to governments. Academics have argued that even the United States is being shortchanged *tens of billions* of revenue dollars every year through customs fraud.

A future TTU network also could assist in providing needed data to better monitor international trading sanctions. It could help provide transparency for international efforts like the abused and corrupted UN oil-for-food program, which was designed to allow Iraq to export oil and import needed humanitarian goods to lessen the impact of sanctions. Approximately $100 billion worth of oil was sold while Saddam and his cronies skimmed off large percentages through kickbacks, bribes, corruption, and smuggling operations. At its base, the misuse of the oil-for-food program was nothing more than the intertwined regional system of trade-based money laundering and corruption.

Although undoubtedly there will be skeptics, and special interest groups will complain, but an international network of TTUs should be attractive to most governments because it will protect the integrity of markets, provide a level playing field, and provide tax and tariff revenue. Regarding privacy concerns and/or the inadvertent release of proprietary information, governments around the world have already been using trade data for years without issue. In this country, Customs and other relevant government agencies mandate and strictly enforce stringent procedures and safeguards to prevent the possible abuse of the data.

In my view, the international War on Terrorist Finance is stalled. I believe one primary reason for this is that U.S. efforts thus far have concentrated on money moving through traditional financial institutions. The results of these efforts have been mixed at best. In fact, in late 2004 I spoke with a representative of individuals based in the eastern Mediterranean who claimed to be involved with insurgency or terrorist attacks in Iraq. He stated that financing for their operations was generally accomplished via cash and the misuse of trade. Financial institutions were not involved.

In another example of trade's link to terror, a legacy U.S. Customs' examination of suspicious trade data in Columbia detected instances of the black market movement of value connected to the terrorist organization, the Revolutionary Armed Forces of Columbia. Given that criminal and terrorist organizations are smart, know to diversify, and increasingly avoid financial-transparency reporting requirements put in place primarily to address the War on Narcotics, it is time America systematically addressed trade-based value transfer. The basic idea of trade transparency coupled with the creation of TTUs is simple and straightforward. The data already exists. As explained in chapter 6, the data mining required simply builds on the pioneering work done by Lou Bock and a few others in Customs. The potential returns could be enormous.

Although both INL and Treasury, my parent agency, wholeheartedly endorsed the TTU initiative, the proposal, almost by definition, dealt with trade and so had to be adopted and implemented by Customs. My former Customs colleagues, including Bock, likewise fully supported and further developed the idea. However, when I proposed the initiative in May 2003 it overlapped with the creation of the new DHS. Indicative of the growing pains within the new department, it took almost two years for the bureaucratic stars to align and for sufficient resources to be devoted to finally initiate the TTU program. The delays further stalled the War on Terrorist Finance. During those two years I kept pushing bureaucratically, and I found allies within Treasury, State, and DHS. Bock and a few others within DHS's ICE continued to demonstrate the promise of the proposal by making cases. At the time this book is being written, DHS/ICE has become an enthusiastic proponent of the TTU initiative. Experienced and forward-thinking managers, investigators, and analysts currently staff the financial section within ICE, where the TTU initiative is located. Treasury and State have provided political backing and initial funding. It is the kind of interagency cooperation of which we should all be proud. I am confident that with adequate resources, political support, and good management the TTU program will pay substantial dividends in the years ahead.

10

Steps Forward

By early 2005 I was in Washington working in main Treasury's new Office of Terrorist Finance and Financial Intelligence (TFI), a great young organization, staffed by very smart and incredibly hardworking people. However, with the creation of the Department of Homeland Security (DHS), Treasury enforcement was a shell of its former self. Its legacy enforcement agencies, including the Secret Service, Customs, and the Bureau of Alcohol, Tobacco and Firearms had departed. TFI's very small staff was left primarily to develop policy. Many of their policy initiatives I wholeheartedly supported, in particular, the desire to attack the misuse of financial "systems" in a coordinated and effective manner. I thought the United States should learn from its mistakes in the War on Narcotics and not spend inordinate resources targeting and investigating the never-ending supply of criminals, but rather use interagency resources and skill sets to better scrutinize and target some of the vulnerable financial systems the criminals employed. Unfortunately, after policy was developed, Treasury had few effective levers to pull or buttons to push to make things happen. As much as I respected the leadership of TFI and appreciated the hospitality of its great young staff, I knew in my gut that it was time to leave. After over twenty-six years of government service, I decided to retire.

On March 1, 2005, I left the Department of the Treasury for the last time. As I walked down the marble steps that face Pennsylvania Avenue, I thought briefly of the history that has taken place on that broad American passageway that runs through the heart of our nation's capital. Reflecting on my very unusual career, I realized how quickly time, events, issues, and people pass by. Along the way, I had some great adventures. I have the satisfaction of knowing that I always tried to make a contribution. And throughout the years, in various positions and government agencies, it was always an honor for me to serve the American people.

✳

Over the last few years I have joined other Americans in watching and listening as the press, independent commissions, and congressional investigating committees examined what went wrong in the events surrounding September 11. As a result of this important work, many necessary and long overdue governmental reforms were introduced. However, the examinations primarily used the institutions themselves as both vantage points and as primary sources of information for their critiques. Unfortunately, there has yet to be a complete, systematic, and programmatic examination of U.S. efforts to combat terrorist financing. This book does not attempt to address the totality of those efforts. Rather it has been offered to the layperson as one insider's perspective into some issues of concern. Undoubtedly the stalled War on Terrorist Finance will be the focus of further examination in the years ahead.

During my career I tried repeatedly to work within the system to promote what I considered were needed changes or new ways of looking at entrenched problems. For a number of reasons—and only a few examples were given in this book—I witnessed a bureaucratic system resistant to reform. After September 11, while still in the government, I too approached some of those same whistle-blower organizations and investigating committees. While all were interested and receptive, their priorities were understandably elsewhere. Terrorist financing seemed to be a small subset of larger issues that needed more immediate attention. I also found that bureaucratic insight and perspective on the subject were lacking. The story I felt needed to be told about the stalled War on Terrorist Finance was complex. It could not be condensed into bureaucratic bullet points and one-page summaries. Nobody seemed to have time for complicated issues.

In part, this book is a natural outgrowth of those earlier efforts to heighten the awareness on remaining issues of concern. As the former communist government in Angola used to say during the height of the Cold War, "*a luta continua*," or "the struggle continues." By using examples from a unique career, which followed the trail from intelligence to law enforcement to the stalled War on Terrorist Finance, I tried to give the reader one public servant's perspective on what it is really like out there, both in the backstreets and in government cubicles.

I have served in the intelligence and law enforcement communities. Both disciplines are trained to collect and report facts, not offer opinions. After retiring from twenty-six years of government service, I feel I have earned the right to publicly express my views on some issues that continue to be of concern. Most of these issues have not yet received a public hearing. Leaving the bureaucracies I served, governed in part by prepublication review, I have regained my freedom of speech. Before I close, I humbly would like to suggest a few additional topics for debate and some suggested steps forward:

Get Serious About Trade-Based Money Laundering

The misuse of trade should be the next frontier in anti-money-laundering programs. Just as a generation ago the United States promoted financial transparency, today it is time to promote trade transparency. International trade is a back door for money laundering, illegal value transfer, customs fraud, tax cheating, and various alternative remittance systems. For the most part, trade bypasses financial reporting requirements. According to an academic study, 70 percent of the dirty money in the United States being laundered overseas today moves out of the United States via undervalued exports.[1] In 2004 it was estimated that over $390 billion moved in and out of the United States via irregularly priced trade goods. Included were dishtowels valued at $153 each imported from Pakistan and bulldozers priced at $1,700 exported from the United States to Columbia.[2] We do not know the certainty of this data because customs and law enforcement have never systematically examined the problem. We do know that America's terrorist enemies have resorted to forms of trade-based money laundering. And trade is a significant crack in the Western financial system.

For a variety of reasons, U.S. bureaucracies have been reluctant to focus on this issue. The competing interests of commerce and enforcement and between liberties and the government's need to know will undoubtedly influence any future debate on how to combat the misuse of trade. Yet just like in the arena of traditional money laundering through financial institutions, compromises can be found, necessary safeguards implemented, and a balance achieved.

By definition, trade is a customs issue. There should not be another debate or interagency rivalry about which agency has primacy and responsibility. DHS/ICE should be given the mandate. The Trade Transparency Unit (TTU) initiative explained in chapter 9 is an excellent start in this regard and deserves full funding and political support. If I have learned anything in years of government service, it is that without adequate money and political backing, any initiative will die a natural bureaucratic death. I would hate to see that happen in the case of developing an international TTU network. In addition, increased staffing and resources should be given to Customs inspectors. Currently, an estimated 2 percent of outbound containers are inspected. Who knows what we are missing and how much value is being transferred via trade? Agents, customs inspectors, and import specialists also all need additional training in recognizing forms of trade-based money laundering. This country is in a fiscal crisis; it desperately needs additional sources of revenue. Increased customs and control at U.S. ports, backed up by increased enforcement efforts in the field, will result in additional fines, penalties, forfeitures, and other revenue simply by better enforcing laws already on the books. A serious crackdown on trade fraud not only would enhance national security but also could substantially increase revenue for the United States.

Personnel Reform in the Federal Government Equates to National Security

I have little experience in government personnel matters. I do know, however, that in the federal government, personnel dramatically impact policy and effectiveness. I believe America's defective federal government personnel system was just as much a contributing factor to the events surrounding September 11 as anything else. Managers need far more flexibility in hiring, rewarding, promoting, disciplining, and removing their workers. I also know that the federal government desperately needs to attract and retain skilled managers and to have the latitude to remove those that prove to be ineffective.

I'm sure the vast majority of my contemporaries will agree that over the years government service has attracted too many mediocrities. Are these the people we want to depend on for U.S. national security? Edward Gibbons wrote in *The Decline and Fall of the Roman Empire* that Rome collapsed when the most talented and well educated of Rome's elites no longer served their time in the Roman cavalry. Although I am not suggesting the imminent collapse of the United States, for national security reasons alone, the United States simply must do a better job of attracting talented and smart young people to serve in the federal government. Pay flexibility is certainly one issue that needs to be addressed to attract the best and the brightest. But the Civil Service continues to suffer from the perception articulated by Ronald Reagan in his 1981 inaugural address: "Government is not the solution to our problem. Government is the problem." Government service must again be made to seem attractive to America's young people.

The foundation for today's Civil Service was laid during the progressive reforms of the late nineteenth century. Regulations were put in place to curb excesses of political patronage. Today troubling political appointments still exist but so do new forms of patronage, including set asides, special preferences, affirmative action, and de facto quotas. The Clinton administration launched an orchestrated effort to combat forms of harassment and glass ceilings, real and imagined, by reconstituting the federal workforce. I personally saw excess reforms happen at Customs and the Financial Crimes Enforcement Network (FinCEN). But personnel engineering to conform to politically correct thought also occurred throughout the federal workplace. In the months before September 11 Central Intelligence Agency personnel were even taken away from their work and forced to participate in such projects as making "diversity quilts." These types of programs are not zero-sum games. A price was paid. Although those on the inside do not want to talk about it, in the years before September 11 such trivialities, distractions, and misplaced priorities definitely contributed to the mission failures in the intelligence and law enforcement communities.

During much of my federal government career, the common refrain among those competing for promotion was, "Merit has nothing to do with it." That type of realistic resignation is a sad commentary. We never have had a national debate on whether or not it is wise to move federal government employment away from being a meritocracy. Although Civil Service reforms have been tinkered with over the years and Civil Service overhaul now seems to be underway in the Department of Defense and DHS, I feel comprehensive Civil Service personnel policy changes should be made part of post–September 11 reforms. Perhaps a new Civil Service Commission could be appointed to work with Congress, federal government employee unions, and other interested sectors. Before making these much needed reforms, there should be an opportunity for an open debate about the kind of Civil Service this country wants and needs.

September 11 taught the United States that specialists should be developed and rewarded. This requires years of dedicated and specialized knowledge development. In that sense, continuity is important. But I feel it would also help to break down bureaucratic cultures and myopic views by increasing opportunities for federal employees, particularly managers, to rotate or have interim assignments in a variety of government agencies and departments. Selected rotations with the private sector could also prove helpful. Having workers who've spent an extended period of time with multiple departments or agencies is extremely valuable for the government as a whole. These well-rounded workers will have a better sense of the larger picture, rather than tunnel vision. They will develop interagency contacts. The employee will begin to think of the government's interest, or better yet, the country's interest, instead of narrow parochial agency interests. And it would be helpful if the law enforcement and intelligence agency service academies increasingly emphasized the concept of national interest as opposed to the prevailing bureaucratic attitude and culture of us versus them. We must begin to take steps to break down bureaucratic turf.

The Federal Work Force Is Crying Out for *ACCOUNTABILITY*

The Federal Bureau of Investigation and the CIA, the two agencies primarily responsible for the prevention of a foreign terrorist attack against the U.S. homeland, failed to prevent the terrorist attacks on September 11. Other agencies also failed in parts of their particular missions. Some commentators believe those agencies include the then–Immigration and Naturalization Service, the Federal Aviation Authority, the State Department's Bureau of Consular Affairs, and Treasury's FinCEN. Although there have been reorganizations and changes in management, in the end most federal agencies indirectly involved with allowing the attacks on September 11 to occur have been given increased budgets, staffing, and authority. Yet in the years before the terrorist attacks, some directors, policy advisers, managers, and lawyers for these agencies and others made decisions that proved just plain wrong. No amount of truth bending and reinventing of history by those involved is going to change these uncomfortable facts. If Congress and investigating commissions don't know who is at fault and don't wish to assign personal blame, many of the rank-and-file in the federal work force do. To my knowledge, not one individual was singled out, fired, resigned, or in any way was held accountable for the events surrounding September 11. The troops are somewhat held accountable by their managers. Likewise, the troops feel that managers should be held accountable for their actions and decisions. In the current discussion about Civil Service overhaul, there has been much talk about giving management more leeway but little acknowledgment about how some in management have failed us. The present federal workplace culture, which allows managers to shirk responsibility, encourages the intellectual and moral cowardliness that contributed to September 11. At the time this book is being written, much of the original leadership of al Qaeda has been destroyed. They are gone. However, some culpable federal government managers in place before September 11 remain. While America's adversaries are learning and adapting, many failed federal management syndromes continue (preoccupation with turf; lack of imagination; fixation on form over substance; dearth of common sense, groupthink, etc.).

Although I was privileged to serve with some truly outstanding leaders and excellent managers, there is no doubt that inept management exists throughout the federal workplace. Workers are sometimes promoted for the wrong reasons, and once in place, incompetent managers are difficult if not impossible to remove. Moreover, because the government does not have a bottom line and more money is always available in the next budget cycle, there is no incentive to remove them. Sometimes multiple links upward in the chain of command are weak or broken, making reporting through the chain of command impossible. And no amount of management training will remedy the situation. Some people simply cannot manage other people and have never learned the important lessons of life at their mothers' knees. Yet burdened with an ineffective or incompetent manager, the federal employee has little recourse. Neither the current grievance systems nor various offices of inspection or internal affairs are set up to deal with managerial incompetence. As a former Customs colleague used to say, "Management protects management. If it didn't, the whole system would collapse."

As part of personnel reform, I suggest the establishment of a few trial, *independent* management accountability boards structured within a department or agency. The units would not take the place of established personnel grievance boards or offices of internal affairs that deal with waste, fraud, and abuse. They would not accept trivial complaints by workers seeking to retaliate against supervisors. But in cases where management is the problem and not the solution, the well-meaning federal employee who is genuinely concerned about the impact of wrong managerial decisions, long-term mismanagement, a broken chain of command, or demonstrated incompetence should have an outlet other than suffering in silence, leaking a story to the press, or approaching an outside whistle-blowing organization. Management accountability boards would also help safeguard and prevent backsliding from many of the reforms introduced after September 11.

Congress Should Get Serious About the Oversight of FinCEN

Speaking of accountability, an honest and complete examination of the record will show Treasury's FinCEN has, for the most part, failed. FinCEN's 2000–2005 Strategic Plan is available for all to see and examine.[3] Compare and contrast FinCEN's articulated plan to the actual record. After peering through the smoke and mirrors, with a few exceptions, FinCEN did not come close to achieving its five objectives of providing investigative case support, identifying financial crime trends and patterns, administering the Bank Secrecy Act (BSA), fostering international cooperation, and strengthening management support. In round numbers, FinCEN's budget over the last five years was approximately one quarter of a billion dollars. The annual appropriations have recently increased. Congress must take its oversight responsibilities seriously and ask the question, "Are U.S. taxpayers getting an adequate return on their investment?"

When FinCEN was first created, the idea of breaking down bureaucratic walls by sharing financial intelligence to assist law enforcement agencies outside of the Department of the Treasury was an "imaginative" concept ahead of its time. For many years I was a very vocal and public advocate of FinCEN and the promise of the young organization. I devoted years of my life to trying to help FinCEN achieve its potential. Current management is trying once again to reorganize. But there are continuing structural, strategic, and personnel failures. FinCEN has never realized its early potential and has drifted dangerously away from its original mission of supporting law enforcement. If we are serious about accountability and examining reasons why the War on Terrorist Finance is stalled, FinCEN's record must be seriously examined and addressed.

Bank Secrecy Act Data—Use It or Lose It

Nobody knows how many individual pieces of financial intelligence, also known as bank secrecy data, exist. The number of forms filed over the last ten years should easily be over 100 million, and each of the forms has multiple fields of information. I am a huge proponent of the utility of this information, having seen firsthand what a valuable tool it can be in supporting law enforcement, not only in the area of money laundering but also in various crimes such as locating fugitives and providing indicators of corruption. Unfortunately, FinCEN, the government agency designated with this task, does not have a centralized, systematic, and successful program to harvest or fully exploit the data. If anything, recent decisions have been made at FinCEN to let others do the work themselves by "empowering" their "customers" and to "accelerate the secure flow of financial information from the industries subject to Bank Secrecy Act requirements to the law enforcement agencies. . . ."

There is nothing wrong with enabling law enforcement to help itself by providing direct access to the data. But in giving segments of this data to specialized agencies, we are not fully exploiting the utility of the database as a whole. There is very little proactive or strategic analysis at FinCEN. Repeated attempts at FinCEN to data mine the whole of BSA information have failed. Individual agencies cannot do this job as they are not interested in the big picture. Even interagency regional review teams under the auspices of U.S. attorneys rightfully concentrate on exploiting only data that is pertinent to them.

Before we propose additional regulations and the commensurate reporting requirements on industry, we should insist that the current data is properly exploited. Anti-money-laundering and counter-terrorist-financing rules and regulations mean major compliance expenses for banks and increasingly broker-dealers, money service businesses, and nonbank financial institutions. There is a growing movement to subject other types of dealers to financial-transparency reporting requirements, including automobile dealerships, travel agencies, insurance companies, real estate companies, accountants, antique dealers, and auction houses. The government is shifting the enforcement burden. If I were in industry, I imagine the costs would be more palatable if I was assured the data was at least being fully exploited. Unfortunately, it isn't. In fact, mandated industry anti-money-laundering compliance programs act as a kind of tax that can retard growth. Until the government demonstrates that financial intelligence is being competently exploited, I suggest there be a moratorium on its further expansion.

Empower the Military in the War on Terrorist Finance

The War on Terrorism is a different type of war for the U.S. military. The front lines extend from remote areas of Afghanistan to building infrastructures in Iraq to the Horn of Africa. However, thus far, the United States has not fully taken advantage of the military's unique presence to obtain information on the ground about indigenous methods of terrorist finance. Since the intelligence and law enforcement communities have not been able to provide effective information in areas of concern—in part because they do not have direct access to many of the areas—perhaps the military could help fill the void. Historically, U.S. law enforcement has found that following the money often leads to the leadership of organized crime. Potentially, following available financial and or value-transfer trails could lead the U.S. military to the leadership of terrorist organizations, allowing the United States to disrupt the ability of its adversaries' command to earn, move, and store financial assets and value. This could hurt U.S. enemies more than tactical victories on traditional battlefields.

At the risk of advocating additional mission creep for the military, I suggest that selected ground units in places like Afghanistan and Iraq be given training in local and indigenous forms of money laundering and terrorist finance. Intelligence reporting requirements should be prepared to assist the grunt in the field. U.S. soldiers and marines can be trained to recognize possible suspect indigenous financial operations sometimes used by our enemies in asymmetric warfare. Information appropriate for U.S. military forces could be prepared to help ground units debrief local sources of information and question prisoners. In short, the military could provide additional eyes and ears on the ground to help the United States collect intelligence on terrorist finance.

Terrorism Is Local

On the domestic front, more emphasis should be put on empowering state and local law enforcement to contribute their on-the-ground expertise to the War on Terrorist Finance. With the decline of state sponsorship of terrorism, terrorists and radical groups increasingly depend on local crime to finance their activities. We already have seen evidence of this in domestic financial investigations into counterfeit goods, stolen baby milk formula, cigarette-smuggling rings, and other crimes. Although Congress has given billions of dollars, some of it for dubious use, to state and local law enforcement in the form of grants to purchase equipment, I feel a small fraction should be spent on training police departments to recognize terrorist finance. Some limited work is being done in this area, but with the proper emphasis we would have tens of thousands of additional sets of eyes and ears of enforcement personnel on American streets that could assist in spotting suspicious financial activity and following the money trail. Federal law enforcement agencies need the local help. The local police officer has intimate knowledge of the area he or she patrols and can better spot suspicious activities. Training in terrorist finance will give the law enforcement officer insight to better ask the next question.

Back to the Basics—A Renewed Emphasis on Enforcement

In 1991 I was at a formal dinner in Italy and seated next to the Italian minister of finance. During a long conversation, he expressed his frustration that Italians did not pay their taxes and asked me why Americans had such a comparatively high rate of tax compliance. My initial answer surprised him. I told him that in my opinion Americans pay their taxes and Italians do not because American police officers enforce traffic laws and their Italian counterparts do not. The statement was made in jest, but it underscored a critical point in our follow-up conversation, i.e., laws, rules, and regulations are next to meaningless without a sufficient level of enforcement to back them up. The perception of adequate and fair enforcement breeds an atmosphere of respect and compliance with the rule of law. New York City's politicans and law enforcement personnel famously discovered that cracking down on graffiti and panhandlers had a ripple effect that carried over to other more serious crimes.

Unfortunately, in the stalled War on Terrorist Finance, the United States has not had adequate enforcement. Rather, U.S. policies place emphasis on new rules and regulations without the commensurate and proverbial "stick." For example, FinCEN is charged with administering the BSA and parts of the USA PATRIOT Act, but it has no compliance officers or investigators. It depends on an alphabet soup of other regulatory agencies to enforce compliance with anti-money-laundering and anti-terrorist-finance guidelines. The results have been mixed at best. Compounding the problem, nonbank financial institutions and sectors of financial-like industries that do not have designated regulators face almost no enforcement at all. And anti-money-laundering regulations for diverse dealers and industries judged to be at risk will increase in the years ahead. Passing a new law or promoting a regulation that gives the political appearance of progress is comparatively easy, but without adequate enforcement, there is nothing to keep the system honest.

Often when I traveled overseas and made public presentations about money laundering to sometimes rather hostile audiences, I would try to diffuse the foreigners' defenses and suspicions by readily acknowledging that the United States, because of its economy of scale and insatiable appetite for narcotics, probably has more money laundering than any other country in the world. Yet to America's credit, the United States also has the strongest and most aggressive anti-money-laundering and counter-terrorist-finance enforcement programs. It has skilled and dedicated law enforcement professionals. As good as America is, however, a recent study showed that money launderers in the United States face a less than 5 percent risk of conviction.[4] While methodologies and statistics of this nature can be open to question, sentencing guidelines change, and undoubtedly many criminals plea bargain to lesser charges, the bottom line in the United States is that for money launderers to be caught and convicted, they have to be either very stupid or very unlucky.

The situation is even worse overseas. Much hard work over the last ten years has put anti-money-laundering laws and infrastructures increasingly in place around the world. Yet with some exceptions, both America's friends and enemies, developed and nondeveloped nations alike, have abysmal records when it comes to anti-money-laundering and anti-terrorist-finance enforcement. There are signs that with the decline of the state sponsorship of terrorism, organized criminal groups are now providing much of the funds that keep global terrorism going. Narcotics smuggling, extortion, counterfeiting, cigarette smuggling, kidnapping, and trafficking in people are increasing sources of cash for terrorism.[5] For success to occur overseas, a new emphasis has to be made to initiate investigations at the street level and follow the financial trail to wherever it leads. Implementation of anti-money-laundering and counter-terrorist-finance programs, initiatives, and political will are the keys. Internationally, I suggest that the Financial Action Task Force and its regional bodies insist that members provide yearly statistics on its anti-money-laundering and counter-terrorist-financing prosecutions and convictions. If there is an honest compilation, the resulting totals may shock and embarrass governments into taking more effective enforcement action.

In this country, I suggest that a new emphasis be placed on enforcing the laws, rules, and regulations that already are on the books, including effective oversight of domestic charities and nonprofit organizations, regulatory compliance for banks and nonbank financial institutions, and law enforcement at the street level, borders, and ports. This will require additional resources. More important, it will require a different philosophical and bureaucratic emphasis.

Reestablish the Interagency Coordination Group

As explained in earlier chapters, from 1996 to 2000 the primary federal law enforcement agencies involved with anti-money-laundering programs established a *working-level* Interagency Coordination Group (ICG). FinCEN hosted the group because it was then thought by the participants to be a neutral and honest broker. The ICG members fostered interagency communication and coordination. Numerous potential bureaucratic conflicts and incidents were quietly resolved because of the group's intervention. The ICG encouraged interagency attention on particular issues and investigations of concern. The ICG members were not political fronts for their respective agencies, but rather senior working-level special agents who just wanted to do the right thing for the U.S. government as a whole. Unfortunately, with new FinCEN management, the ICG was disbanded. Yet it was exactly the type of imaginative interagency coordination effort that was identified as lacking by the 9/11 Commission.

I encourage the formation of a newly constituted ICG with appropriate representatives from the Departments of Justice, Treasury, and Homeland Security. It should not be a permanent group or task force, but rather it should meet informally on a periodic basis to discuss ways to reinvigorate and better coordinate the stalled War on Terrorist Finance. The FBI could use the help. Senior working-level agency representatives who wish to work to better the collective good should be invited and polarizing political lightening rods should stay away. The ICG should meet on neutral grounds.

Open the Pandora's Box of the Department of Homeland Security

In the rush to react to September 11, politicians of both parties hurried to create the new DHS. While the problems and the potential of DHS have been chronicled elsewhere, there can be little debate that the department was populated with agencies that did not get along and sometimes had overlapping missions.[6] As a result, battles over turf, budget, and management systems have continued within the new department. One major mistake in the creation of DHS was charging two separate internal agencies with border and immigration enforcement. Compounding problems in the stalled War on Terrorist Finance, the Customs Office of Enforcement, now part of DHS's Immigration and Customs Enforcement, lost its long-running bureaucratic struggle with the FBI on money laundering and terrorist financing.

In 2004 I spoke to a congressional staffer about the possibility of reexamining the creation of DHS. The response at the time was that Congress didn't want to look too closely at DHS because, "It would be like opening a Pandora's box and nobody wants to see what might fly out." However, recent signs show that Congress is finally starting to become aware of some of the problems and is considering steps to address them.

In conjunction with the overdue review of DHS, I suggest that thought be given to reestablishing the Department of the Treasury's ability to conduct some types of financial crimes investigations. (I am not including Treasury's tax enforcement responsibilities.) For the Department of Justice and DHS, money laundering is a subset of other underlying crimes or "specified unlawful activities." Treasury, almost by definition, focuses on financial matters including international money laundering. Unfortunately, many legacy U.S. Treasury agreements and working relationships with foreign counterpart organizations have been jeopardized. Moreover, the domestic financial industry views Treasury as its natural government interlocutor. Currently, Treasury can assist in making anti-money-laundering and anti-terrorist-finance strategies and policies, but because its enforcement arm was crippled when DHS was created, it lacks the breadth of investigative resources to implement those same policies. Over the last few years the United States has put all of its faith in the FBI's ability to conduct terrorist-finance investigations; a revitalized enforcement arm in the Department of the Treasury also would act as a needed insurance policy.

Tax Evasion and Money Laundering: Two Sides of the Same Coin

According to the Internal Revenue Service, "Money laundering is the means by which criminals evade paying taxes on illegal income by concealing the source and the amount of profit. Money laundering is in effect tax evasion in progress."[7] For the criminal investigator both in this country and overseas, separating money laundering from tax evasion has become increasingly difficult. The methodologies employed in both crimes are often quite similar. One citizen's tax haven can be the same as a criminal money launderer's hidden offshore account. Financial safe havens, promoted by creative lawyers and accountants and proliferated by modern telecommunications, provide ready tax shelters for corporations and rich citizens eager to escape their tax obligations. The result is an eroding of the tax base, which has to be made up by law-abiding citizens.

In the developing world, the unchecked diversion of untaxed billions of dollars is a gaping hole in the international free-market system that we are trying to promote. Corrupt kleptocrats and the elites send scarce money offshore, further impoverishing the poor. Many of the indigenous alternative remittance systems and informal value-transfer systems that were discussed in this book in relation to money laundering and terrorist finance had as their genesis the goal of avoiding the payment of taxes and duties.

Many countries belatedly are recognizing that tax evasion should be considered illicit money under money-laundering statutes. Today, India is implementing new forms of tax reform in large part to go after black money and hawala. Many European governments are tired of seeing their citizens dodge the tax collector by funneling money to jurisdictions with strict financial secrecy. The issue is complicated because a basic principle of international law is that one country does not enforce the tax laws of another. Recognizing the problem, the Organization for Economic Cooperation and Development (OECD) has worked to publicize international tax havens. The OECD also has sought to improve cooperation between tax and anti-money-laundering authorities.

As a former criminal investigator, I think it is hypocritical for the American government to talk tough on money laundering while allowing some of its privileged citizens and corporations to dodge their tax obligations and responsibilities via loopholes. As the IRS knows, tax evasion is a form of money laundering often practiced by the rich. White-collar laundering creates a huge untaxed economy and promotes a kind of capital flight that harms U.S. economic strength and national interests. I urge Congress to ignore special interests and identify and close tax loopholes. Stepped up enforcement of U.S. tax laws also will equate to more effective enforcement of anti-money-laundering and counter-terrorist-finance laws. One of the most cost effective ways of enforcement is to hire more Customs and IRS criminal investigators. Many studies have shown that for every dollar spent on Customs and IRS enforcement, many multiples more are returned to the Treasury in the form of tax and duty revenues, seizures, and forfeitures. I am not advocating intrusive policing, but rather better enforcement of laws already on the books. If tax evasion and money laundering are sometimes cause and effect, it stands to reason that if the United States had meaningful tax reform, there would be less money laundering and possibly fewer vehicles for the financing of terrorism. For example, there has been discussion about replacing the national disgrace called the federal income tax with a uniform flat tax or a national sales tax on personal consumption. With a sales-based tax, you consume and you get taxed. If you don't consume as much, you don't get taxed as much. Both a flat tax and a consumption-based tax would simplify U.S. tax structure and eliminate tax loopholes.

For this brief discussion, ignore the politics of the tax proposals and the economic and social pros and cons. From a money laundering enforcement perspective, if tax loopholes and financial hiding places were made to disappear (along with the army of lawyers, accountants, lobbyists, and special interest groups that makes a living because of a tax system built on doling out political perks and favors), there would be less incentive to hide both legitimate wealth and ill-gotten gains. In a world increasingly without borders, capital is attracted to safe havens. With meaningful tax reform and the resultant closure of tax loopholes, it stands to reason that much of the billions of dollars in offshore accounts that belong to corporations and the wealthy would come back to the United States. I also would argue that with meaningful tax reform—negating many of the reasons for the proliferation of creative financial hiding places—it would become more difficult for criminal organizations to launder as much of their billions of dollars out of the United States. If legal and illegal money currently escaping the United States returned to this country, U.S. financial systems would be more transparent and would allow fewer avenues for hiding money. While acknowledging that this may sound like hyperbole, I urge that Congress consider the benefits to U.S. national security when it studies the need for tax reform.

An Inability to Control Borders Is the Biggest U.S. Security Threat

Although this issue has received attention elsewhere, I would be remiss if I did not also include my view that it is time for this country to get serious about protecting its porous borders. The best foreign and domestic intelligence and an effective means of following the financial trails of terrorism cannot protect the United States when its chief vulnerability continues to be its insecure ports of entry and borders. It is not that difficult for someone determined to enter the United States to do so. The estimated 11 million illegal aliens in this country know that, and so do the terrorists. During the past several years polls have consistently shown that a solid majority of Americans want their government to crack down hard on illegal entry and oppose making it easier for illegal aliens to become citizens. The great majority of American people don't want guest-worker plans, amnesty, or various paths to citizenship. Normally, politicians listen to what the people want. Not in this case. It is obvious that big-business interests whose profits depend on illegal immigrants' labor and prominent Latino-rights organizations have captured some U.S. politicians. It is insulting to the hardworking and brave men and women engaged in U.S. border defense not to have the complete backing of their political leaders. The hard and uncomfortable truth is that every illegal alien in this country broke the law. Every American business that knowingly hires illegal aliens is also breaking the law. America's elected leaders are sworn to uphold the law. Either the laws should be changed or the laws should be fully and seriously enforced. Politicians want to have it both ways, but this time a choice has to be made. The American people should demand that their elected leaders decide the issue based on collective U.S. national security.

❈

Although personally frustrated by the stalled War on Terrorist Finance, I would like to end this book on an optimistic note. America has had some very real successes. After September 11 the U.S. government took specific steps to financially isolate those who support terrorism while simultaneously trying to encourage international financial networks to heighten the risk and the costs associated with funds linked to terrorism. The United States has improved cooperation with many foreign governments, both on intelligence and law enforcement matters, and it is also making progress in capacity building, or helping countries to help themselves. I am confident these efforts will increasingly start paying dividends.

In this country, U.S. law enforcement agencies have worked hard to develop investigations into terrorist-finance networks. After years of unwarranted delay, progress has been made in interagency cooperation and information sharing. As pointed out, money-laundering investigations are long-term and complex. It often takes years to put together significant cases. Although there have been relatively few successful terrorist-finance investigations, I am hopeful there will be more progress in the near future. The American people should be proud of the quiet sacrifices and untiring efforts of their public servants engaged in these efforts. While I do not think America's War on Terrorist Finance has been as smart or efficient as it could be, in fact, there can be no doubt that it is now "harder, costlier, and riskier" for terrorists to raise and transfer funds, both in this country and many others around the world. There are indications that the leadership of al Qaeda is becoming hard-pressed for funding. It also should be acknowledged that the total elimination of terrorist finance is virtually impossible. And thankfully, at the time this book is being written, there have not been any further deadly September 11–like attacks directed against the U.S. mainland.

As said in the introduction to this book, there has been both success and failure in the War on Terrorist Finance. This book has given examples of both. Progress is slowly being made. Like the Cold War, the War on Terrorist Finance is a generational challenge. Similar to the War on Narcotics, this war will not conclude with finality. The issues, the hidden financial trails, and the struggle will continue for years to come.

Notes

U nless otherwise noted, the information contained in this book comes from direct personal knowledge and experience. All quotations are factual and come from personal conversations and interviews with those concerned. Specific information from published sources is cited in the following notes.

Preface
1. George W. Bush, "Remarks by the President in Address to the Nation," June 6, 2002, http://www.whitehouse.gov/news/releases/2002/06/20020606-8.html.

Introduction
1. Peter Greer and Faye Bowers, "Failure of Imagination Led to 9/11," *Christian Science Monitor*, July 23, 2004, http://www.csmonitor.com/2004/0723/p01s03-uspo.htm.

Chapter 1: A Sense of the Street
1. Anthony Boadle, "U.S. Lied About Cuban Role in Angola—Historian," *Reuters*, April 2002, http://members.allstream.net/~dchris/CubaFAQ120.html.
2. "The Intelligence Cycle," *The CIA Factbook on Intelligence* (Washington, DC: Central Intelligence Agency, 2002).
3. Jeffrey H. Smith, "To Find a Spy," *Washington Post*, March 2, 2001, A-25.
4. "The Feds Rely Too Heavily on Lie Detectors," *Washington Post*, April 27, 1997, C-1.
5. William Colby and Peter Forbath, *Honorable Men: My Life in the CIA* (New York: Simon & Schuster, 1978).

Chapter 2: Undercover Agent

1. Dennis V. N. McCarthy, *Protecting the President: The Inside Story of a Secret Service Agent* (New York: William Morrow & Company, 1985), 99.
2. Suzanne Fields, "When Policy Toward Madness Goes Crazy," *Insight Magazine,* September 1, 1997, 48.
3. David Isenberg, "Latest Chinese Warplane Flies With US Technology, US Technology Appears in New Chinese Warplane via Israel," *Asia Times,* December 4, 2002, http://atimes.com/atimes/China/DL04Ad01.html.
4. U.S. Office of Naval Intelligence, *Worldwide Challenges to Naval Strike Warfare,* March 1997, as quoted in ibid.
5. Criminal complaint and affidavit by John Cassara, Criminal Complaint Case No. 89-0800M-01, U.S. District Court, District of Colombia, October 24, 1989.

Chapter 3: The First Step

1. Jack Nelson, "As Crime Spans Globe, INTERPOL Is Catching Up," *Los Angeles Times,* January 4, 1998.
2. Dr. Bocci of the Italian Servizio Centrale Antidroga, Ministry of Interior, "Organized Crime in Italy and Its Link to the International Drug Trade" (paper presented at Interpol Headquarters, Lyon, France, November 29, 1990).
3. John Cassara, "Operation Primo Passo," *U.S. Customs Today,* Fall 1993, 5.
4. Raymond Baker, *Dirty Money and Its Global Effect,* International Policy Report, A Publication of the Center for International Policy, January 2003, 2.
5. Robert E. Powis, *The Money Launderers* (Chicago: Probus Publishing Company, 1992), 9.
6. John Cassara et al., *Criminalità e Finanza* (Bologna: Il Mulino, 1991), 73–75.
7. Vincenzo Salerno, "Remembering Judge Falcone," *Best of Sicily Magazine,* April 2002, www.bestofsicily.com/mag/art48.htm.
8. Robert E. Powis, "Operation Polar Cap," in *The Money Launderers* (Chicago: Probus Publishing Company, 1992), 145–189.
9. Former DEA and FinCEN Special Agent Greg Passic, in conversation with the author, August 1996.

10. R. T. Naylor, "The Underworld of Gold," in *Wages of Crime* (Ithaca: Cornell University Press, 2002), 196–246.

11. "Gold Seized in Colon Free Zone Allegedly Linked to Money Laundering," *La Prensa*, October 29, 2000, monitored by the British Broadcasting Corporation, November 3, 2000.

Chapter 4: We Are All Susceptible

1. "Nation's 'Hot' Spot SoCal Leads Country in Stolen Auto Exports," *Los Angeles Daily News*, November 24, 2004.

2. Timothy Green, *The World of Gold* (London: Rosendale Press, 1993).

3. Anand Giridharadas, "India Hopes to Wean Citizens From Gold," *International Herald Tribune*, March 16, 2005.

4. "Intelligence Operations, Soldiers Shut Out CIA," *Strategy Page*, April 21, 2005, http://www.strategypage.com/htmw/htintel/articles/20050421.aspx.

5. Francis Fukuyama, *The End of History and the Last Man* (New York: Avon Books, 1992).

Chapter 5: All Roads Lead to Dubai

1. Robert Allen, "The Veil Over Dirty Money in Dubai," *Financial Times*, February 25, 2001.

2. Naylor, "Underworld of Gold," 233.

3. Edmund Blair, "Tackling Money Laundering in the UAE," *Reuters English News Service*, November 10, 1999.

4. Hugh Williamson, "Hijackers Got Cash From UAE," *Financial Times*, December 11, 2002.

5. Bill Powell, "The Man Who Sold the Bomb," *Time*, February 14, 2005, 22.

6. "Pak Scientists Hid Money in Dubai," *Times of India Online*, January 25, 2004, http://timesofindia.indiatimes.com/articleshow/msid-444019,prtpage-1.cms.

Chapter 6: Promise and Potential

1. Mary Lee Warren, Deputy Assistant Attorney General, Criminal Division, Department of Justice, Testimony before the Subcommittee on Crime of the Committee on the Judiciary, House of Representatives, 105th Cong., 1st sess. (July 24, 1997); http://commdocs.

house.gov/committees/judiciary/hju58953.000/hju58953_0.htm.

2. Statement of Stanley E. Morris, Director of the Financial Crimes Enforcement Network, before the Senate Subcommittee on International Trade and the Senate International Narcotics Control Caucus, 104th Cong., 2nd sess. (July 23, 1996).

3. "The Egmont Group," *The Report on Crime and Profiteering,* December 1997, 5.

4. Egmont Group, "Information Paper on Financial Intelligence Units and the Egmont Group," September 2004, http://www.egmont-group.org/info_paper_final_oct_2004.pdf.

5. Bureau for International Narcotics and Law Enforcement Affairs, *International Narcotics Control Strategy Report—Money Laundering and Financial Crimes,* March 2005, 56–64.

6. William C. Gilmore, *Dirty Money: The Evolution of Money Laundering Countermeasures* (Strasbourg: Council of Europe Press, 1999), 95.

7. James E. Johnson, Under Secretary for Enforcement, Department of the Treasury, Testimony before the Seante caucus on International Narcotics Control, June 21, 1999; http://www.treas.gov/press/releases/rr3214.htm.

8. FinCEN, *Hawala: The Hawala Alternative Remittance System and Its Role in Money Laundering,* report prepared in cooperation with INTERPOL/FOPAC, undated.

9. Douglas Frantz, "Ancient Secret System Moves Money Globally," *New York Times,* October 3, 2001.

10. Commonwealth Secretariat, "Money Laundering: Special Problems of Parallel Economies" (paper presented at the Joint Meeting of Commonwealth Finance and Law Officials on Money Laundering, London, June 1–2, 1998), 16.

11. "U.S. Customs Database Used to Track Terrorist Financing," *DSstar,* December 11, 2001, http://www.tgc.com/dsstar/01/1211/103779.html.

12. David E. Kaplan, "The Golden Age of Crime: Why International Drug Traffickers Are Invading the Global Gold Trade," *U.S. News and World Report,* November 29, 1999, 42–44.

13. "NIPS Comes of Age," *U.S. Customs Today,* December 2000.

14. FATF/GAFI, "Nine Special Recommendations on Terrorist Finance," http://www.fatf-gafi.org/dataoecd/8/17/34849466.pdf.

Chapter 7: Cracks in the System

1. Quote from a May 1998 U.S. Customs Service briefing paper on Operation Casablanca.
2. The White House Office of National Drug Control Policy as quoted by Michael Kelly, "Minuet in Mexico," *Washington Post,* February 17, 1999, A-17.
3. "Bank of New York Laundering Suspects to Surrender," *United Press International,* February 15, 2000, http://www.newsmax.com/articles/?a=2000/2/15/55945.
4. National Commission on Terrorist Attacks Upon the United States, *Monograph on Terrorist Financing,* staff report to the commission, 2004, 38.
5. John Mintz and Douglas Farah, "Small Scams Probed for Terror Ties," *Washington Post,* August 12, 2002, A-1.
6. Paul Beckett, Carrick Mollencamp, and Michael Phillips, "Withdrawal Pains: In the Financial Fight Against Terrorism, Leads Are Hard Won," *Wall Street Journal,* October 10, 2001, A-1.
7. 9/11 Commission, *Monograph on Terrorist Financing,* 53.
8. Ibid., 25.
9. Douglas Farah, *Blood from Stones* (United States: Broadway Books, 2004), 112–113.
10. Maggie Michael, "Bin Laden Said to Offer Gold for Killings," *Associated Press,* May 7, 2004.
11. "Taliban Offer Reward," *Dawn the Internet Edition,* February 9, 2006, http://www.dawn.com/2006/02/09/int16.htm.
12. Baker, *Dirty Money,* 1.
13. John S. Pistole, "Terrorism Financing: Origination, Organization, and Prevention," Statement by the Deputy Assistant Director, Counterterrorism Division, Federal Bureau of Investigation, to the Senate Committee on Governmental Affairs, 108th Cong., 1st sess. (July 31, 2003).
14. Rita Katz and Josh Devon, "Perilous Power Play," *Centre for Research on Globalization,* May 27, 2003, http://www.national review.com/comment/comment-katz-devon052703.asp.

Chapter 8: Pillars in the Sand

1. Bureau for International Narcotics and Law Enforcement Affairs,

International Narcotics Control Strategy Report—Money Launder-ing and Financial Crimes, March 2005, 8–10.

2. E. Anthony Wayne, "Internationalizing the Fight," *eJournalUSA: Economic Perspectives*, September 2004, 8.

3. UN Security Council, Letter dated 23 August 2004 from the Chair-man of the Security Council Committee, established pursuant to reso-lution 1267 concerning al-Qaida and the Taliban and associated in-dividuals and entities addressed to the President of the Security Coun-cil, S/2004/679, 2004, 12.

4. GAO, *Terrorist Financing: Better Strategic Planning Needed to Co-ordinate U.S. Efforts to Deliver Counter-Terrorism Financing Train-ing and Technical Assistance Abroad*, report to congressional request-ors, October 2005.

5. Peter Reuter and Edwin M. Truman, *Chasing Dirty Money: The Fight Against Money Laundering* (Washington, DC: Institute for Interna-tional Economics, 2004), 143.

6. OFAC, mission statement, http://www.treas.gov/offices/enforce-ment/ofac/.

7. Joseph M. Myers, "The Silent Struggle: The U.S. Strategy to Com-bat Terrorist Finances, Assessing the Fight Against Financial Sup-port for Islamist Extremist Terrorism," *Georgetown Journal of Inter-national Affairs*, December 2004, 3.

8. Personal knowledge of author and review of U.S. Department of State International Narcotics Control Strategy Reports, Money Laun-dering and Financial Crimes Section, years 2002–2006.

9. 9/11 Commission, *Monograph on Terrorist Financing*, 79.

10. Ibid, 10.

11. Caroline Drees, "Steps Against Terrorist Financing Risk Backfiring," *Reuters,* February 23, 2005, http://www.alertnet.org/printable.htm?URL=/thenews/newsdesk/N23395624.htm. Date of late visit: February 25, 2005.

12. "Bank of Mexico Reports Remittances Sent Home by Mexicans Liv-ing abroad Rise to $20B in 2005," Associated Press, January 31, 2006, http://www.moneysense.ca/news/company_news?show news.jsp?content=D8FFTN@GG-ap

13. See note 11 above.

14. Juan Carlos Zarate, Assistant Secretary, Terrorist Financing and Fi-

nancial Crimes, U.S. Department of the Treasury, Testimony before the House Financial Services Committee Subcommittee Oversight and Investigations, 109th Cong., 1st sess. (February 16, 2005).

15. FinCEN, "314(a) Fact Sheet," June 21, 2005.

16. 9/11 Commission, *Monograph on Terrorist Financing*, 4.

17. Alan Cullison, "Inside al-Qaeda's Hard Drive," *Atlantic Monthly*, September 2004, 62.

18. Wayne, "Internationalizing the Fight," 6.

19. A report by the International Organization of Securities Commissions as quoted by Donald Greenless, "Banking in Accordance With the Koran," *International Herald Tribune*, June 2, 2005.

20. Susan Smillie and Hilary Osborne, "Q&A: Islamic Finance," *Guardian Unlimited*, February 15, 2005.

21. Mahmoud A. El-Gamal, Phd., Chair of Islamic Economics, Finance, and Management, Rice University, testifying before the U.S. Senate Committee on Banking, Housing, and Urban Affairs, 109th Cong., 1st sess. (July 13, 2005).

22. *International Narcotics Control Strategy Report*, March 2003, 130.

23. GAO, *Tax Exempt Organizations, Improvements Possible in Public, IRS, and State Oversight of Charities*, report to the chairman and ranking minority member, Committee on Finance, April 2002, summarized by the National Council of Nonprofit Associations at http://www.ncna.org/index.cfm?fuseaction=Page.viewPage &pageID=316.

24. Kenneth W. Dam, Deputy Secretary, Department of the Treasury, Testimony before the Senate Committee on Banking, Housing, and Urban Affairs Subcommittee on International Trade and Finance, 107th Cong., 2nd sess. (August 1, 2002), 9.

25. Juan Carlos Zarate, Assistant Secretary, Terrorist Financing and Financial Crimes, U.S. Department of the Treasury, Testimony before the House Financial Services Committee, Subcommittee on Oversight and Investigations, 109th Cong., 1st sess. (February 16, 2005).

26. UN Security Council, Letter dated 23 August 2004, 16.

27. "Coordinated Efforts Key to Fighting Terrorism, United States Says: Officials Outline to United Nations U.S. Efforts to Freeze Terrorist Funds," State Department press releases and documents, January 11, 2005.

28. "Dealers in Precious Metals, Stones or Jewels Required to Establish Anti–Money Laundering Programs," *FinCEN News*, June 3, 2005.

29. William E. Odom, "Why the FBI Can't Be Reformed," *Washington Post*, June 29, 2005, A-21.

30. Dan Eggen and Julie Tate, "U.S. Campaign Produces Few Convictions on Terrorism Charges," *Washington Post*, June 12, 2005, A-1.

Chapter 9: The Back Door

1. Mariam Nawabi, "Afghanistan's Trade Routes," *Development Gateway*, February 3, 2004, http://topics.developmentgateway.org/afghanistan/rc/ItemDetail.do~382412?itemId=382412.

2. Bureau for International Narcotics and Law Enforcement Affairs, *International Narcotics Control Strategy Report—Money Laundering and Financial Crimes*, March 2005, 66.

3. Fasih Ahmed, "Antiterror Measure Helps Pakistan," *Wall Street Journal Europe*, October 21, 2003, A3.

4. Syed M. Alam, "Afghan Transit Trade," *Pakistan Economist* 34 (2002), www.pakistaneconomist.com/issue2002/issue34/f&m2.htm.

5. Imran Ayub, "Afghan Importers Diverting Goods to Iran," *Daily Times*, November 11, 2005.

6. Robert Charles, "The Afghan Dilemma," *Washington Times*, April 26, 2005.

7. "Trade Transparency Units," in *International Narcotics Control Strategy Report*, 10–12.

Chapter 10: Steps Forward

1. Chris Hamblin, "Imports and Exports: A Black Hole in U.S. Law Enforcement," *moneylaundering.com*, April 7, 2003, http://www.moneylaundering.com/newsarticles/complinet_2003 0407.aspx.

2. Robert Block, "Policing Trade to Nab Terrorists: New Effort Spots Illegal Exports Masking Money Laundering," *Wall Street Journal*, March 11, A-4.

3. FinCEN, *2000–2005 Strategic Plan*, 2000.

4. Champion Walsh, "Study Faults U.S. Policies on Money Laundering, Terror Funds," *Dow Jones Capital Markets Report via Dow Jones*,

December 14, 2004.

5. David Kaplan, "The New Business of Terror: How Organized Crime Is Providing the Cash That Keeps Global Terrorism Going," *U.S. News & World Report,* December 5, 2005, 41–54.

6. Seth M. M. Stodder, "Fixing Homeland Security," *Washington Times,* February 28, 2005.

7. IRS, "Overview—Money Laundering," http://www.irs.gov/compliance/enforcement/article/0,,id=112999,00.html.

Index

About the Author

Mr. John Cassara retired on March 1, 2005, after a twenty-six-year career in the U.S. intelligence and law enforcement communities. His last position was as a special agent detailee to the Department of the Treasury's Office of Terrorism Finance and Financial Intelligence. His parent Treasury agency was the Financial Crimes Enforcement Network, the U.S. financial intelligence unit. Mr. Cassara has particular expertise in the areas of money laundering in the Middle East and the growing threat of alternative remittance systems and forms of trade-based money laundering and value transfer.

From 2002 to 2004, Mr. Cassara was detailed to the U.S. Department of State's Bureau of International Narcotics and Law Enforcement Affairs money-laundering unit to help coordinate U.S. interagency international anti-terrorist-finance training and technical assistance.

During his law enforcement investigative career, Mr. Cassara conducted a large number of money laundering, fraud, smuggling, and diversion of weapons and high technology investigations in Africa, the Middle East, and Europe. While assigned to the Office of the Customs Attaché in Rome, Italy, he directed the first truly international money-laundering task force, called Operation Primo Passo ("First Step"). The innovative operation combated Italian-American organized crime by examining the movement of suspect money between the two countries and represented an early use of financial intelligence to proactively initiate investigations. During his Customs career, Mr. Cassara also served two years as an undercover arms dealer. He began his career with Treasury as a special agent assigned to the Washington field office of the U.S. Secret Service. From 1978 to 1983, he was a covert case officer with the Central Intelligence Agency (CIA). He is one of the very few to have been both a clandestine case officer and a special agent.

Mr. Cassara has been designated a law enforcement "expert" for the Financial Action Task Force (FATF), the Council of Europe's Moneyval, and the U.S. government for international "mutual evaluations." He has lectured around the world on a variety of money-laundering topics. He has addressed the FATF, INTERPOL, the Gulf Cooperation Council, the Italian Gold Institute, the Egmont Group of Financial Intelligence Units, the Federal Law Enforcement Training Center, the FBI Training Academy, the U.S. Treasury, U.S. intelligence agencies including the CIA and NSA, central banks, customs and police services, state and local law enforcement, and scores of money-laundering and terrorist-finance seminars and conferences around the world.